DIVERGENT DEMOCRACY

PRINCETON STUDIES IN
AMERICAN POLITICS

Historical, International, and Comparative Perspectives

Paul Frymer, Suzanne Mettler, and Eric Schickler,
Series Editors

Ira Katznelson, Martin Shefter, and Theda Skocpol,
Founding Series Editors

A list of titles in this series appears in the back of the book.

Divergent Democracy

HOW POLICY POSITIONS CAME TO DOMINATE PARTY COMPETITION

KATHERINE KRIMMEL

PRINCETON UNIVERSITY PRESS

PRINCETON & OXFORD

Copyright © 2024 by Princeton University Press

Princeton University Press is committed to the protection of copyright and the intellectual property our authors entrust to us. Copyright promotes the progress and integrity of knowledge. Thank you for supporting free speech and the global exchange of ideas by purchasing an authorized edition of this book. If you wish to reproduce or distribute any part of it in any form, please obtain permission.

Requests for permission to reproduce material from this work should be sent to permissions@press.princeton.edu

Published by Princeton University Press
41 William Street, Princeton, New Jersey 08540
99 Banbury Road, Oxford OX2 6JX

press.princeton.edu

All Rights Reserved

ISBN 9780691257952
ISBN (pbk.) 9780691257969
ISBN (e-book) 9780691258065

British Library Cataloging-in-Publication Data is available

Editorial: Bridget Flannery-McCoy and Alena Chekanov
Production Editorial: Sara Lerner
Cover Design: Karl Spurzem
Production: Lauren Reese
Publicity: William Pagdatoon
Copyeditor: Melanie Mallon

This book has been composed in Arno Pro

10 9 8 7 6 5 4 3 2 1

To my family

CONTENTS

FIGURES

TABLES

CONFLICT OVER public policy in the United States is age-old, and yet it produces fresh puzzles. Since the Revolution that bore the republic, there have been issues for which people were willing to sacrifice their lives and those of others. But issue positions have not historically cleaved on *party* lines. Even the grievous problem of slavery—which led to civil war—divided the Democratic Party along with the nation at large. And when parties did exhibit clear, alternative issue positions, they were not usually the main basis for electoral competition.

This may come as a surprise to many contemporary observers of American politics, surrounded by distinctions between Democrats and Republicans on matters as wide-ranging as oil drilling and abortion. When new issues arise, parties often take sides; and when existing issues become more salient (e.g., gun policy following a mass shooting), energetic reminders of parties' distinct positions thereon usually follow. We are engulfed, it seems, in a style of divergent democracy.

Why do American political parties engage in fierce competition over issues today? This is not the only way party competition can work. Other means of appealing to voters have emerged around the world and in U.S. history. The far-flung implications of this puzzle motivated me to write this book; and, in the process of doing so, I had a chance to see its fingerprints first-hand all over the country.

My research brought me to many different places with archival records on parties. I've gone to cities and rural towns, international airports and two-lane highways with advertisements for small hotels more than 50 miles away. These trips spanned more than a decade, under quite different political conditions. My first trip in 2010 to the Gerald R. Ford Presidential Library in Ann Arbor, Michigan, occurred during the first term of our nation's first Black president; my last, in 2022, began the day the Dwight D. Eisenhower Presidential Library in Abilene, Kansas, re-opened to researchers after closing for the COVID-19 pandemic (there were balloons, and I think there are photos somewhere of the group of researchers and archivists delighted to resume learning from the vast resources of our national archives).

No matter where or when I traveled, signs of political parties were everywhere. Exclamations of support for the organizations and their candidates, often with ties to their positions on high-profile issues like gun regulation and climate change, were on billboards and bumper stickers I passed on my way to hotels, computer decals and refrigerator magnets sold in airport shops, hats I saw as I walked into local cafes for coffee before starting my day in the archives, and in conversations I overheard while waiting for my order.

At the same time, there was a sense of exhaustion and disdain for parties—on television screens at hotel continental breakfasts, in conversations with restaurant and hotel employees when they learned what I was studying, and so forth. This was familiar—I see it in my home state of New York as well. I imagine readers can conjure their own set of memories and observations from their communities.

This brings to mind Thomas Jefferson, without song or dance but with flair nonetheless. "If I could not go to heaven but with a party, I would not go there at all." So said Jefferson in a letter to colleague Francis Hopkinson in March 1789. To heaven, perhaps not; but to the presidency, indeed. Eleven years after penning this quip, Jefferson won election to the nation's highest office as a member of a party he co-founded.

It would be easy to lament, more than two centuries later, that we're just where we started. Parties remain both disdained and ingrained. While that much is true, a lot *has* changed since the days of Jeffersonian Republicans. A lot has changed in many of our lifetimes. Parties have been constant as a presence, but the ties that bind them to voters have not. Parties appealing to voters through alternative positions across a wide range of policy issues—while evident across the nation today—is not the historical norm. In fact, it's a rather recent development, growing to the current, unprecedented fever pitch over the past half century.

I was surprised to discover in my study of parties that we knew very little about the shift toward issue-based competition, or *programmatic partisanship*, in the United States. We did not even have a way to measure it. It's one of those things in contemporary politics that's so all-encompassing, it's almost imperceptible. I have found, in conversations about this subject, that most people have a hard time remembering or imagining politics any other way.

This book is an effort to build understanding about this important trans-formation in American political life. Parties' strategies for appealing to voters have enormous implications for *how* people relate to politics—whatever their assessment of parties—and we ought to know more about them. I look over a long period to better understand and explain what came before today's dom-inant style of party appeals. And I look around the world for clues as to why the transition to issue-based competition occurred in the United States.

When I started, I aimed to explain why parties became more program-matic. As I worked on the book, I realized it's actually just as much about why U.S. parties were *slow* to adopt this mode of competition. While the rise in programmatic partisanship over the contemporary era may make today's lev-els seem like the primary object of curiosity, we could just as easily flip the puzzle. Political issues are omnipresent in all polities at all times, and polit-ical parties have existed in the United States, much to the founders' dismay, since the nation's early days. With these raw materials, the potential for par-ties to compete using issue positions has always been present. So, why didn't they? Addressing this side of the puzzle led me to the audacious but necessary decision to study the entire period of competition between Democrats and Republicans, 1856 to the present.

Parties may never be popular, and that may be okay. I realize this is a funny statement to make in a book about how parties appeal to voters. But parties don't necessarily need to inspire reverence to serve democracy, organizing conflict in ways that make politics manageable for voters, serving as points of connection between people and government. No known democracy has survived without parties for good reasons. Like it or not, they play many key roles. Perhaps someday, other organizations or institutions will assume these functions, or perhaps not. Either way, understanding how parties appeal to voters, what those connections are made of, and how and why they may change can better position us to evaluate the system we're in, make responsible comparisons to other modes of competition, and set goals moving forward.

Kate Krimmel
June 2023

ACKNOWLEDGMENTS

I ONCE HEARD or read someone remark that whenever they felt weary or stuck while working on their book, they would stop and think about the people who would be in their acknowledgments. I wish I remembered who said that, but alas I will have to settle for an anonymous hat tip for that advice. The many people in these pages have helped me in those moments, among others.

I started thinking about parties and their relationship to policy issues during my transformative years as a graduate student at Columbia University. While this book is not a straightforward revision of my dissertation, which focused more on group-party alliances, it grew out of that work. I realized that I needed a measure of programmatic partisanship to prepare my dissertation for publication and, upon discovering that such a measure did not exist, found myself going down a related but distinct path toward what has become this book.

When I consider my time at Columbia, and my growth and identity as a scholar, my thoughts go immediately to my dissertation chair: Ira Katznelson, who always seems to have a numbered list of thoughtful questions at the top of his head, and who leads with humility and curiosity. He has encouraged me, directly and indirectly through his inspiring work, to be brave, take on big questions, and be mindful of the lens through which I'm examining my subject. The title of the last section of the conclusion ("Onward") is an homage to Ira, who has ended many notes to me with this adventurous directive. It alludes to important things learned and a need to press forward. Ira's guidance over many years has been a gift I can never reciprocate but try my best to honor.

During my time at Columbia and afterward, I have also benefited from tremendous mentorship from Rob Lieberman and Greg Wawro. Conversations with Rob were instrumental in getting me through early stages of my dissertation's development. Rob's support, especially at a time in my career when "messiness" was hard to accept and navigate, helped me build confidence and clarity. Greg has been a source of support and inspiration since I took his class on legislatures in historical and comparative perspective as a second-year graduate student. In that class, and through mentorship on my dissertation and this book, Greg has played a critical role in helping me think about institutions across time and space, and marshal whatever mix of qualitative and quantitative data are necessary to address a question of importance.

I owe a debt of gratitude to the other two members of my dissertation defense committee: Nolan McCarty and the late Alan Brinkley, who read my work with close attention to detail and offered trenchant comments that have shaped my thinking about political parties and history. Nolan also served as my mentor during my predoctoral fellowship at the University of Virginia's Miller Center of Public Affairs and generously included me in Princeton's vibrant intellectual community during my final year in graduate school.

Many people gave their time to read and provide feedback on this manuscript in part or in full, at different stages of its development. Thanks to Ira Katznelson, Matt Lacombe, Rob Lieberman, Eric Schickler, and Daniel Schlozman for reading draft chapters. And many thanks to those who gathered for my book conference at Barnard in the fall of 2022: David Bateman, Dan Carpenter, Devin Caughey, Boris Heersink, Ira Katznelson, Nolan McCarty, Charles Stewart III, and Greg Wawro. It is no small task to read someone's entire manuscript, and they did so with incredible attention to broad strokes and details. The feedback I received from this group of eminent and intellectually generous scholars played a key role in shaping the revision of this manuscript.

Several other people at Columbia have supported me and my work and inspired me with their own: Bob Erikson, Fred Harris, Alex Hertel-Fernandez, Shigeo Hirano, John Huber, Kimuli Kasara, Bob Shapiro, Michael Ting, Yamil Velez, Dorian Warren, Jeff Lax and Justin Phillips (Jeff and Justin have been especially important to my journey, as I learned a great deal from working with them), and the late Charles Tilly (whom I will always remember for the encouragement, "That's a finding, not a problem!" when I had trouble identifying a negative case for an independent study paper).

I have been lucky to have wonderful colleagues, first at Boston University and now at Barnard College, who have provided feedback, support, guidance on the publication process, company on after-work runs, and wonderful work environments. Thanks to Taylor Boas, Dino Christenson, Katie Einstein, David Glick, Doug Kriner, Cathie Jo Martin, David Mayers, Max Palmer, Gina Sapiro, and Graham Wilson (at BU). And thanks to Séverine

Autesserre, Alyssa Battistoni, Sheri Berman, Alex Cooley, Ayten Gündoğdu, Matt Lacombe, Kim Marten, Mike Miller, Eduardo Moncada, and Xiaobo Lü (at Barnard). I am also grateful for the institutional support I have received from BU and Barnard, with particular thanks to Linda Bell, Monica Miller, Debra Minkoff, Randall Reback, Jennie Correia, and Taylor Doran.

I am grateful for the opportunity to present this work in various forums, and for the feedback received. I benefited from thoughtful engagement from participants in the Comparative Politics Workshop at the Graduate Center of the City University of New York (at a particularly tumultuous time, in November 2020), the American Political History Conference at the University of Georgia (2021), the Research in American Politics Workshop at Boston University (2021), and the American Politics Workshop at Columbia University (2022). Special thanks to my discussants at these workshops (Jeremy Pope, Ryan Brunette, Javier Padilla) and at professional conferences. Christina Wolbrecht was incredibly supportive (and patient) with a very early draft of the first chapter of this book, which I presented at an APSA Annual Meeting. And Paul Frymer was the first person to see (and offer very helpful comments on) what is now chapter 4, which I presented at a later APSA meeting.

Thanks also to many people not yet mentioned who have helped me through this work over the years with discussions, feedback, and friendship: Sam Rosenfeld, Dan Galvin, Frances Lee, David Mayhew, Richard Bensel, Matt Grossmann, David Hopkins, Keith Dougherty, Sidney Tarrow, David Karol, Adam Hilton, Julia Azari, Chloe Thurston, Didi Kuo, John Krinsky, Vince Boudreau, Susan Woodward, Kelly Rader, Tom Ogorzalek, Grant Porter, Quinn Mulroy, Shannon Eaves, Monique Mills, Badia Ahad, Jonquil Goode, and Beth Wolf. Special thanks to Nicola Beisel, my undergraduate mentor at Northwestern, who introduced me to original research, encouraged me to pursue an academic career, and has supported me at every step along the way.

This project would not have been possible without invaluable research assistance by Kristen Mansfield, Victor Vuong, Samuel Clark-Clough, Claudia Chung, Marielle Greenblatt, Taylor Faires, Sarish Lone, Annie Iezzi, Madeleine Morales, Heather Loepere, Kate Sosland, and Esther Kardos. As anyone who has done archival research will understand, I am also very grateful to the research staff at the presidential libraries I visited for my dissertation and specifically for this book. This project has also been made possible through institutional support from the American Association of University Women through a Postdoctoral Fellowship and the Miller Center at the University of

Virginia through a Predoctoral Fellowship (thanks especially to Brian Balogh, Jeff Jenkins, and Sidney Milkis).

A big thank you to Princeton University Press for bringing this book to life. From our first exchange, I was energized by the enthusiasm and vision Bridget Flannery-McCoy had for the book. And Alena Chekanov has provided key support for the project, substantively and logistically, throughout this process. Thank you to Eric Schickler, Suzanne Mettler, and Theda Skocpol for including my work in this series, which I have long admired. Thanks especially to Suzanne for incredibly helpful feedback and advice as the guide for my book in the series. And thanks to three anonymous reviewers for supporting the manuscript and offering extremely useful feedback, especially on reshaping the book's front end.

This book is dedicated to my family, who have shaped me in every way and been there with me at my best and worst. To my parents, Lorraine and David Krimmel, who always let me play school instead of house and whose unconditional love is a foundation for everything. To my brother Jeff, fellow scholar (of medicine) with whom I had many conversations about this work in its early stages and who always seems to know the balance of support and grief to deliver at any given moment. And to my brother Mark, who inspires me with his big heart, bold spirit, and commitment to healing others.

Finally, I would be nowhere without the three amazing people with whom I'm lucky to share dinner (even when it's "I don't want that!") every night. My husband, Mitchell, read and commented on this entire manuscript (including the footnotes and appendix—that's commitment), and talked through ideas (the good, the bad, and the ugly) countless times. We navigated life in a pandemic with two young children and no roadmap but much love. I could not have done this without your support. And to our children, Audrey and Juliet: by the time you are old enough to read this book, I hope our democracy is in better condition—stronger, kinder, more resilient. And if it is not, I believe you will help make it so.

ABBREVIATIONS

ACPO   Advisory Committee on Political Organization

ACPP   Advisory Committee on Policies and Platform

ADA   Americans for Democratic Action

AFL   American Federation of Labor

APSA   American Political Science Association

ARC   All Republican Congress

AVC   American Veterans Committee

CIO   Congress of Industrial Organizations

DAC   Democratic Advisory Council

DALP   Democratic Accountability and Linkages Project

DNC   Democratic National Committee

DSG   Democratic Study Group

EA   Encyclopedia of Associations

GDP   gross domestic product

GOP   Grand Old Party

MFDP   Mississippi Freedom Democratic Party

OLS   ordinary least squares

RAC   Republican Advisory Councils

RCC   Republican Coordinating Committee

RCPP   Republican Committee on Program and Progress

RNC   Republican National Committee

SNAP   Supplemental Nutrition Assistance Program

SNCC   Student Nonviolent Coordinating Committee

STM   Structural Topic Model

TPO   Traditional Party Organization

WPA   Works Progress Administration

1

The Puzzle of Programmatic Partisanship

THE WORLD WATCHED with anxiety and bewilderment as the United States grappled with a swelling debt ceiling crisis in the spring of 2023. If Congress failed to raise or suspend the debt limit, essentially denying the U.S. Treasury permission to issue new debt to pay government bills that had come due, the nation would default on its financial obligations for the first time in history. For government employees, contractors, Social Security beneficiaries, bondholders, and many others to whom the U.S. government owed money, this could mean missed payments. More broadly, many economists and financial institutions projected that default would harm the nation's credit rating, weaken its currency, and fling the domestic and global economies into recession.[1]

Amid this high stakes financial environment, some of the sticking points in negotiations between House Speaker Kevin McCarthy and President Joe Biden on legislation to raise the debt limit had remarkably little to do with budgetary politics. Friction on these issues, like adjustments to rules for people to access the Supplemental Nutrition Assistance Program (SNAP, or "food stamps") continued as Congress considered—and ultimately passed into law—the deal struck by the president's and Speaker's negotiating teams.

A program with little budgetary impact (food stamps account for approximately 2 percent of federal spending) appears rather out of place in urgent talks to avoid default on the nation's financial obligations. While the agreement between Democrats and Republicans will affect many people who use or would use SNAP, it will have minimal consequences for the national debt. The nonpartisan Congressional Budget Office (CBO) estimates that changes to SNAP will induce a $2.1 billion change in spending in the *decade* between

2023 and 2033, a minuscule sum considering annual spending currently exceeds $6 trillion.

Congress has performed the ministerial task of raising the debt ceiling 103 times since World War II, and the process was not always so confounding—even with prickly relations between party leaders. Many have pointed to the 1980s, when Republican Ronald Reagan occupied the Oval Office, and Democrat Thomas "Tip" O'Neill served as Speaker of the House. The two exchanged their fair share of jabs. O'Neill used to call Reagan "Herbert Hoover with a smile" and a "cheerleader for selfishness," and Reagan joked that he "liked to keep in shape by jogging three times a day around Tip O'Neill" (who was less svelte than the former actor, as cartoonists loved to point out).[2] And they did not shy away from showdowns over policy. Still, Congress raised the debt ceiling eighteen times during Reagan's presidency without generating a deluge of worldwide headlines. When Reagan first needed Democratic votes to raise the debt ceiling in 1981, the Speaker agreed to help on one condition: that the president write a letter to each Democratic member of Congress asking them to support the effort to raise the debt ceiling, which would insulate them from public blame for this perennially unpopular but necessary legislative action. He did, and they did, and it happened.[3]

Party dynamics are different now, and so by extension is American governance. Raising the debt ceiling has become more acrimonious in recent years, with lawmakers creeping closer and closer to the brink of default before reaching agreements. Further—and of greater import for this book—while attention to nonbudgetary (or barely budgetary) but highly partisan issues amid a brewing economic emergency may seem to defy rationality, it reflects the logic of the party system today.

Global stakes aside, the expression of different views on food stamps by Democrats and Republicans during debt ceiling negotiations is an example of an increasingly common phenomenon: parties competing for public attention and approval through opposing policy positions. Democrats and Republicans have staked out contrasting positions on a wide range of issues, like abortion, LGBTQ+ rights, gun control, environmental policy, and means-tested (i.e., income-qualifying) social welfare programs like SNAP. Party actors amplify these distinctions in various forums, from presidential debates to State of the Union addresses and opposition responses. Such distinctions have even entered venues where they are not germane, like debt ceiling negotiations and their surrounding publicity. Today's parties want voters to know they support different courses of action for the nation.

Issue differentiation reflects what's known as a *programmatic party system*—that is, one in which policy positions serve as a key basis of electoral competition. Parties can use all sorts of tools to compete with one another, an insight dating back to early twentieth-century work by Max Weber, and they do not all involve issue positions. A common alternative to programmatic partisanship (or *programmaticism*) is clientelism, or the exchange of goods, services, or other material benefits (e.g., jobs, known in this context as *patronage jobs*) for political support. Parties might also rely on charismatic candidates to woo voters. Of course, no system—past or present—relies entirely on one type of appeal, but the balance of tools can and does change over time.

The United States today has the most programmatic party system in the world. This may seem obvious and unsurprising to many observers of contemporary politics, who have grown accustomed to watching party leaders spar over issues in a ring that appears to lack basic rules of engagement. It may also seem natural to many who have noticed organized groups with opposing issue positions lining up behind different parties (e.g., gun rights groups tend to support Republicans, while gun control groups tend to support Democrats). From a historical standpoint, however, this level of programmaticism is striking. Rewind to the mid-twentieth century and we'd see the American Political Science Association (APSA), among others, criticizing Democrats and Republicans for excessive programmatic similarity.

Let's return for a moment to Tip O'Neill. His tenure as Speaker of the House, during which Congress raised the debt ceiling with minimal drama even under divided government, provides a historical contrast to the present. Yet he too could marvel at how much party competition had changed. Alongside a personal journey from cutting the grass at Harvard as a kid from a working-class neighborhood in Cambridge to delivering the keynote address at the university's 350th anniversary celebration as a household name, Tip O'Neill's personal and professional life illustrates a larger transformation in the nature of American partisanship.

O'Neill's high-profile policy battles with Ronald Reagan and the Republican Party bore little resemblance to the politics of his youth, in style if not in substance. After his father landed a patronage job as superintendent of sewers, which put him in charge of more than a thousand other jobs, their household became a hub of activity in North Cambridge. "People came to my father with their problems," O'Neill recalled.[4] It was a predominantly Irish immigrant neighborhood, a community of modest means, at a time when there was not much of a government safety net (programs like Social Security, unemployment insurance, and so forth would not emerge until the New Deal). But a clientelistic network of local party machinery stood ready to connect people with various goods and services: unemployment benefits, public jobs, clothing, food assistance, and so forth. After snowstorms, he had around fifty buttons to distribute to people, which gave them access to a day's work shoveling snow for three or four dollars. People would start lining up at five o'clock in the morning on snowy days for the chance to procure one. This is what made Democrats in Tip O'Neill's early years.

It's not so much that O'Neill himself changed—he was a self-proclaimed champion of working-class people at the beginning and end of his career. As a ward leader in Cambridge during the Depression, when machine politics loomed large, this meant handing out snow buttons and winter coats, as well as food baskets for Christmas and Easter; making phone calls to City Hall on behalf of constituents; and other small-scale interactions with his supporters. Over time, as parties developed opposing positions across a wide range of issues and competed largely on this basis, he remained "a true lunch-pail Democrat," in the words of colleague Rep. Rosa DeLauro. And in his own words, in his book *Man of the House*, he proclaimed, "Every family deserves the opportunity to earn an income, own a home, educate their children, and afford medical care. That is the American dream, and it's still worth fighting for."[5] By the time he served as Speaker of the House, what it meant to be a Democrat fighting for such things had changed, as had people's sense of what to expect in exchange for their votes.

This story is bigger than any one policy or politician, even one known for the immortal assertion that "all politics is local" (an insight O'Neill attributed to his father). We can point to many issues embroiled in programmatic politics and politicians who have seen the nature of the party system evolve around them. This shift toward issue-based competition reflects a major development in American political life. How and why did this transformation occur?

Remarkably, we know little about it. One might wonder how such an important development could evade American politics scholars' attention for so long. The answer, I suspect, is that programmatic partisanship has become entangled with the notion of polarization in the American politics literature such that it *appears* to have been addressed by work on that subject. But, it has not; rather, it has been hiding in plain sight.

This book investigates the history of programmaticism in the United States, examining when, how, and why it has changed since the Democratic and Republican parties began competing with each other in 1856. This is vital to understand as we think about the state of representative democracy, a subject about which there is considerable concern and introspection in the United States and in other democracies (and former democracies) around the world. Adam Przeworski's classic and still resonant definition of democracy points toward a "system in which parties lose elections."[6] The nature of party competition tells us about the grounds on which these electoral losses occur, what parties at the elite level (i.e., Republicans and Democrats in Congress) and the mass level (i.e., Republican and Democratic voters) gain and lose and how.

The point is not to idealize any style of party competition. The debt ceiling debacle of 2023 is not flattering for democracy, but neither were many aspects of American clientelism. Political machines were associated with corruption. Boston boss James Michael Curley allegedly had an open drawer in his office where people could leave envelopes full of money (while he stood aside, peering into a mirror) and find themselves entitled to future favors. Tip O'Neill recalled that Curley "liked to brag that he never accepted a donation from a person who couldn't afford it, but that still leaves a lot to the imagination."[7] And not all people had equal access to machine largesse. As in many other dimensions of politics, Black Americans were underserved by machines, which tended to recruit coalitions of mostly Irish, Italian, and eastern European immigrants. (A notorious machine operative of Boston's West End neighborhood apparently met new immigrants where their boat docked, brought them to a site of party registration, and then to a public utility office to find employment.)[8] It's no accident that Shirley Chisholm, the first Black woman to run for president, in 1972, employed the campaign slogan "unbought and unbossed."

The point is to understand, to have a clearer picture of how and why our party system has evolved. Comparing our current system to previous or otherwise alternative styles of party competition can be worthwhile, as long as we're doing so with clear vision and thought. This can help us avoid judgments against unrealistic, glossy standards like nostalgic memories or ideal states. Moreover, by analyzing motivations of key actors and details of the context in which they were operating, we can better understand outcomes we observe as well as paths *not* taken, whether by choice or by chance.

This chapter provides a foundation for the rest of the book. After discussing the concept of programmatic partisanship in more detail, I present a novel measurement strategy for demonstrating changes in issue-based competition over a period of almost two centuries. This measure of programmatic partisanship over time is both a finding of the book and a tool to hone its central puzzle. I proceed to map my approach and argument, as well as consider implications for our understanding of parties and American democracy.

What Is Programmatic Partisanship?

The core principle of programmatic partisanship is an emphasis on policy positions as a basis of competition. Given the complexity of real world party systems, this dynamic is rarely if ever fully dominant or absent, but exists on a continuum. We can think of programmatic partisanship as the extent to which parties attempt to put forth clear, alternative positions on a range of policy issues.

Two criteria warrant emphasis: difference and breadth. For a party to be considered strongly programmatic, its positions have to be *distinct* from those of other parties. If the parties take similar positions on all matters, then issues cannot be used by voters in deciding between the parties in elections.[9] Strong programmatic difference also *extends beyond one issue or set of issues.* Competition that revolves around a central cleavage in society is more factional than programmatic. Take white supremacy in the United States, for example. Slavery, segregation of schools and public spaces, and other tools of racial discrimination and harm undoubtedly involve policy. Such policies can be *part* of a programmatic system, but not its whole. Indeed, if one issue or set of issues is so prominent that it crowds out other matters, it can inhibit the growth of a programmatic system in which parties compete on a range of issues.

This does not mean parties need to—or should—distinguish themselves on every issue. Convergence is appropriate when it serves the public interest, the electorate is in general agreement, or there are not multiple positions befitting a liberal democracy, for example.[10] Exhibiting similar positions on such issues does not undermine issue-based competition; in fact, it strengthens the normative foundation of programmaticism. The parties can engage in pro-democratic competition on a subset of issues facing a polity. They can also be programmatic while expressing moderate positions on many issues, so long as they maintain distinct central tendencies. And a programmatic system has room for parties to place different levels of emphasis on some (but not all) issues; this is, in a sense, an implicit argument about the perceived importance of certain issues.

Variation can exist across parties in the same system. While they may be affected by the same electoral rules, parties within a nation can have different histories and bases leading them to develop on separate paths with quite different features.[11] Looking across nations, the shift toward a programmatic system usually starts with one party, often a new party.[12] When there is imbalance between parties, with one focused more than the other on competition via policy positions, it is harder to achieve clear position differentiation. Yet, even if no party in the system completely satisfies the criteria for programmaticism, it is still possible to observe that one party is more programmatic than another or itself at an earlier point. We can consider a party system programmatic when its major parties are so.

Programmaticism is a characteristic of parties and party systems, not of individual candidates or officeholders. Individuals can be ideological in the sense of holding a set of positions that involve more or less government intervention in the market and society. Indeed, individuals may pursue policy goals even if parties are not programmatic. But no individual can carry out a program alone. A collective statement of policy positions has broader implications for a party system and a nation because it carries more significant potential consequences. Statements by individual politicians have less weight for people's sense of the system as a whole, the currency on which it runs.

As with other concepts, like democracy, scholars have developed alternative definitions of programmaticism, adding different types and degrees of complexity. Additional criteria relate primarily to institutions and legislative behavior.[13] In this book, I employ a definition on the simpler side of this continuum because explication of alternative positions is essential to issue-based competition. Other criteria sometimes included in the definition of programmaticism, like orienting institutions toward position development and following through on positions in office, could be characterized as causes or consequences of position development.[14]

Relationship to Polarization

Programmatic partisanship and polarization are certainly related, both involving distinctions between parties. In fact, they are often conflated. The notion of programmatic difference frequently underlies discussions of polarized voting in Congress. It comes up as a potential upside to polarization, giving voters clear expectations regarding the types of policies each party is likely to pursue in office. This is thought to provide meaningful choices in elections and facilitate a healthy democracy. It also comes up as a potential downside to polarization. Concern has been raised that, under polarized conditions, parties' positions are too far apart for them to find common ground. This is thought to slow the legislative process and produce gridlock.[15]

Yet, programmaticism and polarization are not synoymous. Polarization encapsulates a range of phenomena leading parties to resist connection, which includes but is not limited to programmaticism. There are partisan differences in ideology (*ideological polarization*), displays of in-group/out-group bias along party lines (*affective polarization*), and alignment of party identification with other identities (e.g., race, religion, class, etc.) that stoke anger and prejudice between Democrats and Republicans, motivating political activism while reducing productive cross-party discussion, understanding, and empathy (*social polarization*).[16] These phenomena—along with programmatic partisanship, which involves partisan differences in issue positions—are each a different type of barrier to partisan coalescence. Together, they compose the broader phenomenon of polarization: the set of forces making it more difficult for parties, like repelling magnets, to connect even if other forces (e.g., routine responsibilities requiring bipartisan cooperation like passing the budget and major crises like a pandemic) are trying to push them together.

In sum, programmaticism contributes to polarization, but the existence of polarization does not ensure the presence of programmaticism. It may be a significant feature of polarization at some times in some places, but not others. Studying progammaticism can help us better understand polarization—an important contribution to the American politics literature, given that the rise of polarization is one of the most remarkable features of our time—but existing work on polarization cannot substitute for close analysis of programmaticism.

To understand the growth of programmaticism, we need more direct focus on this phenomenon than the American politics literature has provided thus far. While scholars of mass polarization have examined differences between Democrats and Republicans in the electorate on issues, insights from this literature are insufficient for understanding the puzzle driving this book, because programmaticism primarily involves elites. We have gotten glimpses of elite programmaticism from studies of particular issues (e.g., abortion), but a more comprehensive analysis is needed.[17] None of these works was intended to address the question of why emphasis on issue-based competition varies over time.

Relationship to Clientelism and Other Types of Appeals to Voters

Considering the relationship of programmaticism to other types of appeals helps sharpen its definition. The concept, like most, has a clear center and fuzzy borders. Programmatic appeals are most crisply distinguishable from charismatic appeals, which are based on "unique, idiosyncratic personal qualities of [party] leaders that instill confidence and allegiance in voters," rather than on policy positions.[18]

To separate programmatic from clientelistic appeals, it is useful to specify what is meant by *policy*. Any system could be said to run on policies, considered simply as rules. In this context, however, the term *policy* generally refers to public policy, defined by its scale and rules for distribution. Policy-related goods and services are broad (i.e., collective goods or club goods for large groups like social classes) rather than narrowly targeted. And while benefits from clientelistic linkages are given only to people who have supported the party, benefits from programmatic linkages are not distributed on this condition. Such benefits may or may not be distributed at all, depending on decisions made by those in power. And their distribution may, on average, disproportionately benefit one party's base as a result of differences in demographic composition. But if benefits from a policy are distributed at all, they are not restricted to political supporters.[19]

There are gray areas between clientelism and programmaticism, especially with respect to some distributive policies.[20] As leading scholars of comparative party systems Herbert Kitschelt and Steven Wilkinson (2007b) note, it's relatively easy to identify clientelism when parties are handing out jobs and goodies in exchange for votes, "but much harder to separate from policy linkage where politicians deliver local club goods, such as infrastructure projects. To the extent that specific localities get preferential access to such facilities contingent upon electoral choices of small groups of voters and contributors to parties and candidates, the production of local public goods constitutes the currency of clientelistic politics."[21] In this light, we might consider some "earmarks" or "pork" directed toward particular constituencies in the United States to be clientelistic or at least quasi-clientelistic, for example.

Susan Stokes et al. (2013) offer additional guidance for identifying programmatic distributive policies, distinguishing them from nonprogrammatic types in a manner that cross-cuts traditional ways of thinking about differences between clientelism and programmaticism. For distribution to be considered programmatic, two criteria must be met: (1) "the criteria of distribution must be public"; and (2) "the public, formal criteria of distribution must actually shape the distribution of resources in question."[22] In the case of notorious "earmarks" in the United States, a simple blanket categorization should be avoided. As they note, "Not all bridges are 'bridges to nowhere'—there must be something about the process determining how resources are spent that makes some legitimate and others illegitimate."[23] Attention to rules for distribution can aid this endeavor.

This does not necessarily mean the rules are fair. Indeed, public policies have been implemented according to rules that are deeply inequitable. Policies may explicitly exclude people based on certain characteristics, which sometimes have a logic of equity (as in programs like Medicare aimed at meeting needs of older people, for example) and sometimes a logic of illiberal exclusion (as in New Deal–era programs, like Social Security, that at their inception excluded categories of work performed primarily by African Americans, like agriculture and domestic labor). Public policies can and do evolve over time, becoming more or less equitable. Programmaticism is not wholly just or unjust by definition; rather, it is a style of political competition based on public policy, the normative character of which will be affected by the nature of those policies.

In sum, with sensitivity to nuances relating to certain distributive policies, programmatic appeals can be distinguished from other types by their emphasis on public policy. In addition to clientelistic and charismatic appeals, other types of appeals classified by some scholars as nonprogrammatic include those based on personalism, populism, and identities (e.g., ethnicity).[24] To the extent that voters associate any of these types of appeals with particular policy positions and priorities—as might occur with identity politics, for example— the line between programmatic and nonprogrammatic may blur. To count as a strongly programmatic appeal, however, policy positions should be communicated (through explicit statements or dog whistles), not just left to inference based on identity.

Why Not "Responsible Party Government"?

Readers may wonder why I have chosen to focus on programmaticism, a relatively unknown concept in American politics literature, rather than *responsible party government*, famously discussed in a 1950 report released by APSA, "Toward a More Responsible Two-Party System," and separate works by E. E. Schattschneider and many others. In fact, given the amount of attention devoted to responsible party government over the past seventy years, and the centrality of programmaticism to this concept, readers might wonder why a book on programmaticism is even necessary. To address these questions, it will be useful to step back and discuss the former concept in greater depth; for, to its credit and detriment, responsible party government is many things.

Most broadly, it is a theory of democracy based on the notions of majoritarianism and collective responsibility. The 1950 APSA report devotes significant space to making the case for assessing democracy by the state of its parties. Schattschneider, who chaired the committee that penned the report, also makes this argument in his classic 1942 book, *Party Government*. While parties have been reviled since the nation's founding and continue to be unpopular, they play a critical intermediary role in democracy, organizing conflict so voters face clear, manageable decisions at the polls. When parties offer alternative policy programs, voters understand the stakes of their electoral choices—voting for X party means that policy will head in one direction; voting for Y party means it will head in another. Parties are thus "the makers of democratic government."[25] References to responsible party government will, for some, invoke this argument about parties' key role in democracy.

In addition to serving as a theory of democracy, responsible party government can also be considered a set of processes. The most well-known set describes responsible party government's basic mechanics. Parties stake out alternative positions across a wide range of issues, communicate them to voters, and nominate candidates who will adhere thereto. Once in office, party members exercise discipline with respect to these positions. Voters then assess whether they are happy with the resulting policies and hold the governing party responsible for the current state of affairs. The first stage of this process is quite close to the notion of programmaticism I have described in this chapter, and the stages in toto approximate more complex definitions of programmaticism. But responsible party government goes further than even these maximalist definitions, also describing processes for intraparty democracy that its adherents view as essential to the realization of responsible party government as a model of democracy. For some readers, the notion of responsible party government will bring these processes to mind.

For others, the term responsible party government may conjure the report's rather granular arguments about the types of institutional change that should be enacted to facilitate responsible party government (e.g., parties should have midterm conventions, create party councils to work on policy, etc.). This sweeping, multifaceted nature has been a source of strength and weakness. It likely explains responsible party government's enduring resonance with scholars across the discipline, while also making the concept difficult to apply in a manner that's both precise and true to its scope. Work on this subject has tended to be either very broad, assessing its value as a democratic theory or the extent to which the United States has lived up to this ideal over time, or very narrow, analyzing a specific slice of the concept. The most highly cited works—by far—on responsible party government following APSA and Schattschneider's seminal publications demonstrate this impressive yet awkward range: an intellectual history of the concept by Austin Ranney (1962), who was both student and critic of Schattschneider's; an analysis of lawmakers' responsiveness to public opinion on issues (Miller and Stokes, 1963); and a study of agenda setting by party leaders in the House of Representatives (Cox and McCubbins, 1993, 2005).

In this light, centering my analysis on the notion of responsible party government would be hazardous. While it may involve programmaticism, it also encompasses a range of other processes and phenomena that are outside the scope of my analysis. This may explain why a focused analysis of programmaticism has never emerged from the literature on responsible party government. I could, in theory, start with the notion of responsible party government and amend it. Given its legacy in American politics scholarship, however, this seems unwise. The term is too well known, and it raises a host of ideas that would distract from my analysis. It seems more prudent and useful to start from the idea of programmaticm and build from there.

Programmatic Partisanship over Time

With a discussion of programmatic partisanship's meaning in hand, we can now consider measurement. This is important because a clearer and more continuous picture of variation in programmaticism over time will offer a stronger sense of the puzzle we want to explain. Although we have a general sense that programmaticism is stronger today than it once was, the exact timing and pace of change remain unclear. Many excellent studies examine party positions and their evolution in specific issue areas.[26] But there has, to my knowledge, been little attempt to create a broad, systematic measure of programmaticism in the United States over time. Rather, it tends to be inferred from standard measures of polarization.

Well-established, readily available measures of elite polarization in the United States go back to the nineteenth century, the most common of which relies on DW-NOMINATE scores for members of Congress. These scores, based on lawmakers' coalitional behavior in roll-call votes over the course of their careers, are typically interpreted as measures of ideology.[27] It stands to reason that the distance between the DW-NOMINATE scores of the median Democrat and Republican in each chamber of Congress would increase as the parties become more programmatically distinct. The availability of this proxy may help explain why a direct measure of programmaticism covering a long period has not been developed.

DW-NOMINATE scores cannot provide a basis for a reliable measure of programmatic partisanship, however. While they do gauge intrapartisan cohesion and interpartisan distinction, they cannot tell us what is holding co-partisans together and keeping opposing partisans apart. It could be policy positions, though a significant difference between Democrats' and Republicans' roll-call voting behavior could also emerge without programmatic distinction. In the words of Herbert Kitschelt and Kent Freeze (n.d.), scholars at the helm of efforts to measure programmatic partisanship cross-nationally, "Programmatic cohesiveness of a party is a *sufficient* condition for legislative discipline, but *not a necessary* one: There may be instances of legislative discipline even in the absence of programmatic cohesiveness, because the compliance of legislators with partisan unity is enforced by external institutional incentives and punishments (e.g., side-payments for electoral supporters in a legislator's district)."[28]

Frances Lee (2016b) puts forth a strong argument against interpreting the large difference between DW-NOMINATE scores of the median Democrat and Republican in Congress as programmatic polarization during the Gilded Age. She notes that this period, from the end of Reconstruction through the turn of the century, is characterized differently by political scientists relying on DW-NOMINATE and historians studying Congress at a more granular level. The former view it as a period of high polarization, in which programmatic difference is assumed. In the historical literature, by contrast, "the conventional portrait of the era depicts the two parties as locked in battles over distributive benefits and patronage, with little, if any, programmatic national policy content."[29] They were both parties of limited government, broadly speaking, and neither offered particular stances on major issues of the time. Lee's analysis shows that most congressional action during this period was not about ideology or issues that could map onto ideology; rather, it was largely about distributive policy, patronage, and electoral contests with implications for the distribution of patronage. Even policies that seemed potentially ideological were ultimately distributive. Conflict between parties was strong, which leads to a larger distance between the DW-NOMINATE scores of the median member of each party, but this conflict was not rooted in programmatic differences.

Existing measures of polarization are also insufficient for measuring programmatic partisanship because DW-NOMINATE scores, based on roll-call votes, capture only a sliver of congressional behavior. Most bills introduced in Congress never receive a roll-call vote. And, strikingly, when Clinton and Lapinski (2008) examined legislative enactments and roll-call data from 1891 to 1994, they found that only 5.5 percent of bills signed into law received recorded roll-call votes in both chambers of Congress.

Alternative measures of polarization, like those based on interest group ratings of members of Congress, are also insufficient for measuring programmaticism. While some may be connected to members' behavior on policy issues, these measures are based on a small and nonrandom sample of roll-call votes, covering a limited range of issues. Moreover, they are of limited use in historical analyses because they became common only in the mid-twentieth century.[30]

By developing a more direct measure of programmaticism over the entire course of competition between Democrats and Republicans, we can get a better sense of its trajectory over time. Even if we are reasonably certain that parties are more programmatic than they used to be—it is easy to point to examples of issues on which Democrats and Republicans have taken opposing positions—significant uncertainty remains regarding the timing and extent of changes in programmatic partisanship. We should not assume that it rose at the same time as the difference in DW-NOMINATE scores, or that it has continued to rise, unabated, as have other measures of polarization. A certain degree of programmatic commitment could draw people into a party and solidify their attachments, obviating the need for further increases in programmaticism. There may even be room for programmatic decay without significant penalty.

Measurement Approach

One of my book's central contributions lies in developing a quadrennial measure of programmaticism from 1856, the first year of competition between today's major parties, to the present.[31] I use advancements in machine learning to estimate differences in orientation toward issues overall, comparing national Republican and Democratic platforms on the whole and within topic areas for each year.

Doing so is instructive for a few reasons. Looking within topics enables us to gauge the breadth of issue differentiation, assuring that one set of issues is not driving the overall measure. This strategy also offers a nuanced picture of programmaticism. While the United States is known in the comparative politics literature as a case of high programmatic partisanship, the parties do not disagree on every issue. Thus, measuring party difference within issue areas can offer a sense of the limitations of even a very strong case of programmatic partisanship. Variation in levels of programmaticism across issues also suggests that the measure based on whole platforms is not simply capturing interparty differences in language style or broad ideology.

DATA

I focus on the extent to which Democrats and Republicans express programmatic differences through speech. Party platforms are central in my analysis.[32] They are the official encyclopedic statements of party policy and should be taken seriously as such. It is easy to criticize them as unenforceable "cheap talk" and minimize their importance for this reason, but research has shown an association between platform pledges and lawmakers' actions in the realms of expenditures and policy.[33] Moreover, the energy and anxiety surrounding platform content over the postwar era belies such dismissal. As Paul T. David, scholar of party conventions and long-time professor of government at the University of Virginia, remarked in a 1971 article entitled "Party Platforms as National Plans":

> The platforms involve a remarkable paradox of perception. Editorial writers and some leading politicians, usually of the Legislative Branch, have made it their business for generations to denigrate the platforms as campaign trivia—ephemera to be forgotten as soon as the campaign is over. On the other hand, it is not possible to watch the amount of struggle that goes into any party platform, the thousands of manhours of toil, sweat, and strain that are devoted by people who value their time highly, without concluding that the platforms must be important to some people for some purposes.[34]

Indeed, disagreement over the platform's civil rights plank led to an exodus of southern Democrats from the party's convention in 1948 and a challenge by

Strom Thurmond under the States' Rights ticket to Democratic incumbent Harry Truman.[35]

Finally, there is no other centralized statement of party policy. Party actors make various statements about policy, of course, but the platform is the only official comprehensive statement of party positions. Although it is not the only source of data used in this book, it plays an important role, reflecting its unique standing.

METHODOLOGY

I take a novel two-stage approach to measuring programmatic partisanship through platforms, leveraging the power of machine-learning tools to identify systematic patterns in large volumes of text.

First, I estimate a structural topic model (STM) on party platforms over time at the sentence level, using word co-occurrence to identify topics in the platforms and to calculate the degree to which each sentence relates to each topic. This analysis reveals twenty major topics. They are, in order of prevalence: (1) economy; (2) American dream; (3) foreign affairs; (4) rights; (5) territories and statehood; (6) labor and antitrust; (7) development; (8) businesses and jobs; (9) defense; (10) trade and markets; (11) education; (12) regulation and bureaucracy; (13) healthcare; (14) energy; (15) liberal democracy, at home and abroad; (16) culture, arts, and multiculturalism; (17) land and natural resources; (18) law enforcement and border patrol; (19) transportation and infrastructure; and (20) social welfare.

In the second stage, I take a two-pronged approach to measuring programmaticism, looking at platforms on the whole (i.e., generating one estimate per platform) and within issue areas (i.e., generating a separate estimate for the set of sentences on each issue area in each platform). In both cases, I begin by creating estimates by party and year using a scaling technique called Wordfish, developed by Slapin and Proksch (2008). I take the difference between the estimates for each party as a measure of programmaticism.

A detailed explanation of this methodology, along with validation of the estimates it produces, can be found in the appendix.

Results

Figure 1.1 plots programmaticism over time. The solid line shows raw numbers, and the dotted line is a loess curve (reflecting locally weighted regression) with a 95 percent confidence interval shaded in gray.[36]

Difference between Democratic and Republican platforms

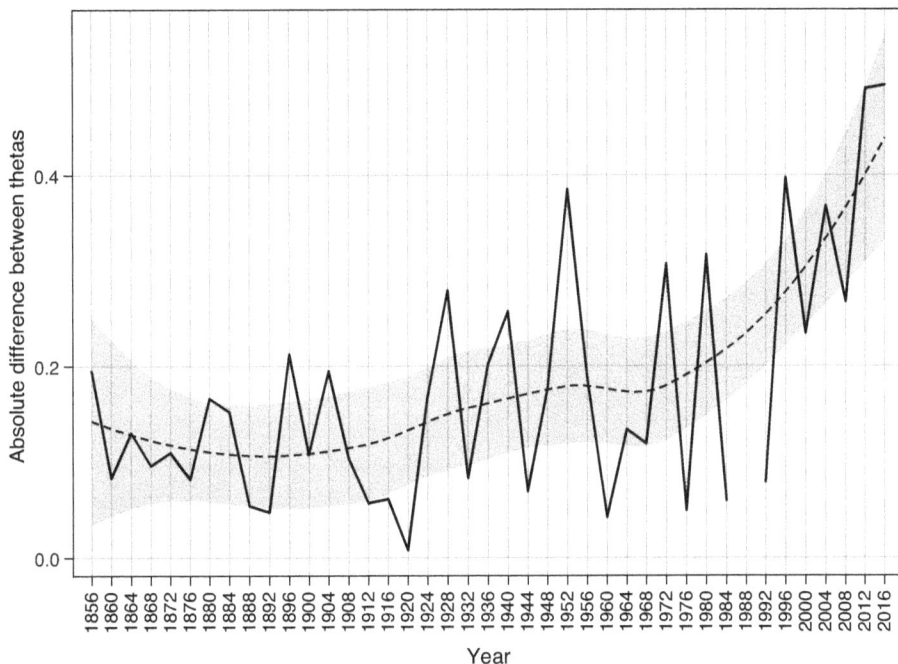

FIGURE 1.1. Programmaticism in the United States, 1856–2016.
This graph plots the difference in Wordfish estimates (thetas) for Democrats and Republicans in each year. It includes all sentences from all platforms with an STM topic probability threshold above 0.1 for at least one topic. The solid line shows raw numbers, and the dotted line is a loess curve (reflecting locally weighted regression), with a 95% confidence interval shaded in gray.

I find differences between the parties' platforms on the whole, as well as within various issue areas, over this entire period. The measure in figure 1.1 is always above zero. This is consistent with John Gerring's classic argument that parties have always displayed some ideological distinction.[37] It also squares with the notion that parties employ multiple tools to appeal to voters, and no tool is likely to be fully dominant or absent at any given time.

Programmatic differences have not been constant, however; their magnitude has varied over time. While the degree of programmaticism can vary significantly from year to year, the loess curve displays a clear trend: an initial, relatively modest increase between the turn of the twentieth century and its midpoint, a flattening or even slight decrease beginning around the 1950s, and a steep increase beginning in the late 1960s that has continued to the present.

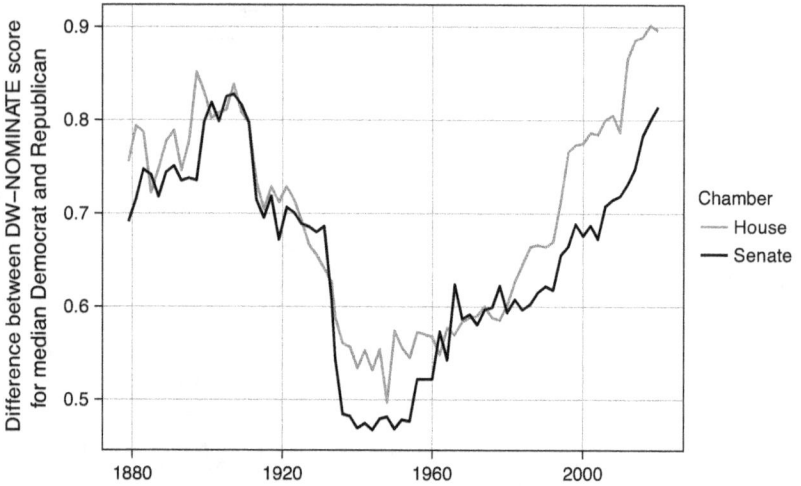

FIGURE 1.2. Polarization in the United States Congress, 1879–2020. This graph uses data from Voteview (Lewis et al. 2023) to plot the difference between the first dimension DW-NOMINATE score for the median Democrat and Republican in each chamber of Congress in each year.

This trend is interesting in its own right, and in relation to standard measures of polarization. Measured with DW-NOMINATE, as figure 1.2 shows, polarization in the United States follows an infamous U-shaped curve, with high levels in the late nineteenth and early twentieth centuries, low levels in the mid-twentieth century, and a steep increase beginning in the early 1970s.[38] Programmaticism has risen sharply, along with the difference in ideology between Democrats and Republicans in Congress, in the contemporary era. But comparing figures 1.1 and 1.2 makes clear that the field's standard measure of polarization should not be used as a proxy for programmaticism, which was not high in the late nineteenth and early twentieth centuries.

As a robustness check, I broke the data into four periods and ran separate Wordfish models on each one to make sure that the trend shown in figure 1.1 is not an artifact of changes in the meaning of words. Figure 1.3 shows that the trend remains substantially similar. There is some more undulation in the loess curves in this graph than in figure 1.1, but the steep and consistent rise in programmaticism clearly does not occur until the contemporary era. And though there is a small rise around the turn of the twentieth century, this graph still does not come close to following the U-shape of the field's standard measure of polarization.[39]

Difference between Democratic and Republican platforms

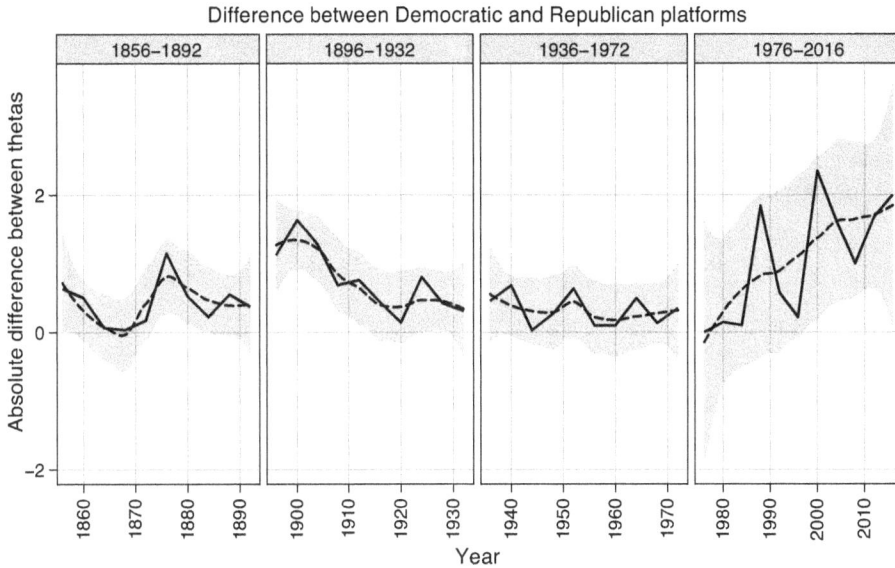

FIGURE 1.3. Programmaticism in the United States, separate models by period. This graph plots the difference in Wordfish estimates (thetas) for Democrats and Republicans in each year, with separate models for different periods. It includes all sentences from all platforms with an STM topic probability threshold above 0.1 for at least one topic. The solid line shows raw numbers, and the dotted line is a loess curve (reflecting locally weighted regression), with a 95% confidence interval shaded in gray.

Figure 1.4 plots differentiation within each issue area.[40] We can see an increase in programmaticism in the contemporary era across many important issue areas, like business and jobs, culture, energy, social welfare, and rights. In 2016, for example, the parties espoused divergent views on rights. For Democrats, rights meant those for women (including support for the Equal Rights Amendment and abortion), workers (including the right to collective bargaining), LGBT individuals (including same-sex marriage), and voters (with explicit emphasis on the importance of the Voting Rights Act and reduction of barriers to voting), and so forth. For Republicans, rights meant Second Amendment guarantees, right-to-work laws, opposition to abortion, support for traditional family values, and definition of marriage as a union between one man and one woman. A century earlier, in 1916, the parties had expressed much more general and similar views on the need to protect the rights and safety of citizens at home and abroad, as well as specific endorsement of suffrage for women through action by the states.

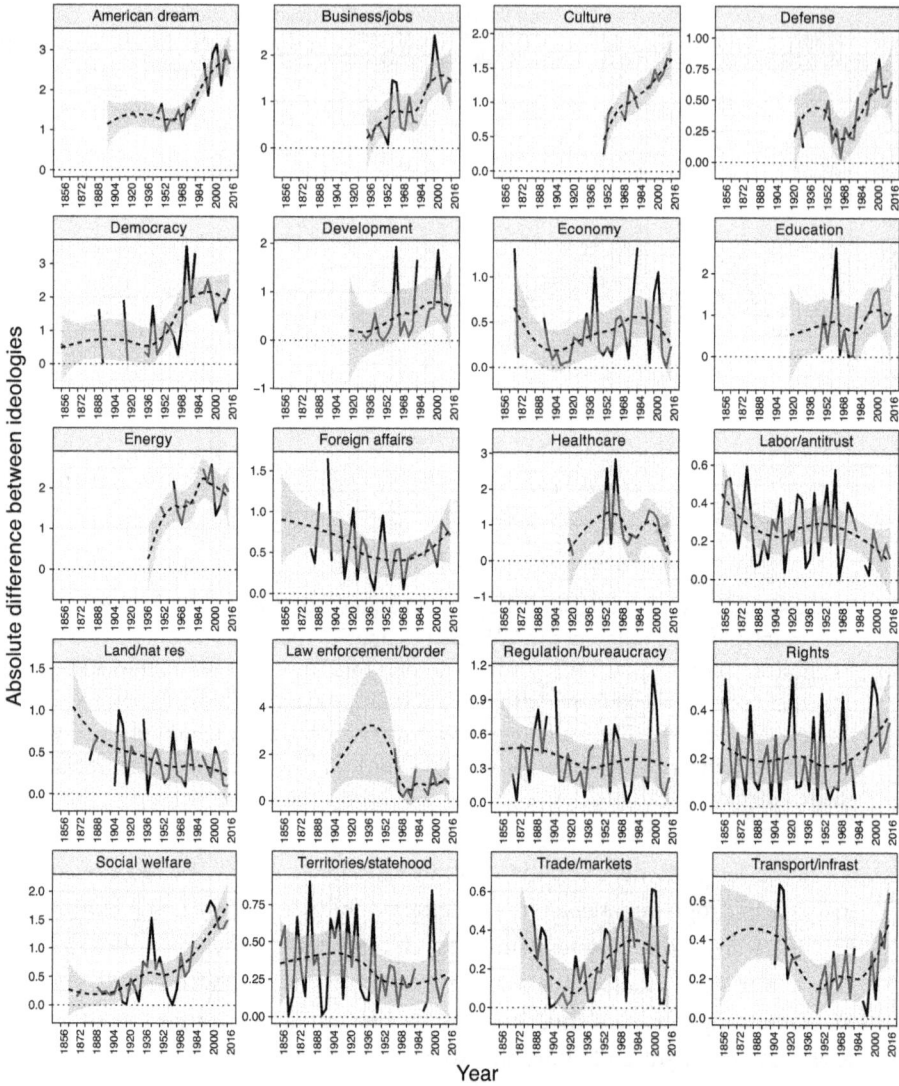

FIGURE 1.4. Programmaticism in the United States by topic, 1856–2016.
This graph plots the difference in Wordfish estimates (thetas) for Democrats and Republicans in each year by topic. All quasi-sentences with topic probability thresholds above 0.1 for the topic are included. The solid line shows raw numbers, and the dotted line is a loess curve (reflecting locally weighted regression), with a 95% confidence interval shaded in gray.

There is considerable variation across issue areas. This is noteworthy, given that the United States is considered an exemplar case of programmatic partisanship from a comparative perspective. Even in the world's most programmatic system, the parties don't differ substantially on all issues. In some cases, the timing reflects the overall trend, with the major rise beginning around the late 1960s. In other cases, the trend begins earlier. In some areas, distinctions between parties actually declined, in ways that meet expectations. For example, in land and natural resources, this decline reflects a growing settlement consensus. In labor, it reflects an increasing neoliberal consensus. The fact that variation exists across issue areas, both in the baseline level of programmaticism and in the trajectory over time, suggests that the overall estimate of programmaticism shown in figure 1.1 is not simply capturing differences in vague ideology or language style.

As we interpret these results, it's important to keep in mind that this is a measure of programmatic difference, not an absence of clientelism. Even if they have an inverse relationship, these two types of tools can and do coexist, and they are not the only instruments in parties' toolboxes. A low level of programmaticism in a given year does not necessarily indicate a high level of clientelism in that particular year.

The Puzzle of Programmatic Partisanship

This analysis sharpens the puzzle of programmaticism. Why has it risen to historic heights over the contemporary period? And why wasn't the earlier, if less dramatic, rise sustained? These questions are related; answering the second can offer valuable insight into the first. We have as much to learn from relatively low levels of programmaticism earlier in American history as from its rise in recent decades. By taking a long view, we can see not only what ultimately sparked and facilitated the steep rise of programmaticism in the contemporary era, but also what depressed attention and squelched attempts to increase it earlier.

A long-term study of the United States is also well positioned to contribute to American and comparative literatures, given what we know about programmaticism's relationship to development. Figure 1.5 plots GDP per capita at purchasing power parity (PPP) in 2008 against a DALP cross-national measure of programmaticism from 2008 to 2009.[41] The dashed line shows the

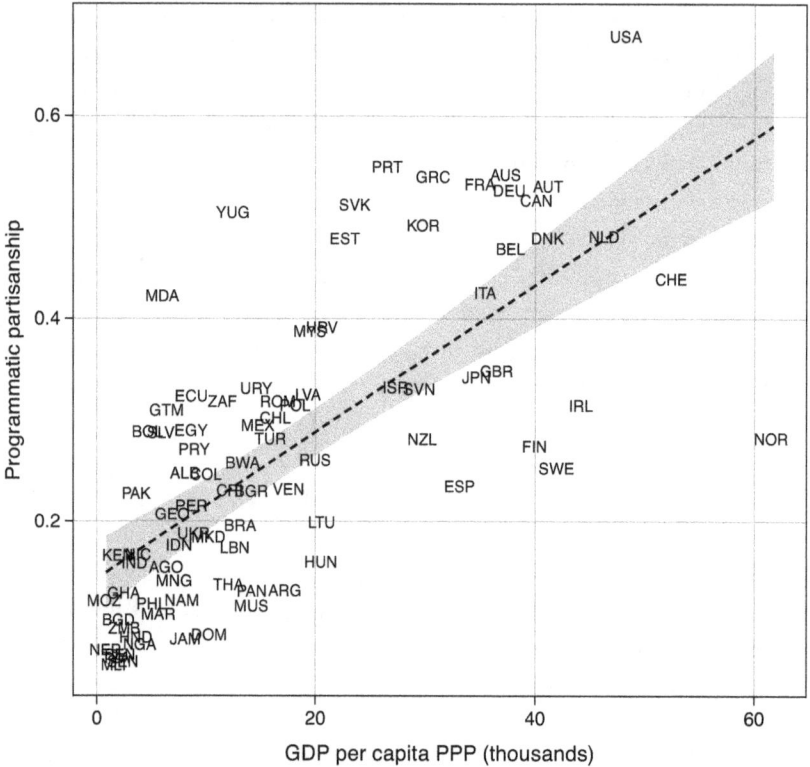

FIGURE 1.5. Economic development and programmatic partisanship.
The measure of programmatic partisanship comes from the Democratic Accountability and Linkages Project (DALP), and GDP data come from the World Bank.
The dashed line shows the linear relationship with a 95% confidence interval
shaded in gray (adjusted r-squared = 0.49, $N = 88$). A similar graph appears as
figure 2.1 in Kitschelt and Wang (2014).

linear relationship, which is strong and positive: more affluent nations (e.g.,
the United States in the top right corner) tend to have more programmatic
parties than do poorer nations.[42]

The United States stands out as an interesting case in this regard. While it
is far above the line in figure 1.5, indicating higher levels of programmaticism
than its wealth would predict, my measure of programmaticism shows that it
did not begin its steep rise until the late 1960s, well after it had achieved a relatively high level of economic development. This further deepens the puzzle,
as it suggests that the United States has been both a "late bloomer" and an
"overachiever" in its programmatic development. Why?

Book Structure and Central Contributions

This book offers fresh perspective on the puzzle of programmatic partisanship. Much of the existing literature on issue-based competition has been cross-national, focusing especially on new democracies and developing nations in the contemporary era. We can gain new insight into this subject by examining a single case over a long period, following American parties as the nation grew from a relatively new, embattled democracy with an industrializing economy and largely clientelistic parties to an advanced postindustrial democracy with the most programmatic party system in the world.

In doing so, my analysis centers on party organizations, as there has been far more research on issue differentiation in the electorate and Congress.[43] This choice may raise questions among American politics scholars accustomed to the subfield's conventionally dismissive attitude toward party organizations. It is clear from work by comparative scholars, however, that programmaticism bears an important relationship to clientelism, which was historically carried out in the United States primarily by local party organizations (e.g., the Curley machine in Boston) at a time when the national party organizations (the Democratic and Republican National Committees, or DNC and RNC) were relatively meager and inactive.

Moreover, party organizations serve as custodians of the official encyclopedic statements of party positions: the platforms. This renders them particularly interesting in the study of programmaticism. And while the national committees may lack traditional sources of power, they play an important organizational role in the process of position development. Other institutions, like Congress, enter the narrative at various points, as there has been some cooperation and complementarity across institutions. But the book centers primarily on party organizations. Future work can and should examine the rise of programmaticism from other angles, as such a complex phenomenon is inevitably multicausal.

Chapter 2 offers a theory of programmatic partisanship in the United States, building on a foundation of important work predominantly by comparative scholars on modes of appealing to voters. My theory contributes to existing knowledge by focusing specifically on factors facilitating the development of programmaticism. Perhaps because programmaticism has long been treated as a foil for clientelism, work on the former tends to focus on explaining the decline of the latter. Evidence indicates that the two linkage types do, indeed, have an inverse relationship.[44] Thus, in considering factors that

influence the growth of programmaticism, it makes sense to pay careful attention to factors leading to a reduction of clientelism. The negative association
between these two linkage types, however, is far from perfect.[45] The decline
of clientelism does not guarantee the rise of programmaticism. To understand
the latter, we need explicit theories thereof.

Didi Kuo (2018) provides a strong foundation on this front in her study
of shifts toward programmaticism in the United States and Britain in the late
nineteenth century, emphasizing the role of capitalists in demanding both reliable policy and an increase in bureaucratic capacity necessary for policy implementation. Others have also noted that a certain degree of political development, including but not limited to bureaucratic professionalization, is needed
for programmatic appeals to be credible to voters.[46] But this argument is typically presented as a reason clientelism develops or endures, rather than as
part of a theory of programmaticism in particular. Moreover, these studies—
including Kuo's—focus on institutions facilitating policy implementation.
While this is certainly important, it leaves a vital aspect of programmaticism
uncovered: factors influencing parties' ability to develop policy positions in
the first place. Institutions designed for implementation will not necessarily
be helpful for the task of position development.

To understand the steep and sustained growth of programmaticism in the
contempoary era, we need a theory that covers position development. My
argument is rooted in the notion that developing party positions across a wide
range of issues is labor-intensive and risky. In a large, diverse nation with
a complex economy and only two major parties, inevitable contradictions
arise between the preferences of different coalition subgroups. Parties may
not even be sure of the ideal position with respect to each group. There
is no crystal ball for this—the party needs to gather and weigh information to figure it out. Even after parties do this work, announcing issue positions can cause intractable problems. Unlike organizations relying primarily on material incentives (e.g., distributing jobs, benefits, etc.), which can
"divide the dollar" between members, organizations running on "purposive"
(i.e., nonmaterial, goal-oriented) incentives face more constraints in resolving
internal conflicts.[47]

Developing a party program is hard. Parties have criticized each other for
policy actions (and inactions) since the dawn of the republic, but that is not
the same as putting together a set of policy stances underpinning the party. As
former Speaker of the House Sam Rayburn was known to say, "Remember,
any jackass can kick over a barn door. It takes a carpenter to build one."[48]

He was not talking about developing a party program, but the sentiment still applies.

Institutions are needed to facilitate this process. I focus specifically on party organizations, which can both hinder and help the process of position development. Drawing on comparative work showing an inverse relationship between clientelism and programmaticism, I argue that sustained programmaticism was unlikely to arise while local party machines remained strong in the United States. Machines would have reason to resist a shift toward programmaticism. Moreover, I argue that programmaticism will tend not to be a first-line tool for parties. They could, in theory, attempt to fire on all cylinders; but this is unlikely to happen in practice, given the challenges and risks involved in party position development. So long as they are able to rely on another strategy (e.g., clientelism), parties will tend not to turn in full force to programmatic tools. Thus, I theorize that local party machines constrained the development of programmaticism in the United States, even as it experienced economic development that would have predicted a turn toward issue-based competition.

Yet, party organizations can also have the opposite effect. I argue that national party institutions, which were weak until the second half of the twentieth century, ultimately played an important role in promoting programmaticism. Some degree of policy differentiation may arise naturally; at least some politicians, after all, are thought to be drawn to office to affect policy, and groups of like-minded politicians may be drawn to the same party. Such organic party position development has limits, however. Differentiation across a wide range of issues requires institutions for gathering information about policies and groups' preferences, as well as for resolving conflicts. This imperative only intensifies as a nation becomes larger and more complex, with more issues facing the federal government. In this sense, programmaticism is a moving target; it will tend to become more challenging as the state develops and widens its scope. This helps explain why the initial growth of programmaticism, discussed by Kuo (2018) and shown in figure 1.1, was not sustained.

The growth of national party institutions for policy development during the mid- to late twentieth century provided an important foundation for the steep rise of programmaticism seen in the contemporary era. They may not be as powerful as some parties in other nations, and their strength and autonomy may be underwhelming in some respects—provoking a characterization of "hollowness" from prominent party scholars Daniel Schlozman and Sam

Rosenfeld—but their growth over time remains notable and impactful.[49] The barebones national organizations of the nineteenth and early twentieth centuries, with their lack of stable staff and tendency to disband between elections, could not have made the critical contributions to issue position development that the stronger and more professionalized DNC and RNC would offer later.

To recap, I have argued thus far that (1) theories of clientelism's decline are useful for understanding variation in programmaticism but cannot substitute for explicit theories of the latter; and (2) additional work on programmaticism is needed to cover the challenge of position development. Further study is also needed because existing theories relating to the United States have not sufficiently considered the role of *racial orders*, a term coined by Desmond King and Rogers Smith (2005), in the history of programmaticism. Since the founding of the United States, two orders—sets of institutions, organizations, and people—have been wrestling for control of the nation's present and future: a *white supremacist* order and an *egalitarian transformative* order. Although the specific institutions and actors may have changed, and some have even switched sides over time, the orders have been omnipresent and have shaped almost all aspects of our nation's politics in some way. Thus, King and Smith (2005) argue that nearly all studies of American politics should consider the role of racial orders. This imperative seems especially relevant to understanding something so fundamental to the nature of electoral competition as programmatic partisanship.

I argue that racial orders have shaped the trajectory of programmaticism in at least two important ways. First, they extended the life of nonprogrammatic practices. Major New Deal programs were tailored to the preferences of southern lawmakers, key players in the white supremacist order.[50] Among the mechanisms allowing these programs to discriminate against African Americans was the decentralization of program implementation, so that local bureaucrats and private firms committed to white supremacy could use the discretion afforded to them to direct benefits from New Deal programs primarily toward whites. While these policy design features were meant to exclude African Americans, they also rendered benefits from New Deal programs more vulnerable to nonprogrammatic distribution, under Stokes et al.'s (2013) criteria, than they would have been otherwise.

More broadly, I argue that the white supremacist order long depressed support for the very notion of programmaticism. Parties and their responsibilities are not described in the Constitution. This deliberate omission, rather than squelching impulses for their rise as the founders had hoped, instead facilitated centuries of disagreement about what exactly parties are and what they should be doing. Academics are not the only ones who have faced this challenge—proponents of programmaticism also had to contend with the question of whether taking positions across a wide range of issues constituted behavior befitting parties.[51] Those benefiting from the white supremacist order had strong reasons to resist this interpretation of parties' purpose.

Programmaticism bestows power in party leaders to manage party position development. While this may sometimes amount to a service, when high stakes issues fundamental to democratic functioning—like major franchise restrictions—remain substantially unresolved within parties and the broader polity, it can feel threatening to some party members. In the United States, southern lawmakers were likely to oppose the very notion of programmaticism so long as Jim Crow laws buttressing white supremacy were the status quo. Such contentious conditions would make programmaticism difficult to cultivate; party positions are more like orchids than weeds. With the passage of the Civil Rights Act of 1964 and Voting Rights Act of 1965, the stakes of programmaticism changed substantially, opening space for programmaticism to develop.

My theory helps explain why programmaticism rose sharply beginning in the late 1960s, after the civil rights revolution and substantial fizzling of political machines. It also addresses some of the nuances of the puzzle of programmaticism, such as why its earlier rise was limited and unsustainable, and why its more significant, steady rise occurred well after the nation's level of economic development would predict. In this light, it is not surprising that the modern rise has been sharp—there was a great deal of pent-up demand.

Chapter 3 analyzes the relationship between clientelism and programmaticism in the United States over time, showing how and why the former endured for so long and hindered the latter's growth. Chapters 4 and 5 trace the history of programmaticism through the lens of party organizations, examining the theory I outline in chapter 2 and learning inductively from the process of reading primary materials from 1856 to the present. This illuminates not only who and what ultimately facilitated programmaticism's contemporary rise, but also who and what hindered earlier attempts to increase it. I trace the history of when and how parties increased their emphasis on position development, how and why the process for position development became more advanced and institutionalized over time, and who pushed and who resisted these efforts and why, drawing on transcripts of Democratic and Republican

National Conventions and party committee meetings, oral histories, archival materials collected at various presidential libraries, historical newspapers, and secondary sources.

This book's uncommon but complementary mix of methodologies reveals systematic patterns in party attention to issue development and differentiation on matters of policy, as well as important factors that constrained and facilitated the growth of programmaticism in the United States over time. It also elucidates important institutional roots of the distinct but related phenomenon of political polarization. Remarkably, a large literature on the origins of contemporary polarization has developed with almost no attention to the fact that the United States transitioned toward a different type of party system over time. By examining the rise of alternative party positions and changes in the process by which they were created, this book offers new insights— from an institutional perspective—into a trend that's generally considered ideological.

More specifically, it contributes to the way in which we think about the role of racial politics in facilitating polarization. The realignment of the South after the civil rights revolution is an oft-cited factor in the rise of polarization, as the Democratic Party lost its conservative contingent, and southerners made Republicans even more conservative.[52] This rather mechanical explanation for polarization misses a critical way in which racial orders contributed to its trajectory. The white supremacist order did not just oppose civil rights for African Americans and eventually abandon the party that adopted and effectuated a pro–civil rights stance—its steadfast commitment to preserving Jim Crow laws long constrained acceptance of the notion of programmaticism more broadly. This is a sobering example of the ways in which racial orders can powerfully shape the nation's politics well beyond the scope of what we might consider "racial issues."

After the fall of Jim Crow laws, racial politics would continue to shape issue-based competition. The parties became more distinct on issues surrounding the rights of Black Americans, turning these issues into fuel for programmaticism in some respects, raising questions about boundary conditions for this style of party competition in a liberal democracy. Institutions and agents of racial oppression also retained the power to disrupt programmatic competition. When civil rights have become very salient, there are instances when Democrats and Republicans have each taken steps back from programmaticism.

In addition to contributing to our understanding of polarization and racial politics, this book also intervenes in a high-profile debate among American politics scholars about the very nature of parties: are they, as in the traditional view, coalitions of office seekers or coalitions of policy-demanding groups, as argued by a new "group-centered" theory of parties? Rather than choose between these options, I argue that we need to move toward a more dynamic conceptualization of parties.

Toward a More Dynamic Conceptualization of Parties

Traditionally, parties were thought to be coalitions of office seekers. V. O. Key (1942) famously complicated this view by breaking the monolith into three distinct but interconnected pieces: parties in government, parties as organizations, and parties in the electorate. Parties are not one-dimensional entities whose operations we can observe on one plane, he argued; to fully understand them, we need to analyze all three dimensions. In John Aldrich's classic 1994 book *Why Parties?*, he refines this framework, replacing parties in the electorate with parties in elections, arguing—as had Schattschneider (1942) before him—that parties in the electorate are better conceived as consumers of party messages than as components of parties. Either way, this framework encourages us to think of elite-level parties as collections of individuals aiming to win office and govern in a way that maximizes their ability to win office in the future, as well as institutions built in this pursuit.

Over the past decade or so, a fresh view of parties has risen to prominence. This group-centered theory (also known as the UCLA school) argues that political science has been guided, or rather misguided, by a distorted characterization of parties. Political parties are not simply teams of ambitious office seekers, as scholars have typically portrayed them; rather, parties "are best understood as coalitions of interest groups and activists seeking to capture and use government for their particular goals, which range from material self-interest to high-minded idealism."[53] This coalition develops a party program reflecting the wishes of its policy-demanding members and works, usually successfully, to ensure the nomination of candidates who will adhere thereto. Bawn et al. (2012) refer to this theory of parties as "group-centric." It is more than this, however. Policy-demanding interest groups are not merely important to parties in this view; they are inherent. They compose parties.

What the UCLA school describes is a conceptual fusion of parties and interest groups.

This school of thought has taken a major step forward in advancing scholarly and popular discourse on parties by shedding new light on the critical role of interest groups in contemporary party politics.[54] And yet, there is reason for caution in pushing forth at full speed with the school's conception of parties as coalitions of policy-demanding groups. The closeness of group-party relationships varies a great deal over time and even at particular historical moments—too much, I have argued, to justify breaking down the conceptual wall between parties and groups.[55] The overlap between them is something we should measure empirically, not assume theoretically.

Of course, if I am to insist on defining parties and groups separately, I must face the question of how to distinguish between them. In contrast to parties, interest groups are traditionally thought to be focused on achieving particular policy outcomes. Schattschneider defines special interests in contrast to common interests, as the former are "shared by only a few people or a fraction of the community; they exclude others and may be adverse to them."[56] When people with shared characteristics or values endeavor to enact new policies or preserve existing policies serving their common interests, they become *interest groups* in the political sense. Thus, two features distinguish parties from groups: their goals and their scope. Parties are concerned primarily with winning elections, while groups are concerned primarily with policy outcomes. And groups are relatively homogenous, while parties bring many interests together. Parties must do so in order to build winning coalitions in elections.

In the most widely cited articulation of group-centered theory, *The Party Decides*, Marty Cohen, David Karol, Hans Noel, and John Zaller point to Schattschneider as the UCLA school's closest ancestor. While they do share the notion that groups are "the raw material of politics," they depart sharply in their vision of group-party fusion.[57] Schattschneider spent much of his career championing parties, arguing in his classic *Party Government* (1942) that strong parties were essential for democracy and cautioning against interest group power. Since parties must mobilize broad majorities, while groups guard unrepresentative minorities and "[sing] with a strong upper-class accent," group power ultimately hurts the populace.[58] Not only did he see parties and groups as distinct types of institutions, he argued that they had an inverse relationship. He even went so far as to say "pressure groups thrive on the weaknesses of the parties."[59] This concern undergirds *Party Government* and the 1950 report by the APSA Committee on Political Parties, which he chaired.

Other leading scholars of the mid-twentieth century, like David Truman (1951) and V. O. Key (1942), distinguished clearly between parties and groups. At this time they argued that groups and parties generally avoided close relationships. The alliance between organized labor and the Democratic Party was an obvious exception; but even the leading scholar of this partnership, J. David Greenstone (1969), argued that it was unusual for the period. In this context of group bipartisanship, the traditional distinction between parties and groups in terms of goals and scope is quite straightforward.

The growth of programmaticism complicates matters and cautions against rigid conceptualization of parties in either direction. As parties increasingly use policy positions as a means of electoral competition, distinguishing them from groups based on goals becomes more difficult. In other words, programmaticism leads parties to appear less traditional and more like the UCLA school's conceptualization of parties. Just as Matt Grossmann and David Hopkins (2016) argue that we should not assume symmetry between Republicans and Democrats, so too should we avoid assuming that parties at time 1 are the same kinds of creatures that they are at time 2.[60] A careful study of programmaticism can affect how we think about not only what parties *do*, but also what they *are*.

To be clear, I maintain a distinction between parties and groups throughout the book. While the line between parties and groups may soften with the growth of programmaticism, it does not dissolve. It is still possible to identify organizations and people using the party label (e.g., the Democratic and Republican National Committees, members of Congress, etc.), and organizations and people using group labels (e.g., the National Rifle Association and its president). These labels retain meaning, even in a period of high programmaticism, to their members and from an academic perspective. Parties remain, on average, broader in scope and driven more by reelection than policy, relative to groups.

Nonetheless, this distinction is not fixed. Rather than trying to adjudicate between the traditional view of parties and the new group-centered theory, it will be more productive to put these two schools of thought on opposite ends of a continuum and think about parties' positions on that continuum at different times. This will help us move toward a more dynamic conceptualization of parties.

Divergent Democracy up Close and in Context

The United States has not received much attention in existing scholarship on programmaticism, and programmaticism has not received much attention from scholars of American politics. The study of programmaticism in the United States can shed new light on the growth of polarization, one of the most important and highly discussed subjects of our time, and on our conceptualization of parties. And an in-depth case study of the United States over time can help us better understand the relationship between development and programmaticism more broadly.

A richer and more nuanced understanding of programmaticism can also help us better evaluate governing systems, particularly the state of divergent democracy we see in the United States today. Programmaticism is often treated as a measure of progress for a party system. It is thought to be important for representation, facilitating accountability, as argued in APSA's 1950 report and in more recent work in comparative politics.[61] Programmaticism increases incentives to provide public goods and is generally associated with "more efficient policymaking and greater levels of social legitimacy."[62]

Although programmatic systems tend to be associated with higher quality democracies than clientelistic systems, on average, scholars have cautioned against overgeneralization on this front.[63] Moreover, I argue, it is possible that the best outcomes may be achieved at a level of programmaticism short of the maximum. Divergent democracy can go too far. We should treat programmaticism as a macropolitical indicator to monitor the health of democratic systems, as discussed in more detail in chapter 6. As with macroeconomic indicators, like unemployment, it can be too high or too low. Identifying the healthy range for programmaticism is beyond the scope of this book; indeed, it is the project of a literature rather than any one study. But precise conceptualization and measurement over time are important steps in this direction.

2

What Constrains and Facilitates Programmaticism?

THE STUDY of programmatic partisanship is both old and new. As a concept, it has long been recognized. Attention to clientelism, one of its primary alternatives, goes back decades. This work engages the notion of programmatic partisanship, if largely as a foil. Mid-twentieth-century work on responsible party government discussed the concept of programmatic partisanship more directly, if not by this name. But our understanding of why parties shift toward programmaticm remains inchoate. Existing scholarship has provided some clues and, to a more limited extent, some answers to the question of what constrained and facilitated programmatic partisanship in the United States over time, but additional work is required. In particular, we need to better understand what influences parties' ability to develop the kinds of alternative policy positions that are central to programmaticism. This is the focus of my theory, to be detailed in this chapter.

First, though, we should consider what we *do* know, beginning with foundational research on the inverse relationship between clientelism and programmaticism documented by comparative politics scholars.

Programmaticism and Clientelism

The relationship between programmaticism and clientelism is often treated as a conceptual matter: clientelistic politics are not programmatic, and vice versa. In the words of Cheeseman and Paget (2014), leading scholars in this area, "programmatic politics is the antithesis of clientelistic politics." Clientelism has even been operationalized by low levels of programmaticism.[1]

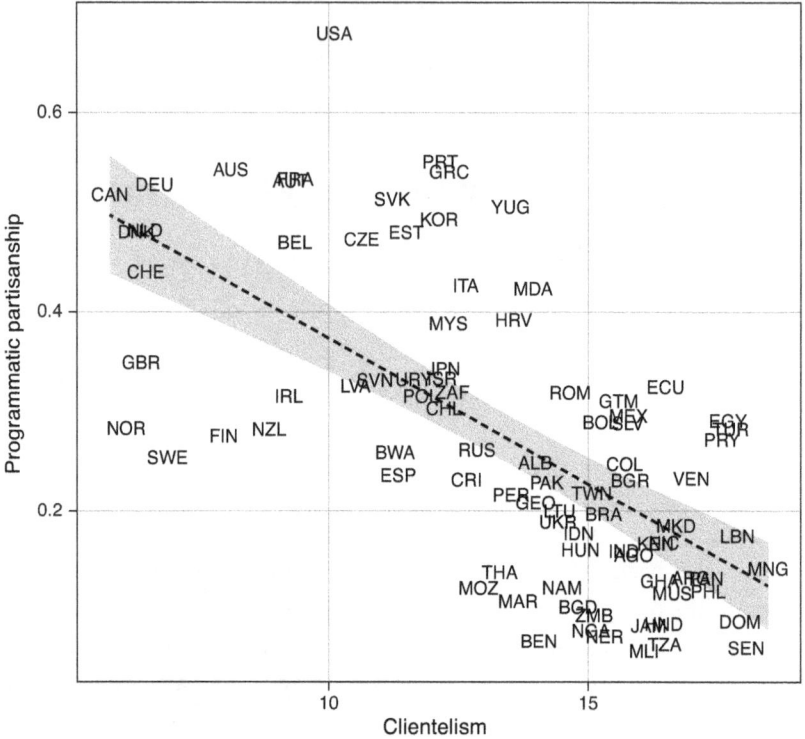

FIGURE 2.1. Clientelism and programmatic partisanship.
The measures of programmatic partisanship and clientelism come from the
DALP. The dashed line shows the linear relationship, with a 95% confidence
interval shaded in gray (adjusted r-squared = 0.43, $N = 88$). This relationship is
statistically significant at the 0.001 level ($t = -8.16$).

There are good reasons for this. From a technical standpoint, clientelism
is notoriously difficult to measure, so a proxy is often necessary. From a normative standpoint, programmaticism has long been considered a measure
of progress for a party system, a sign of maturity, and clientelism has long
been considered the opposite. And from an empirical standpoint, looking
cross-nationally, these two types of appeals have an inverse relationship.[2]

Figure 2.1 illustrates this negative association, using data from the Democratic Accountability and Linkages Project (DALP) from 2008 to 2009.[3] The
dashed line shows the linear relationship, which is statistically significant at
the 0.001 level, with a 95 percent confidence interval shaded in gray. The
United States (in the top left quadrant) exhibits a moderately low level of
clientelism relative to other nations, and the highest level of programmaticism

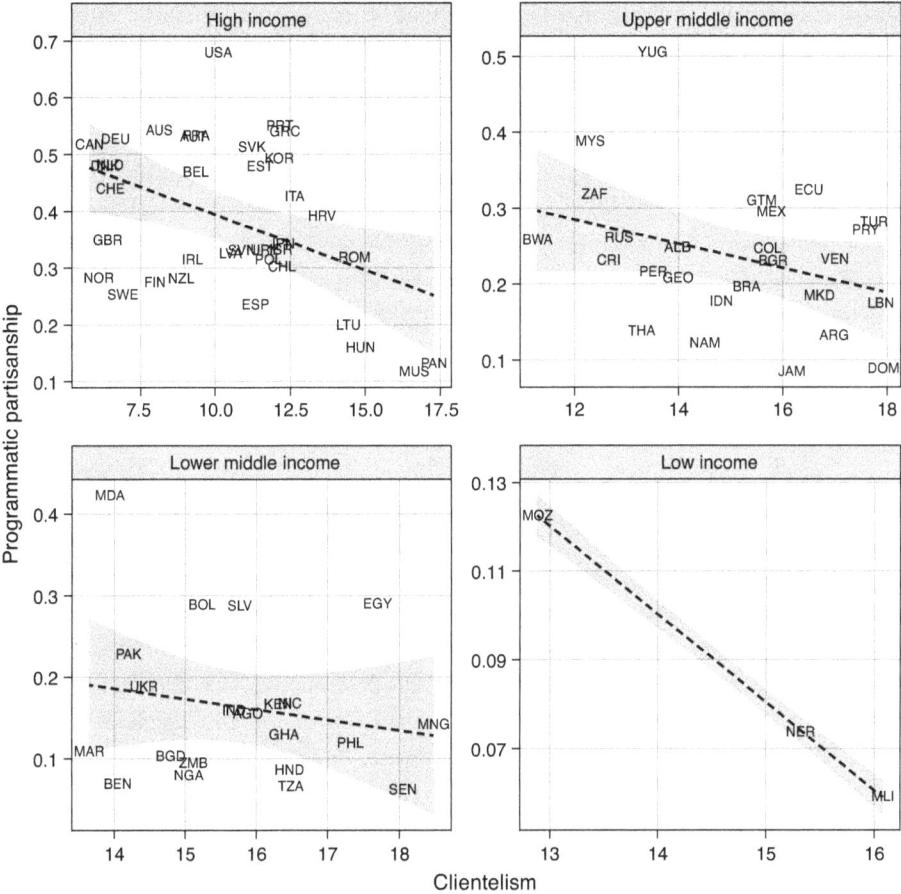

FIGURE 2.2. Clientelism and programmatic partisanship, by income group. The measures of programmatic partisanship and clientelism come from the DALP, and GDP data come from the World Bank. The dashed line shows the linear relationship, with a 95% confidence interval shaded in gray.

in the world. The negative correlation between clientelism and programmaticism remains significant even if we focus only on high income nations like the United States, as shown in figure 2.2, which replicates figure 2.1 for economic subgroups using 2008 data from the World Bank. For the high income group, the relationship is statistically significant at the 0.05 level.[4] This cross-national evidence is bolstered by case studies of countries with high levels of clientelism and low levels of programmaticism (e.g., the Dominican Republic, India) and countries in which parties became more programmatic over time as clientelism declined (e.g., Brazil, South Korea, Ukraine, Zambia).[5]

The inverse association is not perfect, of course. Scholars widely acknowledge that no country relies completely on one type of appeal to voters. All countries in figure 2.1 display some degree of clientelism, whatever their level of programmatic partisanship. (In fact, the scale for clientelism doesn't even start at o for this graph because there are no cases between o and 5.) And many countries show moderate levels of clientelism and programmaticism (e.g., those around the center of the graph). Finally, there are different types of clientelism and various definitions of both clientelism and programmaticism, complicating broad generalizations about their relationship.[6]

Nonetheless, the evidence for a negative association between these two types of appeals is strong and robust enough to be relevant to any study of programmaticism. Cross-national evidence suggests that the relationship is especially pronounced in countries with high levels of clientelism. The top-right quadrant of figure 2.1 is sparsely populated, and many countries are clustered in the bottom right corner. No country in the DALP dataset exhibits high levels of programmaticism and clientelism.

For my purposes, this suggests that programmaticism was unlikely to develop under the clientelistic style that long dominated U.S. party politics through institutions like the Jacksonian spoils system and political machines (e.g., Tammany Hall). This notion is stated more succinctly in the clientelism constraint hypothesis. Research on American clientelistic institutions indicates that they shared many of the same properties and tactics as those in other nations, so there is little reason to believe that the United States would be exceptional.[7]

Clientelism Constraint Hypothesis: *Clientelism long constrained the growth of programmaticism in the United States.*

Path dependence, in multiple forms, can help explain this dynamic between clientelism and programmaticism in the United States. The core of the clientelism constraint hypothesis suggests an inverse relationship over time between these two modes of appealing to voters. It also acknowledges clientelism's durability in the United States. This part of the clientelism constraint hypothesis is axiomatic; it's not really falsifiable given that we know clientelism lasted for a long time in the United States. Nonetheless, if we want to understand programmaticism's trajectory over time, it would behoove us to consider not only why clientelism and programmaticism have an inverse relationship, but also why the former lasted for so long.

To begin, I argue that clientelism involves *increasing returns*, the signature feature of the economic model of path dependence. Once an institution starts down a particular path, positive feedback mechanisms can make it difficult to switch courses even if the initial push down that path was arbitrary or the conditions affecting the decision to move in that direction fade. This can lead to puzzling and often suboptimal outcomes. Patronage networks have all four characteristics that make an institution likely to confer increasing returns: "large set-up or fixed costs," "learning effects," "coordination effects," and "adaptive expectations."[8] Though patronage networks may have a reputation for unearned might, they are still costly and complicated to establish.[9] Once created, political actors grow accustomed to working with them, more people are incentivized to use them as they grow more popular, and many worry about losing out on benefits if they risk trying another system (i.e., one based on purposive incentives). These incentives apply to both politicians and voters. Together they "adapt their strategies in ways that reflect but also reinforce the 'logic' of the system."[10] Moreover, those in power can use their positions to reinforce the system that facilitated their rise.

Path dependence can also help explain why the system shifted away from clientelism. Mechanisms of reproduction and positive feedback in path-dependent processes offer clues regarding the circumstances under which change can occur, specifically when the mechanisms are disrupted. Path dependence can "also lend insight into the distinctive ways that different countries are affected by putatively common international forces and trends."[11] These forces may impact the mechanisms of reproduction in some places at some times and not others.

In addition to the economic model of path dependence, made prominent in political science by Paul Pierson (2000a), the sociological model can also help explain the relationship between clientelism and programmaticism in the United States over time. Here, institutions are thought to be grounded in society rather than in the behavior of individuals and firms, as in the economic model. Kathleen Thelen (1999, 386) explains:

Institutions . . . are socially constructed in the sense that they embody shared cultural understandings ("shared cognitions", "interpretive frame") of the way the world works. . . . This means that even when policy makers set out to redesign institutions, they are constrained in what they can conceive of by these embedded, cultural constraints.

Clientelism is both a political and a social phenomenon, as it's premised on personal relationships between politicians and voters or sometimes community leaders. In a clientelistic system, politicians are not simply representing their constituents in an abstract or aggregate manner that we may think about today—machine operatives engaged in one-on-one conversations and exchanges with voters. This allows for the development of *shared cognitions* about politics. Moreover, because machines tended to build coalitions of working-class and new immigrant communities—people who had not traditionally been close to the political system—they were particularly likely to wield cultural power over their constituents. They were, after all, key agents of political socialization for these communities.

Thus far, I have focused mostly on clientelism's durability, for which the notions of *increasing returns* and *shared cognitions* are helpful. To understand the inverse relationship between clientelism and programmaticism, we can turn to another concept associated with path dependence: *political space*. Put simply, material incentives left limited room for issues to matter in political competition. Once a space is occupied by certain actors, it is difficult for others to enter. Surveying work on political space and its role in path-dependent processes, Pierson (2000b) notes that "actors arriving later may find that resources in the environment (for example, potential supporters) are already committed to other patterns of mobilization" (81). This phenomenon confers a significant first-mover advantage, which helps explain why some groups and institutions are more powerful than one might otherwise expect. I am invoking the notion of political space in a slightly different way. My argument is not about *who* mobilizes voters, but about *how* they do so. Once a party has an effective set of tools for mobilizing a winning coalition of voters, they have limited incentives to invest heavily in others.[12] And they are especially unlikely to employ a tool like programmaticism that involves large upfront costs and carries new risks.

Mona Lyne (2007) observed this "crowding out" dynamic in a study of Brazil from 1945 to 2002. "When voters opt for a quid pro quo," she argues, "they necessarily forgo their ability to pass judgment on overall policy." Movement away from "direct exchange" can unlock new possibilities, even if clientelism endures at lower levels and in subtler forms.[13] Indeed, "[e]ven when voters heavily weight the delivery of non-excludable locally targeted goods (often labeled pork or particularism), they do not relinquish the possibility of also looking at overall outcomes in making their choices."[14] Clientelistic practices can still constrain the growth of programmaticism to some degree under such circumstances, but they are not prohibitive.

Just because a decline of clientelism—especially the quid pro quo variety—opens space for programmaticism to rise does not mean it will, of course. In figure 2.1, there is much more dispersion around the line when clientelism is low than when it is high. In other words, programmaticism is usually low in countries with high levels of clientelism, but there is more variation in programmaticism when levels of clientelism are low.[15]

In sum, it is clear that in addressing the question of why programmaticism has varied in the United States, we should pay attention to explanations for changes to the level and nature of clientelism. To understand programmaticism, however, we cannot rely entirely on theories of clientelism. Although the decline of clientelism may open political space for issues to matter in electoral competition, it does not guarantee that programmaticism will rise. We need to think explicitly about programmaticism.

We can begin by considering existing theories, drawn mostly from comparative politics literature. This work often differentiates between the *demand side* and *supply side* of these tools. In other words, what makes people more accepting or even demanding of clientelistic goods and services in exchange for votes, and what makes parties more or less able to deliver them? What increases demand for public policy, raising the importance of policy positions in electoral politics, and what affects parties' ability to deliver policies and positions thereon? Thus far, existing literature has primarily provided insight into factors that influence clientelism and the demand side of programmaticism, leaving a need for more work on the supply side of programmaticism. My theory's most significant contribution lies in this area.

Modernization as an Explanation for Programmaticism

It has long been thought that modernization—economic growth and attendant phenomena like urbanization and education—would lead countries away from clientelism and toward programmaticism. Researchers have examined various aspects of development and found meaningful relationships with party appeals.

Economic Growth and Change

The theory that economic growth facilitates movement toward issue-based party competition clearly has some credence.[16] As noted in this book's first chapter, there is a strong and positive correlation between economic development and programmatic partisanship (see figure 1.5). This relationship holds even after accounting for many other features of nations, such as democratic experience, population, and regime stability. There is also a strong, positive relationship between GNP and programmaticism at the party level, controlling for many factors, including incumbent status, party size, and authoritarian legacy.[17]

This pattern is unsurprising given the long-established relationship between clientelism and poverty.[18] At low levels of economic development, demand or at least tolerance for clientelism is higher among the populace. Clientelistic benefits—goods and services that are generally modest in monetary value, public sector jobs, and so forth—are more appealing to lower income voters than to higher income voters. There is, in more technical terms, a diminishing marginal utility of income.[19] This dynamic has been noted by scholars studying various nations, including Japan, Brazil, Mexico, and Argentina. Poorer voters are also thought to be more risk-averse, preferring the certainty of clientelistic benefits to the possibility of policy benefits.[20]

Given that higher income people tend to be more numerous in higher income nations, development can change the balance of demand for clientelism and programmaticism among the populace. Higher income voters are more likely to privilege public goods over clientelistic benefits, enjoy the experience of voting for a party they feel aligns with their preferences, and place more value on living in a higher quality democracy with less corruption associated with clientelistic exchange.[21]

This helps explain why responding to rising incomes by offering more valuable clientelistic benefits tends not to be a successful strategy for parties. With a fixed pool of available resources, there is a trade-off between provision of clientelistic and public goods. Increasing benefits can also make clientelism prohibitively expensive, creating intolerable levels of public debt and straining a nation's economy. Under these circumstances, resistance to clientelism tends to rise from middle-class and wealthy citizens, business elites, and even parties themselves.[22]

Demand for programmaticism can arise not only from higher income people, but also from the context of economic development. The move toward industrialization created new problems, like managing sanitation and public health in urban areas, which raised demand for policy responses.[23] People also "realize that sophisticated economies need general policies that permit the infusion of public and large-scale club goods such as infrastructure, education or health care" and may also see the need for politicians to manage an advanced economy, heightening demand for macroeconomic policy.[24] Thus, economic development can increase pressure on parties to engage in programmatic competition.[25]

Certain types of business innovations can also facilitate programmaticism. In an interesting contribution to our thinking about clientelism versus programmaticism, Lyne (2007) and Magaloni, Diaz-Cayeros, and Estévez (2007) argue that voters face a collective action problem: they might all be better off under governance by a programmatic party, but they worry that if they support the programmatic party while most others support the clientelistic party, they will lose out on all benefits. This can give clientelism an especially strong grip on a party system. Clientelism has a weakness, however, in that it is essentially a zero-sum game (i.e., a job I give to one person I cannot give to another). With certain innovations, industries can experience economic growth that is not zero-sum in this manner (Lyne, 2007). When this happens, programmaticism can gain an edge, offering more to voters than clientelism does.

Economic context can also increase the credibility of, and thus demand for, programmatic appeals. Public policies generally require money, which in turn requires a reasonably strong tax base.[26] And policy implementation requires a minimum degree of institutional development that very poor nations tend not to have. This is at once a "supply side" and a "demand side" explanation for the association between poverty and clientelism: resource-poor nations are ill equipped to implement public policies well, and, knowing this, voters prefer their relationship with politicians to be based on something other than policy positions. With development, this dynamic can change.

Major economic events can also affect the balance of support for clientelism and programmaticism. Kitschelt and Wang (2014, 53) have argued that economic crises could boost programmaticism, especially during periods of transition from one type of economy to another. When existing models of economic growth seem outdated or irrelevant, there may be more demand for parties to articulate new, alternative economic policies, leading to more programmatic partisanship.

Demographic Changes Related to Development

Other demographic changes related to modernization are also important. Urbanization tends to decrease support for clientelism and increase demand for programmaticism. This dynamic has been observed in studies of various nations, including Britain, Mexico, Italy, Austria, and Japan.[27] Population growth more broadly is also thought to strain clientelism.[28]

Demographic changes are thought to have this effect for a few reasons. To some extent, it may be related to higher levels of wealth in urban areas. These areas also tend to be more heterogeneous, rendering coalition maintenance more challenging. This, along with population growth, makes it more difficult for party organizations to monitor clientelistic exchanges.[29] Strong monitoring is not essential, however; clientelism has persisted in many nations even when innovations like the secret ballot have made monitoring more difficult.

Role of Brokers

Stokes et al. (2013) bring many of these explanations together but offer a more specific mechanism by which modernization affects parties' strategies for appealing to voters. Clientelism requires a great deal of information. To manage this problem, they argue, parties need brokers.[30] In the United States, these were typically precinct captains. Yet, party leaders naturally worry about the extent to which they can rely on these agents, as "brokers are interested in extracting rents from their parties and in having their parties win elections." Stokes and colleagues present evidence that party leaders worry about this problem, and that brokers "are able to threaten party leaders with a withdrawal of blocks of voters whom they control."[31] When this relationship becomes too risky and inefficient for party leaders, they may prefer to rely on government bureaucrats to help them appeal to voters. This dynamic, Stokes et al. argue, is at the heart of understanding movement away from clientelism.

Stokes et al. (2013) identify four factors that influence party leaders' thinking in this area. The first, which they call "returns to scale," reflects the notion that clientelism becomes less efficient as a country's population increases and constituencies get larger. Programmaticism, being more scalable, thus becomes more attractive. The second factor involves monitoring, a challenge in any principal-agent relationship. Parties' ability to monitor their brokers can be affected by institutions like the Australian ballot, though Stokes and colleagues note evidence that "ballot reform is an indicator of shifts away from clientelism, rather than a cause."[32] Sociodemographic features like urbanity can also come into play, as monitoring brokers in small towns and rural areas with tighter-knit communities is easier than in large cities.[33] This helps explain why the urbanization that generally accompanies industrialization and economic growth is associated with movement away from clientelism. They also offer a novel theory of the association between poverty, their third factor, and clientelism. "Because the responsiveness of voters to electoral bribes diminishes with income," they argue, "brokers may have greater incentives to extract rents or engage in other politically wasteful activities when voters are on average richer."[34] This diminishes the efficiency of clientelism and enhances programmaticism's relative appeal, since "the responsiveness of voters to programmatic appeals does not diminish with income." Finally, they point to the "costs of programmatic communication." Party leaders rely on brokers largely to communicate with voters, but as literacy and mass media rise, leaders can more easily communicate directly with voters. This reduces their reliance on brokers and, by extension, clientelism. The industrial revolution was influential in this regard, and modern technological advances in communication have been as well.

Limitations of Modernization Theory

For many reasons, modernization has a meaningful relationship with party strategies for appealing to voters. Indeed, at least a modest degree of development appears all but necessary for programmaticism—the top left quadrant of figure 1.5 (low GDP, high programmatic effort) is sparsely populated.

Development is not a wholly satisfying explanation for variation in party appeals, however. Case studies have shown that clientelism persisted for much longer than early modernization theorists expected in some nations, like Italy, Belgium, Japan, Australia, Austria, Greece, and the United States.[35] And, as figure 1.5 shows, many nations are considerably less programmatic today than you would expect based on their level of economic development, like Spain, Sweden, and Norway. More broadly, dispersion around the line in that figure is much greater at moderate and high levels of development than at low levels. In other words, it appears that a certain degree of economic development is necessary but insufficient for programmatic partisanship to rise. Modernization theory does not explain why some moderate and high income nations exhibit much more programmatic partisanship than others, nor does it specify a threshold beyond which programmatic transitions should occur.[36]

In sum, attention to modernization is important for understanding programmaticism, but it is not the only factor to consider. Its relationship to programmaticism is complex, and it leaves critical questions unanswered.[37] Institutions also warrant attention.

Institutional Theories of Programmaticism

Democratic Experience and General Institutional Strength

Institutions are thought to influence clientelism and programmaticism in a few ways. Most broadly, scholars have argued that weak states will struggle to make credible policy commitments, given their limited capacity to implement them.[38] This dynamic is thought to affect new democracies, which have not yet had an opportunity to engage in the costly process of building institutional capacity. Weak states also have greater tendencies toward corruption. Both factors push the needle in new or otherwise weak states toward clientelism.[39] This can have a feedback effect, as clientelistic parties tend not to provide effective oversight of policy implementation, further entrenching clientelism.[40]

As with economic development, the decline of clientelism and the rise of programmaticism are not simple functions of democratic institutions. While research suggests there is a relationship between democratic experience and programmaticism, it is not linear. Parties actually tend to get more clientelistic over the early period of a democratic regime's development, as stronger institutions can facilitate delivery of goods to political supporters. But after a certain point, the relationship between clientelism and the age of the democracy becomes negative, on average.[41]

Bureaucracy

Bureaucratic institutions are thought to be especially important. This factor received early attention in Martin Shefter's influential work and has gained additional credence through subsequent research.[42] Examining Germany, Britain, Italy, and the United States, Shefter (1977) argued that the relative timing of democratization and bureaucratization affected the type of party system states adopted. In the United States, where mass enfranchisement occurred before a professionalized civil service developed, clientelism took hold. Under these conditions, parties were able to pillage the civil service for their own political gain. Path dependence tended to make these systems sticky. People used their positions to shape the institutional environment in ways that maintained their power. And from a more sociological perspective, "the mobilization of the masses into politics permanently changes the perceptions, expectations, and norms of political actors—the very language of politics" (12).

Change is possible in path-dependent processes, and this has been true in both bureaucracies and party systems. In later work, Shefter (1994) argues that shifts in the relative power of parties and bureaucracies have implications for the nature of the party system. When both are strong, "responsible parties" may emerge. Robust bureaucracies can allocate social welfare benefits, reducing voters' reliance on machines. They can also implement policies, increasing the credibility of programmatic appeals.

Of course, this raises the question: what incentivizes and allows states to strengthen and professionalize their bureaucracies? Existing literature provides a few answers. A certain degree of economic development can make a difference, as noted earlier, since it expands the tax base, affording governments more resources to build state institutions. Modernization also made clientelism's brokers less reliable for party leaders, heightening incentives to change the system.[43] External pressure can also make a difference. In the United States, Shefter (1994) points to the role of middle-class reformers and politicians (e.g., Progressives), and Kuo (2018) shows that businesses pushed party leaders to adapt the party system to accommodate the needs of modern capitalism.

Relative Strength of Parties

The relative strength of parties can also affect modes of competition. Political competition is negatively associated with clientelism.[44] This pattern has been noted by scholars examining nations across the development spectrum. Magaloni, Diaz-Cayeros, and Estévez (2007), in their study of Mexico, find evidence for this relationship even controlling for the well-known relationship with development. In Kitschelt's 2007 study of four cases in which clientelism endured beyond what economic development would predict (Austria, Belgium, Italy, and Japan), he notes that all four have histories of fascism.[45] Even after fascism declined, these countries experienced eras of dominance by "a single or two-party coalition hegemony/duopoly in government."[46] He points to an increase in electoral competition—and more specifically, the decline of "the dominance of Christian (or Liberal Democrat) center-right parties"—as one of two major factors, along with the decline of industries involved in clientelistic relations, in the weakening of this linkage strategy in these nations.[47]

Several scholars have noted an interactive relationship between political competition and development. This has been evident in Japan, for example—a country where clientelism lasted well beyond expectations based on economic development alone. As Ethan Scheiner (2007) notes, "Seeing clear displeasure with clientelism among urban voters and the more developed sectors of the economy, along with the strong presence of an opposition that competed with the ruling party in cities, Japan's leaders made a greater effort to scale back the clientelistic system."[48] In a different context, studying variation in clientelism across the eighty-nine regions of the Russian Federation after the fall of the USSR, Hale (2007) finds higher levels in regions with low levels of electoral competition and economic development.[49]

Other Institutional and Social Considerations

The classic clientelistic exchange involves repeated quid pro quo exchanges between politicians and voters, which will be most efficient when monitoring is easy. Movement toward the secret ballot makes this more difficult, leading to a loss of efficiency for clientelism. It is not prohibitive, however. Political actors are sometimes able to manipulate the system to undermine ballot secrecy (e.g., by having their operatives work at polling places).[50] Scholars have identified certain institutional and social factors that allow clientelism to endure under these conditions. When monitoring cannot occur at polling places, it can take on subtler forms. As Hicken and Nathan (2020) summarize, "Four alternative solutions have been identified: scaring voters into believing the ballot is not secret, distributing revocable benefits that align clients' and patrons' incentives, relying on pre-existing social norms and obligations, or engaging in collective monitoring."[51]

We can take a few lessons from this for the U.S. case. First, movement toward the secret ballot would likely reduce the strength of clientelism somewhat but may not cause its demise. Because U.S. machines tended to mobilize new immigrants, socializing them into politics, they would be likely to have more power over their constituents than the average politician would have over the average constituent. It is plausible that many people would believe machines could monitor their political behavior even if they could not, and that they would feel an obligation to the machine that incorporated them into politics in a new nation. Moreover, tight-knit immigrant neighborhoods would be prime spaces for social norms and obligations to reinforce loyalty to the machine even if the ballot were secret. Moreover, to the extent that patronage jobs remain available and local governments maintain wide latitude to use public contracts as clientelistic currency, voters' and machines' incentives align such that monitoring is unnecessary.[52] The fine-grained level at which election returns are reported could also allow clientelism to endure beyond the secret ballot's adoption by facilitating collective monitoring.[53]

This helps explain clientelism's durability in terms of the power that machines have over voters, but the opposite dynamic should also be considered. Politicians can be afraid to withhold benefits because voters expect them and may punish politicians for "exiting" clientelistic relationships.[54] Politicians can end up in a Prisoner's Dilemma, wherein everyone would be better off if they stopped offering these payments, but individually they are disincentivized from doing so. This can serve as a mechanism reinforcing path dependence.

General Contributions and Limitations of Existing Work

Modernization theory, along with work on the inverse relationship between clientelism and programmaticism, gives us a sense of when we can expect "windows of opportunity" for programmaticism to crack open, to borrow a term from John Kingdon's classic work on public policy creation, and how wide that space might be, so to speak.[55] Movement away from low levels of development and from high levels of clientelism both seem to create opportunities for programmaticism.

Intercurrence, a concept introduced by Karen Orren and Stephen Skowronek (2004), can help explain why. Any given polity has multiple orders—sets of institutions, actors, norms, and so on and there are often tensions between them. These tensions, which can stem from different purposes and eras or contexts in which they were created, can generate conflict that provides opportunities for change. More specifically, intercurrence "produces contradictions for agents, entrepreneurs, and leaders to exploit and alternatives for them to imagine."[56] It "directs researchers to locate the historical construction of politics in the simultaneous operation of older and newer instruments of governance, in controls asserted through multiple orderings of authority whose coordination with one another cannot be assumed and whose outward reach and impingements, including on one another, are inherently problematic." It emphasizes both institutions and agents as sources of pressure and resistance that make political change often incremental as well as "partial and uneven."[57]

Drawing again from Kingdon's theory of policy creation, just because a window opens doesn't mean anything will happen—the players involved need to be ready to take advantage of the opportunity. In Kingdon's theory, this means having a viable policy proposal in hand. For programmaticism, it means having the institutions necessary for programmatic development. This analogy should not be overstretched, as the window of opportunity created by clientelism's decline will not necessarily be time-limited in the same way that policy windows tend to be. Nonetheless, it underscores the point that opportunity, while important to understand, is only part of the story.

Theories of programmaticism are needed to understand when and why some party systems move through the window of opportunity. We know a fair amount about the demand side of this question from existing work on factors leading voters, capitalists, and even party leaders to press for a programmatic approach. The literature on the supply side is smaller and, while rich with respect to its particular subjects of study, focused more on institutions facilitating policy implementation than institutions facilitating parties' ability to develop policy positions. This critical part of the process seems to have been overlooked, perhaps taken for granted, and is the focus of my theory.

Contributions and Limitations of Existing Work with Respect to the United States

The U.S. case underscores both the value and the limitations of existing theory on modes of appealing to voters. We can begin with modernization. Economic growth, population growth, and urbanization trends are all generally consistent with the notion of programmaticism increasing over time, as it has, and sitting at a historic high today, which it does. Moreover, Stokes et al. (2013) present evidence that factors associated with modernization—rising incomes, population growth, urbanization, and a rise of literacy and mass media—strained clientelism's brokers in the United States, pushing it toward programmaticism.

These findings offer important contributions to American politics literature, in terms of not only programmaticism, but also polarization. Although it may be possible to achieve polarization without programmaticism—and thus, it's critical to distinguish between these concepts—programmaticism leads to polarization, as defined broadly in chapter 1.[58] Alternative issue positions make parties more distinct and make it more difficult for them to connect. It's also clear that the modern rise of polarization in Congress, as measured by differences in DW-NOMINATE scores, has corresponded with the rise in programmaticism documented in chapter 1. Although there is a substantial literature on the origins of contemporary polarization, modernization has been largely neglected as a contributing factor. It is an important addition to this literature as well as to discussions about whether and how to respond to polarization because modernization trends are unlikely to decline over time. This may cause stickiness in programmaticism, and thus in polarization.

Modernization theory alone cannot account for variation in programmaticism in the United States, however. While the modernization hypothesis fits this case in broad strokes, there are obvious limitations to this explanation when we consider the nature of programmaticism's rise in more detail. The United States was a latecomer to programmaticism, relative to its level of development. The modernization literature doesn't specify a threshold beyond which counties turn toward issue-based competition, so it's a little hard to say what counts as "late." Nonetheless, the characterization seems reasonable given that the United States experienced profound economic growth starting in the 1930s, and programmaticism did not begin its steep rise until approximately four decades later. Moreover, Stokes et al. (2013) note that the United States shifted toward programmaticism later than Britain, lending credence to the perception that its transition was delayed.

Attention to economic distress reinforces this notion. The nation's most severe economic downturn, the Great Depression, which began in 1929, was not associated with a significant rise in programmaticism. This is particularly notable, given how many other major changes were considered and enacted at the time. As Ira Katznelson (2013) shows, the United States experimented with many new ideas—including some, like European-style economic planning, that were quite radical for the United States—and created many new programs and agencies during the New Deal era that followed the Depression.[59] Yet, its parties did not engage in a significant shift toward programmaticism.

Shifts in the nature of the economy, with the decline of certain industries and the rise of others, could play a role in changing perceptions about the relative merit of different tools for political competition. In particular, the shift toward a knowledge economy would likely be associated with the kind of non-zero-sum growth discussed by Lyne (2007) that can facilitate movement toward programmaticism. This would be a rich subject for future research, with studies designed to address this particular dynamic. It would advance our understanding of rising demand for programmaticism, though it would still leave us needing better explanations for the supply side.

Political competition may have contributed to the sustained nature of programmatic development over the contemporary era. The United States has experienced its longest stretch of two-party competition, in terms of shifts in control of Congress and closeness of presidential contests, between 1980 and the present.[60] This explanation would be more convincing in combination with other factors, however, as the United States experienced other, albeit shorter, periods of heightened two-party competition. One possibility, based on existing work, is that the interaction between political competition and economic development has been powerful in the contemporary era. Nonetheless, political competition in the sense of shifts in party control or closeness of presidential elections is most compelling as a reinforcing mechanism. It cannot explain why the modern rise started in the late 1960s.

A broader view of political competition could prove useful. As Robert Mickey (2015) argues, southern states were "authoritarian enclaves" within a broader democratic system from the 1890s until the early 1970s. The democratization of these enclaves could help explain the rise of modern programmaticism. This explanation, however, calls for more attention to the role of racial politics in shaping the nature of party-voter linkages, a subject that has received limited attention in the small body of extant work on programmaticism in the United States.

Institutions have great potential to help explain why programmaticism has increased in the United States over the contemporary era, and why earlier rises were more modest and less sustained, given that the pattern of growth in programmaticism suggests an "unlocking" of sorts in the late 1960s. After a long period of incremental or no growth, programmaticism rose sharply in the contemporary era. This suggests that forces were holding it back, and then released or at least loosened their grip. Institutions are known to have this power. New institutions could also support new activities. Thus, institutions have potential to explain both what hindered the growth of programmaticism as the United States developed and what ultimately facilitated it.

Bureaucracies are clearly important, given their centrality to policy implementation; however, they are not the only institutions requiring attention. The strengthening of U.S. bureaucracies over the last three decades of the nineteenth century does not seem to have created an environment sufficiently conducive to the growth of programmaticism (see figure 1.1). The rise in programmaticism at this time was modest in comparison to the contemporary rise, and it did not last. Moreover, the New Deal era brought an explosion of

U.S. bureaucratic capacity with no commensurate rise of programmaticism. Thus, while Shefter and Kuo have offered critical insights into the supply side of programmaticism, additional work is needed.

The supply side of programmaticism has two key parts: the ability to implement policy and the ability to develop strong, alternative party positions on policy issues. The former does not lead automatically to the latter, though it can enhance the latter's credibility. I build on Shefter's and Kuo's work by considering what constrains and facilitates parties' ability to develop issue positions. This can help us better understand variation in programmaticism in the United States, and potentially in other nations as well.

Indeed, a supply side theory of programmaticism can help address an important problem in the literature on nonprogrammatic partisanship identified by Hicken and Nathan (2020) in a recent *Annual Review of Political Science* article. They explain that for decades, scholars have been fixated on the "puzzle" of clientelism's persistence in the face of institutional innovations like the secret ballot, now common in the developing world as well as in advanced industrialized democracies, and other phenomena that make monitoring difficult. The premise of this puzzle is flawed, as it makes an implicit comparison between clientelism and some readily available, efficient alternative that often does not exist in the real world. We need to learn more, Hicken and Nathan argue, about the actual alternatives parties face and how their costs compare to the costs of clientelism. Sticking with clientelism can be a perfectly rational choice, even if monitoring challenges render it extremely inefficient, if parties do not have a more efficient alternative available to them. Rather than following the red herring of understanding clientelism in the absence of monitoring—which may not be a puzzle after all—we need to better understand other tools. One of the four key questions Hicken and Nathan identify for future research is "What Are the Realistic Alternatives to Clientelism?" An explicit theory of programmaticism can speak to this question.

A Supply Side Theory Focused on Position Development

I begin by presenting a set of axioms regarding party position development before generating hypotheses explaining variation in programmaticism. I characterize these statements as axioms because they are unlikely to be falsified; most reasonable people would accept them as truths. Yet, they are worth highlighting because they have been overlooked in American politics literature, and they provide an important foundation for my theory of programmaticism.

The Process of Party Position Development

My theory is grounded in the notion that the process of developing party positions across a wide range of issues is labor-intensive and risky. Such positions do not materialize out of thin air—they have to be figured out. This can be challenging for a number of reasons. To begin, there are many questions and issues on which a party could take a position at any given moment. The "policy primordial soup," to borrow another term from Kingdon's (1984) classic work on policymaking, is thick and voluminous. As government, society, and the economy grow more complex, the number of political problems and questions rises. Thus, while modernization may create demand for policy positions and facilitate the government's capacity for policy implementation, it can actually make position development more challenging. Parties need to sort through the "soup" so to speak, to choose issues on which to take positions. The bigger the "pot," the harder this is. And, of course, they also need to figure out what positions to take.

Ideologies—conceived as general orientations toward the role of government in society and the economy, measured on a left–right spectrum—may provide guidance on some issues, particularly for the Republican Party, which is structured more by ideology than the Democratic Party (Grossmann and Hopkins, 2016) Intellectuals and writers have also connected positions on various issues, as Hans Noel (2013) has shown, constructing ideologies— conceived here as sets of issue positions that are bundled together and shared by many people in a political system—that have influenced partisans and contributed to the growth of contemporary polarization. But not all issues map onto ideologies, whether they be left–right or otherwise. Even if they did, parties may not want to adopt all parts of ideologies crafted by intellectuals, who do not face the same kinds of electoral incentives and constraints.

This brings us to the inevitable topic of electoral strategy, and the first axiom: *Different parts of the party's coalition may disagree about what the party's position on a particular issue should be, or whether they should even take a position at all.* Even if we assume elite party members are motivated entirely by elections, it is not always clear what position is ideal for these purposes. There are often contradictions between what different parts of a party's electoral coalition—their existing coalition or the one they would like to develop—prefers with respect to an issue. This is inevitable in a large, diverse nation with only two major parties. For example, there have been many disagreements between labor and civil rights groups on Democratic Party policy and between the Christian Right and other parts of the Republican coalition.[61] It is not even always clear what each individual coalition group prefers.

The party will often need to gather and weigh information to figure all of this out. This brings us to a second axiom: *The process of developing a party position on an issue carries significant informational costs, always political and sometimes technical as well.* Parties need to know what each part of their electoral coalition wants, how much they care, and what the penalty would likely be for going against its wishes on the issue. In other words, they need people to do the kind of work that whips do for bills in Congress. They may also need to gather technical information on the policy area. Only after considering these factors can party elites know what issue position, if any, makes the most sense.

Complicating matters, "the party" is not one simple entity that relies on one brain to make decisions about matters of electoral strategy. It is rather more like a multiheaded creature: as Key famously argued, there is a party-in-government, a party-as-organization, and a party-in-the-electorate. While the party-as-organization (itself not a unitary actor) is formally responsible for developing and publishing the party's platform, it is not the only one with an interest in it. Members of the party-in-government, who run under the party's label, also have a horse in the race. Even within the party-in-government, the American separation of powers system makes it so that there are multiple actors' preferences to consider.

Even if we assume they are all motivated primarily by electoral concerns, disagreement is likely because their electoral considerations are different. Presidents, senators, and members of Congress have different term lengths and are therefore elected on different schedules. The length of time until their next election may affect their willingness to take a risk with a particular issue position and their balance between shorter and longer term strategizing. They also have different constituencies, with members of Congress representing districts that are smaller and typically more homogenous than the states that senators represent, and certainly smaller and more homogenous than the entire nation that the president faces in elections. Thus, when different parts of the party's coalition have conflicting preferences regarding an issue, these different key players may come to disparate conclusions about what position (if any) the party should take. This leads to my third axiom: *The process of developing a party position on an issue requires conflict resolution among different parts of the party's coalition, as well as among key players with authority over the party brand.*

I have focused in this book on party platforms, which party organizations could theoretically just write and publish themselves. A presidential candidate might also pressure the organization to present their own set of policy preferences as the party's platform. But there are two problems with this. First, it would come with a risk of public dissent from other key players, undermining the platform. Second, it is not likely to be durable. If the candidate steamrolls, rather than trying to resolve conflicts with dissenting players, the resulting positions are likely to be unstable. Thus, durable programmaticism is unlikely to be achieved under these circumstances.

Once all this work is done, announcing a party position carries risks of alienating certain party members. Even after engaging in conflict resolution, some members of the party will disagree with the ultimate position taken. As Clark and Wilson (1961) argue in their classic work on organizational incentives, this is a challenge in organizations driven by "purposive" incentives. While organizations operating primarily on material incentives, like clientelistic parties, can resolve conflicts by "dividing the dollar," it's more difficult for organizations running on nonmaterial, goal-oriented incentives to settle internal conflicts. Compromise is less straightforward and sometimes impossible.

Importance of Institutions for Position Development

Given the difficulty of developing positions across a wide range of issues, I argue that an institutional perspective can provide valuable insight into the growth of programmaticism. The process described above is intricate, and institutions can ease the challenges of information gathering and conflict resolution. Parties could, of course, try to do this on an ad hoc basis; however, that is unlikely to lead to stable programmaticism. By routinizing processes and defining roles, institutions can make the process more efficient and thus more sustainable.[62]

My theory reflects the important but nuanced role of institutions, focusing on two types in particular: (1) party organizations, given their historical role in clientelistic practices and responsibility for platform development; and (2) racial orders, given their far-reaching and often subtle power over American political life.[63]

COMPLEX ROLE OF PARTY ORGANIZATIONS

Party system institutionalization is thought to be necessary for the growth and durability of programmatic partisanship. In turn, programmaticism is thought to reinforce a party system's stability. As Nic Cheeseman and Dan Paget (2014) explain:

> When parties are stable and consistent in their approaches to elections, they can build stronger and more consistent policy positions, and stand a better chance of developing more effective links to citizens on this basis. Likewise, programmatic parties can structure politics in ways that help to institutionalize party systems. Institutionalization and programmatic politics are thus likely to be mutually reinforcing.[64]

But, I argue, the relationship between party institutions and programmaticism is likely nuanced. More specifically, it may depend on the type of party institutions. As noted earlier, programmaticism was unlikely to grow in a strong and durable manner so long as party machines, which operated primarily on the local and sometimes state level, remained strong. When parties can rely on material exchanges, they are unlikely to engage in significant programmatic partisanship. This is consistent with arguments made by Schattschneider (1942) and the 1950 report of the APSA Committee on Political Parties, which he chaired, about the parties' lack of incentives in the mid-twentieth century to take strong, alternative policy positions. In this sense, party institutions can inhibit programmaticism.

Notions of political space can help explain why, but this is probably not the only reason programmaticism was slow to develop in the United States. Given the high upfront costs and risks involved in programmaticism, I argue that it is unlikely to be a first- or even second-line tool for parties. They will tend to require quite strong incentives to use it. Other items in the toolbox for electoral competition, like charismatic appeals, carry lower costs and fewer risks and can more easily be paired with clientelism and each other.

Party institutions can also have the opposite effect. This notion is stated more specifically in the national party strength hypothesis.

National Party Strength Hypothesis: *The growth and professionalization of national party organizations will tend to facilitate movement toward programmaticism.*

As with movement away from clientelism, this shift is not strictly causal. Such growth should not always be expected to produce issue-based party competition everywhere. But, I argue, there are good reasons to believe it provided a critical foundation for the sharp and sustained growth of programmatic parties in the United States in the contemporary era, and potentially in other places as well.

It takes a lot of work to develop strong, durable party positions across many issues. The information gathering, discussion, cooperation, and bargaining involved in this process requires significant institutional capacity, in terms of both human and organizational resources: staff with a reasonable level of pay and job security, offices, pens and pencils, computers, phones, and conference rooms where discussions can take place. It requires the ability to gather large groups of partisans together to hammer out compromises, which in turn requires money (for hotels, meals, etc.) and staff to coordinate such events. A lot of this work is difficult and unglamorous. Paltry, unstable national organizations are not capable of performing this work sustainably. Subnational party organizations are not well positioned to perform this work either. Even if they wanted to devise a set of unified party positions, they would face significant collective action problems if they tried to do this without a central authority capable of managing the flow of work and conflict. Outside groups can help with position development, but they also need a coordinating body to manage the flow of work and help adjudicate conflict.

In sum, it is difficult for parties to formulate positions across a wide range issues in the absence of reasonably strong national party organizations. Reinforcing this notion, Rafael Roncagliolo Orbegoso, former minister of foreign affairs of the Republic of Peru and member of the Board of Advisers for the International Institute for Democracy and Electoral Assistance (IDEA), noted that the organization's research on parties in the Andean nations showed that weak organizational capacity rendered many of them unable to sustain a programmatic orientation. When they "faced their responsibilities with a poor capacity to develop and communicate policies and programs," he argues, this "had the effect of hollowing politics out."[65] When parties are more institutionally stable, they are better positioned to carve out positions and build relationships with voters based on programmatic appeals.

One might question the importance of national party organizations, given that they have limited power to enforce positions. Indeed, relative to party leaders in government, party organizations have few carrots and sticks. But, dismissing them for this reason would reflect a narrow view of their power.

As noted earlier, developing party positions requires a great deal of work, a lot of which is arduous. Party organizations may not be the only entities capable of doing this work, but their ability and willingness to do it or not will have significant consequences.

Moreover, they are the entities best suited for this work. As custodians of the national party platforms, the RNC and DNC are presumably responsible for creating institutions and processes geared toward position development for the platforms. Such institutions can help get programmatic competition off the ground and smooth development of new positions, reinforcing the rise of issue-based competition. National party organizations are responsible for thinking about the entire party, across branches of government and the nation. So positioned, they should be more likely to work toward resolving existing conflicts (e.g., between Congress and the president) than introducing new conflict into an issue area. While they may not necessarily serve as neutral arbiters between Congress and the presidency, they are unlikely to bring a third position to the table. Thus, their participation is likely to guide the party toward more consistent positions.

Involvement by the party organization can also increase durability. As the player best positioned to think and speak ecumenically, it will have incentives to bring various coalition members together to develop positions. When varying perspectives are included in the discussion, the position that emerges is likely to be more durable. It will reflect a compromise that more people had a hand in creating and are therefore more invested in. Indeed, research by scholars in Austria indicates that inclusive processes are likely to increase acceptance of platform positions.[66]

It would be too much to say that national party organizations are *necessary* institutions for programmatic development. They are not the only organizations that could ever possibly perform the work of position development. What's most important is the work itself. If other groups can perform the research and conflict resolution tasks described above, they could buttress programmaticism.

This is probably more feasible later in the process of programmatic development and maintenance. At the time the United States began its durable rise in programmaticism, alternative organizations that might come to mind, like think tanks, did not exist in the manner they do today. They may help with position development now, and many are indeed party aligned. Once there is a basic programmatic foundation, it's presumably easier for think tanks to find their place in the system. But national party organizations, given their unique standing, remain particularly well positioned to help a nation transition toward a more programmatic party system.

Another institutional explanation that's related to, but distinct from, the role of party organizations involves what Desmond King and Rogers Smith (2005) call *racial orders*. These are specific types of *political institutional orders*, defined as "coalitions of state institutions and other political actors and organizations that seek to secure and exercise governing power in demographically, economically, and ideologically structured contexts that define the range of opportunities open to political actors."[67] This encompasses institutions (both governing and nonstate institutions at the national and subnational level) and their features and outputs (e.g., laws, rules, processes, norms), along with the people who populate them at any given time.

Since the founding, there have been two racial orders—distinguishable from other political institutional orders by their focus on race—competing for control over the nation's present and future: a *white supremacist* order and an *egalitarian transformative* order.[68] While they have evolved in terms of content and composition over time, and some institutions and actors have even switched sides (e.g., Andrew Johnson, Harry Truman) or maintained relationships with both (e.g., Franklin Delano Roosevelt), these orders have been so powerful and omnipresent that "the nation has been pervasively constituted by systems of racial hierarchy."[69] In this light, King and Smith argue that "no analysis of American politics is likely to be adequate unless the impact of these racial orders is explicitly considered or their disregard explained." Racial orders particularly warrant attention with respect to a matter so central to the nation's politics as the nature of party-voter linkages.

To be clear, the idea that ethnicity—a concept related to race—can affect party-voter linkages is not new, particularly to comparative scholars. Existing work shows that ethnicity often forms a basis of clientelistic linkage. This has been the case, for example, in Russia, India, and many African nations, as well as the United States.[70] In addition to facilitating solidarity and trust, ethnic groups sometimes have networks that can be used to implement clientelism, rendering this type of system more efficient and less costly.[71] Conditions of high intergroup economic inequality tend to push a nation toward clientelism, especially when parties have relationships with ethnic organizations.[72]

Ethnic politics can also affect the nature of party competition by affecting policy provision. High intergroup inequality is associated with less support for and enactment of redistributive policy, as well as fewer public goods.[73] This does not just reflect the preferences of higher income voters; poor ethnic groups in highly unequal societies have reason not to trust government to provide for them and thus prefer clientelistic benefits.[74] Programmaticism will be less likely to develop under these conditions, since it tends to involve the provision of public goods, and often redistributive policies as well.

Building on this work, I posit that the potential for antidiscrimination legislation can also prove powerful. Movement toward programmaticism could decrease intergroup inequality through various mechanisms, including the redistributive and public goods policies that have received a lot of attention in the comparative literature, as well as through legislation explicitly mandating equality in treatment by public and private entities and individuals, access to public goods and services, and the franchise. For dominant ethnic groups, this could make programmaticism appear threatening. If parties compete via policy positions, sparks from that friction could undermine the existing hierarchy.

There is another factor to consider as well: the way in which racial orders map onto the party system. When they cross-cut parties, meaning there are substantial intraparty divisions on issues of racial inequality, the political environment will be less auspicious for programmaticism. It will be harder for parties to commit to issue-based competition when they know it will be difficult and risky to face internal conflict on policies regarding racial inequality.

Together, these factors lead to the following hypothesis regarding the United States.

Racial Oppression Hypothesis: *Institutions and agents committed to racial oppression delayed programmatic development in the United States, particularly as racial orders cross-cut parties and fundamental barriers to political equality (e.g., franchise restrictions) were the status quo.*

There is ample evidence that white supremacists long had this kind of power and the motivation to use it. Indeed, the white supremacist order has typically been the more powerful of the two racial orders over the course of U.S. history.[75] Among other things, it affected decisions about territorial expansion—influencing the literal shape of the nation—and had a profound impact on New Deal policies that built the modern American state, directing benefits from social welfare programs (including seemingly universalistic programs like Social Security) disproportionately toward whites.[76] Moreover, a great deal of research indicates that southern members of Congress prioritized protection of Jim Crow laws maintaining white supremacy in the South above all other issues.[77]

Thus, it stands to reason that southern members of Congress—key players in the white supremacist order—would have resisted the notion of programmaticism. So long as issue-based competition could involve positions threatening Jim Crow, the stakes of programmaticism would have been too high. And given the challenges attending position development across a wide range of issues, I argue that such resistance would have been very difficult to overcome.

This highlights a challenge that programmaticism is likely to face: legitimacy. While scholars may, on the whole, tend to argue that programmaticism offers better accountability and other superior democratic outcomes, there is no rulebook for political practitioners—or academics, for that matter—stating this. Parties are conspicuously absent from the United States Constitution, meaning that their purpose and powers have always been far less defined than those of the executive, legislature, and judiciary, even though they have been almost as omnipotent in the nation's political history. This has led to centuries of disagreement over what parties are and what they should be doing, not only among scholars (e.g., the debate between the traditional and group-centered theories of parties discussed in chapter 1) but also within parties themselves. The notion that parties should be taking positions across a wide range of issues, that this was conduct befitting parties, was not a foregone conclusion.[78] It was an idea that needed to gain legitimacy. In the face of resistance from a critical mass of party members, this would present an uphill battle of its own, on top of the challenge of actual position development.

Notably, the racial oppression hypothesis states that the white supremacist order delayed—but did not ultimately prohibit—programmatic development in the United States. This is because the passage of the Civil Rights Act of 1964 and the Voting Rights Act of 1965 profoundly changed the stakes of programmaticism. Jim Crow laws were no longer on the table. While white supremacy and discrimination against African Americans have both endured—the nation's two racial orders march forth, as they have since the founding, though not without some evolution in substance and relative strength—the civil rights revolution led to major changes in African

American rights. These included franchise protection, a critical building block for other political changes.

The racial oppression hypothesis may bring to mind the well-known argument in American politics that southern realignment following the civil rights revolution led to polarization.[79] When the South transitioned from a Democratic to a Republican stronghold, the region's former party lost its conservative contingent, and its new party became even more conservative, on average. This rather mechanical argument is not wrong, but it is incomplete. Members of the white supremacist order did not simply defend legally sanctioned racial oppression and move away from the Democratic Party after it led the effort to pass civil rights legislation, breaking a long-standing deal that southern Democrats would support New Deal legislation so long as their co-partisans did not threaten Jim Crow laws—their commitment to maintaining white supremacy delayed movement toward issue-based competition for the party system as a whole. This had far-reaching consequences for many issues not directly associated with race. In sum, the role of white supremacy in the trajectory of polarization in the United States is more complex and even more significant than existing literature suggests.[80]

The realignment of the South after the civil rights revolution reduced the degree to which the white supremacist order cross-cut parties, smoothing a path for continued programmatic growth. That's not to say there are no barriers. Racial orders never perfectly map onto parties, so times of heightened salience for racial inequality may strain programmaticism. While this may not roll back the system, it could make parties more hesitant to emphasize issue-based competition.

Conclusion

A phenomenon as complex as a shift toward programmaticism is inevitably multicausal, and understanding it fully in the United States—not to mention in the world—is the work of a literature, not a single book. In this chapter, I have offered a theory that builds on existing work and provides a foundation for additional work.

This chapter's central emphases and contributions are as follows. First, the inverse—though imperfect—relationship between programmaticism and clientelism suggests that theories focused on understanding variation in clientelism can be useful for understanding programmaticism, but explicit theories of the latter are also necessary. The decline of clientelism creates opportunities for programmaticism to rise, but does not guarantee that it will. If there is insufficient demand for issue-based competition, or parties are ill equipped to engage in such competition, programmaticism will not ensue, at least not strongly.

Most existing work on programmaticism focuses on the demand side, considering what puts pressure on parties or otherwise incentivizes them to use this tool. My theory contributes to a small but growing literature on the supply side, moving beyond this literature's focus on policy implementation—an important but insufficient explanation for the growth of programmaticism on its own—to consider institutions necessary for parties to develop alternative positions across a wide range of issues. In so doing, I have argued that party institutions have had a complex relationship to programmatic development in the United States, with local party machines playing a constraining role and national party organizations playing a facilitating role. Finally, I hypothesize that racial orders are a critical institutional consideration in the United States. So long as Jim Crow laws were the status quo, members of the white supremacist order would have strong incentives to resist a shift toward issue-based competition. And given the difficulty involved in party position development, such resistance would be hard to overcome, especially at a time when racial orders cross-cut parties. The white supremacist order delayed not only civil rights for African Americans, but the shift toward programmaticism more broadly. This is an important and sobering example of the power of racial orders to shape the nation's politics far beyond the borders of what might be considered "racial issues."

To be clear, I am not arguing that the United States shifted from a state of pure clientelism to a state of pure programmaticism. No system is fully programmatic, as in "a civics textbook caricature of democracy."[81] States rely on a mix of voter-party linkages, and both clientelism and programmaticism should be considered on continuums.[82] There has never been a total absence of programmaticism in the United States—parties have always tended to stand for something, even if they did not display the range of positions seen in the contemporary era.[83] And though traditional party machines no longer proliferate in the United States, patronage did not completely disappear after the late 1960s, and more subtle forms of nonprogrammatic distribution of goods and services have endured.[84] Indeed, this is another legacy of racial orders in the United States. By insisting on tailoring New Deal programs to exclude African Americans—a strategy achieved largely through decentralized implementation that left significant discretion to state and local officials—the white supremacist order also made these policies more vulnerable to nonprogrammatic distribution, extending the life of clientelistic practices in ways they may not have intended.[85] Despite all these complexities, however, there has been a shift toward greater programmaticism over time in the United States. My theory endeavors to help explain this important development in the nation's party system.

3

The Dance of Clientelism and Programmaticism

THIS CHAPTER PRESENTS a historical analysis of clientelism and its relationship to programmaticism over time. One might wonder if another account of clientelism in the United States is needed, given the existence of many rich studies of party machines and excellent overviews of this literature.[1] Indeed, the present chapter owes a great deal to this work. Nonetheless, the history of clientelism in the United States warrants close attention in this chapter from the perspective of this book's central purpose: to understand what hindered and facilitated the growth of programmaticism.

Two questions rise to the forefront of this pursuit. First, did clientelism constrain the growth of programmaticism, as posited by the clientelism constraint hypothesis presented in chapter 2? In other words, to what extent does a long historical analysis of the United States reveal the kind of inverse relationship between clientelism and programmaticism observed in cross-national studies? Second, why was clientelism so durable in the United States, and what ultimately led to its decline? Addressing this question can help us understand why the steep growth of programmaticism did not occur until the contemporary era.

This chapter employs multiple strategies for assessing the clientelism constraint hypothesis. One obvious approach is to compare the trajectories of clientelism and programmaticism. At the extreme, my expectation is clear: the ultimate fall of clientelism as a major tool should open a window of opportunity for significant programmatic growth. Accordingly, I examine the timing of clientelism's dissipation relative to the beginning of programmaticism's steep growth over the contemporary era. This analysis lends credence to the clientelism constraint hypothesis, as both occurred in the late 1960s.

While that period is clearly important, we can learn from more than just the dramatic changes contained therein by taking a longer and more nuanced view. When clientelism weakened at earlier points in American history—bending but not breaking—were there upticks, if not surges, in programmaticism? In this case, the prediction based on existing work is less clear, given the well-established positive relationship between modernization and programmatic partisanship.[2] Decreases in clientelism may be associated with programmatic effort only once a nation has reached a certain level of development. Given how little we know about the threshold beyond which modernization facilitates programmaticism, a historical analysis of the United States has great potential to contribute to existing knowledge. This serves as both a plausibility test for the clientelism constraint hypothesis, broadly speaking, and an opportunity to identify potential boundary conditions thereon.

Building on the bird's-eye perspective offered by comparing their trajectories, we can gain additional insight into the relationship between clientelism and programmaticism by zooming in on significant episodes of opposition to the former. While I have argued that clientelism was subject to path dependence, this does not mean that the path was smooth or its continuation guaranteed. The "losers" of particular institutional arrangements do not always accept that status. By examining disputes between them and the "winners" of such arrangements, as well as the challenges that new ideas and forms of politics face in trying to find a place within established institutional orders, we can better understand how and why change occurs amid the inertial forces of path dependence. The parties we see today, like all institutions, are "enduring legacies of political struggles."[3]

Several groups have challenged American clientelism, most notably Mugwumps, Progressive reformers, managerial capitalists, New Dealers, and the New Politics movement. Amid each of these challenges, were there glimmers of programmaticism? If so, what form did they take and why didn't they (in the first four cases, at least) lead to a sharp, sustained increase in programmatic partisanship? If not, can we tell why not? And finally, to what extent and in what ways do we see changes in these dynamics over time? Answering these questions can help explain why the inverse relationship between clientelism and programmaticism, while strong and robust, is imperfect.

These questions invoke both structure and agency. While studies of American political development may be known best for their focus on institutions, they have also uncovered the role agents can play as interpreters of existing rules and norms, and as advocates for change. Their power can stem from outright strength as well as the ability to offer innovative ideas and creative solutions to problems.[4] For party systems in particular, shifts toward programmaticism likely rely on strong political entrepreneurs to guide the process.

Of course, it's also important to consider the context in which these entrepreneurs were operating. Throughout this analysis, I keep an eye toward the functions that clientelism served at various points in American history. In the tradition of American political development, I also consider the role of timing and sequence in explaining clientelism's durability. I find evidence of path dependence, ways in which the process of party development—on its own and in relation to the state—conferred increasing returns to clientelism. This helps explain why the dramatic rise of programmatic partisanship did not occur until the late twentieth century despite the nation's relatively high level of economic development before this period.

I also identify factors that ultimately created a more auspicious environment for reform movements. The party system was one of many institutional orders—in addition to the economy, welfare state, and bureaucracy, for example—developing along with the nation. Each had its own logic, but they also influenced each other. Thinking about the party system as a player in the intercurrence of multiple orders can help us understand its development. Modernization may not have caused a shift toward programmaticism in a strictly determinitive manner, but it did lead the party system to outgrow the clientelistic path it had been traveling for a long time.

As is often true for institutions, changes in the party system were slow, partial, and riddled with contradiction. Even when institutions "ingrained in an earlier era encounter new and antithetical purposes later on"—a phenomenon that's bound to occur over the course of a nation's history—it's rare for older orders to be completely displaced by newer ones. Indeed, "insofar as all political change, even at critical junctures, is accompanied by the accumulation and persistence of competing controls within the institutions of government, the normal condition of the polity will be that of multiple, incongruous authorities operating simultaneously."[5] This has been evident in the party system's evolution.

In sum, the analytical history presented in this chapter serves more than one purpose and reflects more than one method of analysis. I engage in a traditional style of analysis, assessing the plausibility of a defined hypothesis, and learn inductively from the process of considering the history of clientelism through the perspective of my book's central question. Moreover, I aim to evaluate the clientelism constraint hypothesis as well as identify potential contingencies and boundary conditions surrounding it. While unorthodox relative to the standard scientific model of research, this strategy offers the flexibility necessary to address big questions about which we have relatively limited knowledge. It is also well positioned to handle the challenge of engaging with a puzzle that requires explaining both institutional stability and change.

The chapter's analytical narrative strategy borrows from both rational choice and historical institutional traditions and, like any compromise, is bound to disappoint strong adherents to each individual tradition. An analytical narrative "represents an attempt to construct explanations of empirical events through analyses that 'respect the specifics of time and place but within a framework that both disciplines the detail and appropriates it for purposes that transcend the particular story.' "[6] History in this case is not merely a story but an analytical tool that can be used to evaluate theories.[7] Because it's meant to answer a particular question, the history will not be comprehensive with respect to every case or era under analysis. The payoff comes through its ability to reveal more generalizable patterns.

In addition to the analytical history described above, this chapter employs quantitative tools to evaluate the plausibility of the clientelism constraint hypothesis. I take advantage of cross-state variation in historical machine strength and contemporary party distinctions. In theory, legislatures in states with machine legacies would lag behind others in terms of party differentiation. I find support for this observable implication of the clientelism constraint hypothesis, as my analysis reveals less platform distinction and polarization today in states that still had strong party machines in the late 1960s, relative to states that did not. While this is not a perfect test, it lends credence to my hypothesis.

None of these analyses may be entirely persuasive on their own, but these very different strategies are powerful when their results point in the same direction. In combination, they offer strong support for my hypothesis that clientelism constrained the growth of programmaticism in the United States.

An Analytical History of Clientelism in the United States

A Tradition from the Beginning

While famously associated with political machines like New York's Tammany Hall, clientelism predated them in the United States by over half a century.

Notwithstanding the fact that electoral bribery was illegal under common law as well as many state constitutions, party competition based on material rewards (e.g., jobs, goods, etc.) was common at the beginning of the republic. Political appointees of early presidents were drawn from a narrow elite group of political supporters. Candidates also engaged in democratically dubious "treating," offering incentives like money and alcohol at the polls.[8] Even the revered George Washington—viewed by many as a benign "patriot king" who could guide the nation down the path to democratic stability during its uncertain early years—had earlier "purchased 160 gallons of liquor for electors in his election to the Virginia House of Burgesses."[9]

These were individual acts, not intended to bolster party organizations. Indeed, though parties arose in the 1790s, soon after the nation's founding, it would be several decades before party organizations would emerge in significant form. The notion of legitimate opposition was not yet accepted in the republic's formative years. Many who ran under partisan labels (e.g., Thomas Jefferson, James Monroe) viewed parties as vehicles of persuasion, temporary means to a partyless state.[10] Under these circumstances, there would be little incentive to invest in party organizations or engage in strong, durable programmaticism—politicians were not envisioning much less planning for party competition beyond the short term.

Political context also pushed early party leaders toward clientelistic more than programmatic appeals. Having just escaped British colonial rule, the American founders were understandably suspicious of centralized authority. While there was disagreement regarding the appropriate balance between national and subnational power—reflected in the names of the era's two major factions, the Federalists and Anti-Federalists—this conflict was contained within a narrow range of considered outcomes. Grave concern about tyranny stemming from excessive centralized authority is reflected in the Federalist Papers, which aimed to build support for the Constitution, and in the nation's "belt and suspenders" separation of powers horizontally (between executive, legislative, and judicial branches) and vertically (between national and subnational governments). In this context, the concept of taking positions on a wide range of policy issues at the national level was unlikely to graze the imaginations, much less shape the actions of party leaders.

At this point, it would be easy to indulge in a sigh at the founders' expense, claiming that their fear of parties and attempted suppression thereof led to undemocratic party practices. This judgment, however, rests on the assumption of a counterfactual in which the founders devised opposing policy positions and competed on this basis, a grossly unrealistic scenario for the time. The meager national government of this era was not well positioned to provide public goods or to implement other types of public policy, and could not have made credible promises in this area.

Political culture among elites and eligible voters—a limited subset of the adult population at this time—was also inimical to issue-based party competition, even if we consider the "multiple traditions" present in the United States since its founding.[11] Programmaticism would not attract those immersed in the American liberal tradition famously described by Louis Hartz (1955), which privileged rugged individualism, private property, and freedom from government interference. Public policy tends to expand rather than contract the size of government. Neither would it appeal to those preferring an illiberal ascriptive tradition, given that the nation "freed" by revolution still enslaved African Americans and restricted the rights of women, Native Americans, immigrants, and others outside the circle of white property-owning men. Considering this status quo, public policy was more likely to spell trouble than triumph for those with an illiberal vision for the nation.

The Jacksonian Party (and Spoils) System

In the 1820s, a cadre of middle-class leaders associated with Andrew Jackson pursued a set of reforms that "created a party-centered political system in the United States."[12] These changes, while transformative in some ways, would fortify rather than diminish the strength of American clientelism by institutionalizing what had been a relatively ad hoc practice. This geographically based mass-mobilization effort shifted power away from the Jacksonians' elite rivals, who'd had a firm grip over political power in the prior era.[13] Reformers constructed stronger party organizations, eventually debuting the infamous *spoils system* in 1828, under which they exchanged bureaucratic positions, mostly unskilled jobs at this time, for political support from working-class voters.[14] A portion of these bureaucrats' salaries were then directed toward the party organization to support its activities.[15] Between 1828 and 1840, similar changes occurred on the other side of the partisan aisle.[16]

This reflects broader patterns, according to classic work on party competition by Martin Shefter (1977, 1994). When the development of internally mobilized mass-based parties predates the development of an administrative state, countries tend to rely primarily on clientelism. Externally mobilized parties do not have access to state resources, and thus need to find other ways to build their party, whereas parties mobilized from within the political system (e.g., those in the United States) are not forced to find such creative solutions. And in the absence of a strong, professional administrative state, politicians can pillage public resources. Essentially, Shefter argues, patronage is irresistible for politicians unless someone or something stops them.

Clientelism also served myriad functions at this point in American history. Beyond well-known benefits like procuring money and labor to help parties mobilize for elections, the Jacksonian spoils system aimed "to legitimate the presence of these novel partisan organizations in a deeply antiparty political culture."[17] This new system was generally seen as democratizing, making government more accessible to average people, not just the elites at its helm during the founding period.[18] Paradoxically, the Jacksonian system legitimized parties, which appear to be necessary for liberal democracy—no known case has endured in their absence—as well as illiberal partisan practices.

Clientelism is also a useful tool for governance under conditions of low economic and political development.[19] For one thing, patronage helped to populate state offices. Distributive clientelism, enacted in part through private bills in Congress directing money and contracts to particular people and businesses within lawmakers' constituencies, also facilitated growth of the nation's infrastructure and economy at a time when the national government had limited administrative capacity to implement public policies.[20] Clientelism was a particularly useful tool in the United States, given its elaborate separation of powers. As Stephen Skowronek argues in his classic book, *Building a New American State*, "By mid-century, administrative patronage had become a key element in supporting the prerogatives of party elites and in facilitating their collective action within America's fragmented institutional system."[21]

The Jacksonian system was decentralized, which may seem counterintuitive since actors associated with a president spearheaded its creation. Given continued distrust of centralized power, however, Sidney Milkis (1993) argues in *The President and the Parties*: "It is not surprising ... that the partisan organizations that arose during the Jacksonian era—Democratic and Whig parties—assumed a form that centered partisan responsibility and practices in the Congress and state government."[22] In any event, as I discuss in more detail in chapters 4 and 5, a decentralized party system is unlikely to encourage issue-based competition at the national level.

By 1856, then, as the Democratic and Republican parties began competing with each other, clientelism was entrenched, and substantive interparty differentiation uncommon. In fact, patronage played a key role in Republicans' transition from a movement to a stable party, and this came at the expense of emphasis on public policy.[23] They were not alone—their Democratic rivals and Whig predecessors also "routinely sidestepped the nation's most pressing policy issues because such controversies jeopardized an often precarious electoral status and threatened the satisfaction of parochial aspirations and acquisitive appetites."[24] Generations of voters had been socialized into politics via clientelism by the mid-nineteenth century, whatever their party affiliation. This system and the less formal clientelistic tradition that predated it would have powerful legacies.

Rise of Political Machines

Clientelism's grip on American politics tightened through the end of the nineteenth century. An additional reason, beyond path dependence, for the persistence of American clientelism despite changes like modernization that normally weaken it was the system's ability to evolve along its path. In the wake of the Civil War, "fierce competition for the presidency and Congress led to greater efforts to strengthen state parties and find ways to cater to the demands of a society in upheaval."[25] American clientelism thus transitioned from the relatively simple Jacksonian spoils model into a more sophisticated party machine model.[26] Machines took on a "managerial" quality, "shar[ing] more in common with the business enterprise or the military organization than with the antebellum spoils organization."[27] This made clientelism a more powerful tool for parties.

In the stereotypical machine, a kingpin (e.g., Tammany Hall's Boss Tweed) oversaw a hierarchical party organization that maintained power over a city by using material incentives (e.g., public jobs, contracts, liquor licenses) to lure and threaten voters, and resorting to electoral malfeasance when those tools proved insufficient. In the case of New York, ballots were notoriously seen floating in the Hudson River, snaking along the city's west side. In actuality, there was considerable variation across machines—some were run by elected officials, some not; most did not rely heavily on corruption, but a few did; some were factional, wherein several ward-level bosses exerted monopolistic power over their own jurisdictions but had to compete with each other for municipal resources; and some were at the state rather than city level. They were unified, however, by their heavy use of material goods and services to garner political support.[28] As in the Jacksonian model, it was common for a percentage of public employees' salaries to be directed toward the party organization, providing critical financial support for its activities. These levies could be quite substantial. "By the 1870s," Kuo notes, "civil service workers at the federal and state levels had to donate as much as 10 percent of their incomes to campaign war chests."[29]

Another commonality was their tendency to avoid issue competition. In a classic work on machines, Raymond E. Wolfinger (1972) notes that policy issues "are irrelevant to this political style and more an irritant than anything else to its practitioners." Among many examples, he cites "one student of Chicago politics [who] said that for the Democratic organization there, 'Issues are obstacles to be overcome, not opportunities to be sought.'"[30] This was not a fertile environment for programmatic growth, to say the least.

While more prevalent in some areas of the country (e.g., the Northeast) than others (e.g., the West), this new form of American clientelism was widespread. Examining thirty large American cities between 1870 and 1945, Brown and Halaby (1987) find that slightly more than half had a machine at the beginning of this period, and the trend shot upward over the next few decades, peaking around 80 percent in the mid-1890s before gradually declining to approximately 50 percent by 1945.[31]

In the eminent words of Skowronek (1982), the United States had developed "a state of courts and parties."[32] Given the structural contrast with peer nations, particularly those in Europe, the United States was often wrongly characterized as stateless, and a "sense of statelessness" pervaded the polity. But there was in fact a state in the feisty former British colony, buttressed largely by clientelistic party organizations.[33] The development of strong bureaucratic institutions would come much later, in a protracted struggle between old and new orders.

Notably, Civil War pensions facilitated the rise and durability of this iteration of the state. These benefits became associated with patronage politics, sapping support for other welfare state programs that could potentially undermine clientelism.[34] Machines pounced on the opportunities that war pensions offered. More broadly, these pensions were not distributed fairly or evenly—politicians used them to gain favor with particularly important constituents, like applicants in electorally important (e.g., swing) states. This legacy undermined public confidence in the idea of a welfare state. People worried that machines would seize patronage opportunities from potential benefits like unemployment insurance, reducing program efficacy while fortifying clientelistic organizations that many viewed as corrupt. Moreover, doubt abounded that the state was capable of administering such programs. This is a good example of how history can constrain future choices. Clientelism delayed the development of a type of program that would ultimately undermine machines. There is a sociological element here, too—people were introduced to the idea of social welfare programs through Civil War pensions that turned out to be highly inefficient and prone to corruption. That impression was sticky.

Challenges to Machines from Development and Reform Movements

It was not all smooth sailing for machines during their heyday in the second half of the nineteenth century. As in other nations, industrialization sowed restlessness with the existing governing structure's meager capabilities. As reformer Carl Schurz argued, the republic's "bucolic stage has long since been passed," and governing institutions had to evolve alongside a changing economy.[35] Pressure also came from businesses needing well-functioning political institutions, from the post office to regulatory bodies.[36] The federal government had grown in size and scope far quicker than in professional capacity.[37] Friction between these multiple orders sparked an opportunity for institutional change. Demand for a career civil service system to manage the tasks of modern governance arose in the United States along with other advanced industrializing nations (e.g., Great Britain, Canada, Japan, Prussia) in the late nineteenth century.

Yet, the United States stood apart from its peers in a key way: "In America," argues Skowronek, "the modernization of national administrative controls did not entail making the established state more efficient; it entailed building a qualitatively different kind of state."[38] This required time and fortitude, as reformers struggled to undermine the entrenched power of subnational parties with strong patronage networks and little interest in policy or administrative capacity. Even when change occurred, reformers did not get to build a new system from scratch. Institutions are rarely dismantled entirely; rather, new institutions are built alongside existing institutions, creating tensions and contradictions.[39]

Resistance to American clientelism began in earnest with a faction of northeastern Republicans, known as Mugwumps, who aspired to eviscerate the spoils system.[40] These elite activists aimed to regain power they had lost with the rise of machines, whose coalitions tended to center on working-class and new immigrant communities. Without patronage, Mugwumps hoped political leaders would pay more attention to public opinion. This would increase their own influence, as the movement was composed largely of "journalists, patricians, and professional men who were opinion leaders in their communities."[41] Leveraging their media ties, they attacked machines through publications like the *Nation* and *Harper's Weekly*, putting forth political cartoons depicting machine bosses as animals, usually tigers, and themselves as heroes defeating the fearsome beasts (see, for example, the cartoon in figure 3.1, from the popular Mugwump publication, *Puck*).[42]

Along with qualms about machines' purported lack of principles, Mugwumps also found their incorporation of new immigrants unsettling. Perpetuating a pattern that has repeated inexhaustively throughout American history, middle- and upper-class Anglo Americans found the presence of "others" in the polity alarming and worked to limit their power.[43] Among their complaints was a rise of Irish nationalism in Boston.[44] Mugwump propaganda often depicted the "Irish Biddy," a derogatory caricature of an Irish servant woman, exerting emasculating power over local politicians (see, for example, the cartoon in figure 3.2).

More formally, Mugwumps attempted to challenge the nation's patronage-based system through civil service reforms in the 1870s and 1880s. This type of reform has been a go-to strategy for movements aiming to reduce clientelism because professionalizing the civil service would reduce its value as a source of patronage, stifling organizations like political machines.[45] If their reforms were enacted, the Mugwumps claimed that "political competition no longer would center around a struggle for the spoils of office; rather, it would involve the clash of principles."[46]

This argument nods to the tension between clientelism and programmaticism and reflects desire for more attention to policy issues; but the Mugwumps' vision was not squarely programmatic. While shared advocacy for abolitionism drew them to the Republican Party during the Civil War era, their goal was not to boost Republicans' chances of beating Democrats using issue positions.[47] They generated more intraparty conflict than Republican fodder for interparty competition, often protesting presidential candidates and appointments they considered unacceptable.[48] They also clashed with their party's mainstream on various issues. These "tempermental outsiders" even discussed dissolving the two-party system.[49] Though this idea never gained traction, it's safe to say the Mugwumps were not serving as strategists for Republicans in competition with Democrats.

FIGURE 3.1. Mugwump depiction of machines as tigers.
"In at the Death," *Puck*, November 7, 1894. This figure originally appeared in *Puck* magazine, a popular Mugwump publication, and was reprinted in Thomas (2001). Source: Library of Congress.

Their tenuous relationship with their party grew explosive in 1884 when they supported Democratic candidate Grover Cleveland over the scandal-ridden Republican James G. Blaine, of whom they had long disapproved. To be clear, this was not a case of a group finding its natural home. While Mugwumps worked more with Democratic leaders after the 1884 election, it was an uneasy partnership. Neither Democrats nor Republicans at heart,

FIGURE 3.2. Mugwump depiction of Irish influence over machines.
This cartoon originally appeared in *Puck* magazine on February 21, 1883, and was reprinted in Thomas (2001). It bore the caption: "Another One Gone Wrong. New York's Mistress: 'Want a new Charter, do you? Take care, or I'll put you up there with the others!'" Source: Library of Congress.

they were not well-positioned to persuade either to change the nature of party appeals.

Indeed, "Mugwumpery was above all an escape from party."[50] They valued their autonomy, eschewing the notion of party loyalty or discipline. They also wanted voters to become more independent, supporting "whichever party nominated the best man."[51] The value they placed on political independence was reflected in their decision to establish one of the nation's first interest groups, the National Civil Service Reform League, "an organization that worked outside party channels to secure the enactment of the policy it advocated, and which was prepared to endorse candidates regardless of party who pledged to vote correctly on this single issue."[52]

Mugwumps' power as a programmatic force was also limited by their failure to develop a coherent, well-considered substantive agenda beyond reforming the civil service, reducing tariffs, and shifting toward the gold standard. Once these issues were no longer at the forefront of the national agenda, many moved toward Progressive causes.[53] The movement also heralded free market forces without developing a plan to manage the era's high levels of poverty and inequality, positing, to the detriment of their credibility, that incomes would naturally rise over time. Moreover, they railed against corruption stemming from wealthy citizens' outsized impact on politics, a stance that sat uneasily with their own status as upper-class elites as well as with their opposition to redistribution.[54]

Reflecting their checkered but still disruptive history, as well as anti-intellectual sentiments and politicians' desire to discredit civil service reformers, Mugwumps evoked derision across the political and geographic spectrum. Despite their nontrivial role in civil service reform, they were "regarded less as professional pioneers than they were as a political nuisance—unwelcome irritants to the settled habits of the public mainstream."[55] In the parlance of path dependence, they were trespassers on the party system's established path. Evincing their strained relationship with Democrats despite their support for Grover Cleveland, Senator Zebulon Vance (D-NC) called the Mugwumps "sickly, sentimental, Sunday-school, 'Goody-two shoes,'" and Senator David B. Hill (D-NY) dismissed them as a "brainless set of namby pambys." On the other side of the aisle, prominent Republican Whitelaw Reid referred to the Mugwumps as a group "living in the sewer."[56] Insults often took on a sexual tone, questioning the Mugwumps' masculinity. A notable example was "Kansas Republican Senator John Ingall's characterization of them as the 'third sex' of American politics, headed for extinction for lack of both virility and fertility." In a similar vein, owing perhaps to their relationship with both parties, they were called "political hermaphrodites." Feminization was also common, as "'Miss-Nancy,' a popular synonym for effeminacy, found constant employment along with doggerel about dainty, delicious 'political flirts.'"[57] For example, the cartoon in figure 3.3 depicts Mugwumps as both feminized and sexually ambiguous, reflecting their embattled relationship with the party system.

FIGURE 3.3. Feminization of Mugwumps.

This cartoon originally appeared in the *Judge* on August 9, 1884. In reprinting the cartoon, Makemson (2004, 186) notes: "In Hamilton's 'Small Favors Thankfully Received' . . . Curtis sported anything but high fashion, wearing the clothes of a middle-aged housewife, complete with droopy socks and tattered, oversized slippers. Curtis offered a small morsel of an 'Independent Vote' to a battle-scarred, emaciated Democratic cat, which replied, 'It ain't much, but it is a god-send to my starving stomach.'" George William Curtis was the editor of Mugwump publication *Harper's Weekly* and would later serve as chair of the National Civil Service Reform League. Source: Archive.org.

In sum, while Mugwumps gained support from some wealthy societal elites, they were not strong political entrepreneurs for programmaticism during their run, from the Ulysses Grant administration through the end of the nineteenth century; and, insults aside, they were not a particularly formidable movement. Based primarily in cities in New York, Massachusetts, and Connecticut, they had limited influence in a primarily rural nation. And despite their high levels of education, they never managed to create strong organizations. Indeed, Muwgumpery "was not an organization but a mood."[58]

Their efforts contributed to the passage of the nation's first civil service reform, the Pendleton Civil Service Act of 1883, but the law did little to reduce patronage.[59] It applied to only some civil service jobs, the federal bureaucracy continued to grow after the law's passage, and very little civil service reform occurred on the state level.[60] This was a major limitation, given the party system's decentralization. Even though "almost 100,000 federal employees were placed under merit rules" in the last few decades of the nineteenth century, "the parties had no less federal or state patronage available to them in 1900 than they had had in 1883."[61]

The Pendleton Act and the Civil Service Commission it created lacked strong, committed entrepreneurs in government to assert and defend their power. The merit system had some utility for politicians, helping to manage appointments in a growing state. But, as Skowronek aptly notes:

> Established governmental elites had not sanctioned a governmental reconstruction. Neither the Half-Breed Republicans nor the Democrats rallying around Grover Cleveland gave any indication that they were now willing to blaze the path the reformers had charted. The merit system was born a bastard in the party state. The support it had gained among the party professionals was that of another weapon in the contest for party power.[62]

The law operated within an entrenched system hostile to its goals. It aimed to reduce parties' power, but "its fate was in the hands of officials who were nothing if not good party men." The underresourced Civil Service Commission released reports condemning patronage, but politicians generally did not heed its advice. In this, we can observe increasing returns in action, as people in power used their power to protect their position. It was a step away from clientelism, but one with limited ability to weaken the system in the short term. In fact, by making civil service somewhat more productive, the law may have delayed the development of a new type of party system.

While many scholars date the growth of a professionalized administrative state to the New Deal, important developments occurred under pressure from groups and circumstances, particularly industrialization, during the late nineteenth and early twentieth centuries. After the turn of the century, "the doors of power opened to those who saw a national administrative apparatus as the centerpiece of a new governmental order."[63] This era saw the establishment of institutions like the Bureau of the Budget and the General Accounting Office (GAO), which would have enduring importance for the goal of heightening the new American state's efficiency.

Central to this effort were Progressives, described in a classic work by James Sundquist (1983) as "one of the most dynamic reform movements of the country's history."[64] Like the Mugwumps, Progressives were a movement of people who found themselves shut out of politics, in this case by a rise in one-party dominance following the 1896 election. If civil service reform weakened machines, "the field would be clear for the reformers to assume power by relying on the organizations and institutions that they controlled—the nonpartisan press, chambers of commerce, civil associations, and so forth."[65]

Progressives shared the Mugwumps' drive to upend the extant party order and deployed some of the same arms against machines. In fact, the Mugwump movement was one of three that provided a foundation for what would become the Progressive movement, along with the Populist movement associated with William Jennings Bryan and social reformers aiming to improve the lives of the poor.[66] These diverse bases gave the Progressive movement breadth and strength, but also rendered it somewhat diffuse and sometimes devoid of clear leadership despite its association with many strong political personalities like Theodore Roosevelt and Robert La Follette.

Progressives were determined to weaken parties. This was a unifying theme for the movement's distinctive parts. Government could and should operate more like the private sector, unburdened by inefficiencies attending party politics, they argued. The extant civil service was not well positioned to support the private sector or to discipline it when necessary, as illustrated in the Progressive cartoon in figure 3.4. To ameliorate these problems, and to serve nativist impulses, this group of mostly middle- and upper-class professionals (e.g., doctors, lawyers, business owners) pursued electoral and civil service reforms. Indeed, Progressives sought not only to wrest power away from machines, but also to secure their social and political dominance over machines' constituencies, composed largely of working-class and immigrant communities.

FIGURE 3.4. Jack and the Wall Street Giants.
This cartoon, titled "Jack and the Wall Street Giants," originally appeared in *Puck*, 56, no. 1402, 1904. Source: Library of Congress.

Progressives had a clearer vision for reform than their predecessors. Through forums like *Atlantic Monthly, Harper's Weekly*, and the *Nation*, they "created a national intellectual community for the first time and provided a national forum where positive and concrete proposals for institutional reform could be aired and debated."[67] Incorporating an "intellectual vanguard of university-trained professionals" into the policymaking process—cited by Skowronek as "America's single most valuable state-building resources," even though they did not hold political office—Progressives came up with tenable proposals, equipping them to take advantage of a window of opportunity whenever it opened.[68] Borrowing ideas from European states with sensitivity toward domestic challenges and institutional idiosyncracies, Progressives "could, in Woodrow Wilson's words, take 'the cosmopolitan what-to-do' and provide an 'American how-to-do it.'"[69] Their plans appealed to many groups who would benefit from a more competent, professional bureaucracy, magnifying the movement's power.

Of particular note were many businesses that had grown impatient with the inefficiencies of clientelism, as Didi Kuo documents in *Clientelism, Capitalism, and Democracy*. The nation's transition from smaller-scale capitalism, symbolized by a large number of family-owned businesses, to managerial capitalism had important implications for businesses' needs from government and, by extension, their preferred method of party competition. "It is not simply the case that wealthier societies are less hospitable to clientelism than poorer ones," Kuo argues. "Instead, capitalism creates a distinct class of economic actors who require different outputs from government. As corporations grow and markets expand, businesses need effective bureaucrats, neutral administration of policy, and predictable party positions, all of which are either lacking or weak in the context of clientelism."[70]

A key reform involved replacing party ballots—printed by party organizations, listing only their own candidates, and clearly recognizable by color—with the Australian (aka "secret") ballot, printed by the government and listing all candidates' names. This new type of ballot, adopted in some form by every state between 1888 and 1892, made voters' decisions more difficult for parties to monitor. This undercut quid pro quo arrangements described above, "deal[ing] a blow" to American clientelism.[71] Outright vote buying became less common by the early twentieth century, at least outside the South.[72]

The strike to clientelism was not fatal, however. Parties could still pay certain voters to stay away from the polls.[73] Moreover, while the power of "a shot of whiskey, a pair of boots, or a small amount of money" at the polls may have declined, patronage remained a valuable tool.[74] As Stokes et al. (2013) note, "Voters who received benefits or public-sector jobs were accountable to machines that were deeply networked organizations, their tentacles reaching through ward and precinct captains into working-class neighborhoods, churches, and meeting halls."[75] Moreover, if the incumbent lost the election, civil servants knew they could lose their jobs. This aligned their incentives. Machines also enjoyed an intangible power over immigrants they had socialized into politics.[76]

Progressives and managerial capitalists made some headway in achieving civil service reforms like competitive bidding for public contracts and merit-based hiring, firing, and promotion practices. The number of federal employees falling under civil service law rose over time, reaching 80 percent by the early 1920s.[77] This would have positive feedback effects, as merit civil service employees became a constituency that worked to protect their status by lobbying Congress.[78] Unsurprisingly, they generally opposed the patronage system. Amendments to the Federal Corrupt Practices Act in 1925 built on Progressive reforms by outlawing the exchange of employment for political support, protecting public employees from campaign contribution requests by public officials—historically intended and perceived to be coercive—and punishing those who offered and accepted electoral bribes.

These reforms were far from ideal, however. They did not extend to the subnational level—civil service reform would not begin to proliferate in the states until the 1930s. This was a critical limitation at a time when the locus of party power was entrenched at the subnational level. Moreover, civil service laws themselves cannot stop the flow of patronage, as they require people with sufficient motivation to enforce them. This would eventually come from external pressure and a gradual change in norms accompanying generational replacement.[79]

Progressives' relationship to programmaticism is complex. They were not aiming to increase issue-based party competition. In fact, they did not desire such competition in any form—they wanted to dampen parties' role in American politics writ large. And commitment to policy positions did not motivate Progressives; unlike the Mugwumps, they "did not want to play the role of intransigent ideologues" (though some, like La Follette, were more policy motivated).[80] Rather, they aimed to render government more managerial and efficient, making cities run more like private businesses. Perhaps for this reason, they did not develop a clear partisan alliance, nor did the national parties take alternative stances on matters of importance to them. In fact, not only did the parties respond in similar ways, they also "responded at about the same time and to about the same degree, so that no sharp distinction could be drawn between them."[81]

Progressives also left complex and somewhat dissonant institutional legacies, helping to achieve electoral and civil service reforms that would undermine machines while establishing reform regimes in many cities that were, according to important work by Jessica Trounstine (2008), similar to machines in key ways. Trounstine groups both types of regimes under the heading of *political monopolies*, which maintain political power via bias and coordination, reducing the need for high quality representation. They used different strategies—machines employing government resources to gain political support, and reform regimes inhibiting opposition groups' ability to express dissent—and tools, machines relying largely on patronage and corruption, and reform regimes controlling access to information, erecting suffrage barriers, and annexing territory to advantage incumbents, for example; but they shared an illiberal sense of electoral security. Under these circumstances, there was little incentive for issue-based electoral competition. In fact, Progressive regimes may have caused a step back in this sense because they extended the reach of monopolistic regimes to cities that did not have machines, like Dallas, Phoenix, and San Jose, among many others. While they might, in theory, have tried to lure nonnative and working class constituencies away from machines through policy appeals, this was neither their strategy nor their aspiration; instead, they tried to disenfranchise these communities and establish their own noncompetitive regimes.

Countervailing these forces, however, Progressive reforms provided an important foundation for programmaticism by creating a stronger and more professional bureaucracy (i.e., with defined jobs, benefits, etc.) that was more capable of implementing public policy. Pressure for these changes came from managerial capitalists as well.[82] Progressives also forged a stronger relationship between the executive and societal elites, the kind of voters who tend to generate demand for programmaticism.

These changes, while important, were not completely transformational. The system evolved under pressure from reformers, including Progressive-minded presidents like Theodore Roosevelt, but reformers had to contend with the entrenched system they had inherited, sometimes dismantling but often building new institutions alongside existing ones. In short, they created an administrative system, but it didn't work particularly well—this was the "paradox of Progressive state building."[83] Frustratingly, "Machinery for the attainment of efficiency proliferated, but 'the system as a whole [was] ill-geared.'"[84] This problem would not resolve easily in the short term, especially given that reformers' influence declined as the country entered an era containing two world wars and a global depression.

Clientelism's trajectory over time reflects the partial success of Progressives and managerial capitalists. Machines became less common between the late nineteenth century and mid-twentieth centuries, though they were still a significant presence in 1945, the end of Brown and Halaby's (1987) period of study. Indeed, patronage-based party organizations remained relatively prevalent into the 1960s.[85]

Scholars have validated this pattern with an alternative measure of clientelism: contested elections to the U.S. Congress, defined by "the filing of proceedings to bar the right to a seat of a Member-elect based upon a question concerning the electoral process."[86] The House's first committee, the Committee on Elections, was tasked with settling these disputes, indicating their prominence in the republic's early years. While not a direct measure of clientelism, it's a reasonably good proxy because "most contests concern electoral fraud, irregularities, and improper ballots or ballot counting."[87] Contested elections are used to measure electoral abuse in other countries, and they offer data that are generally consistent across states and time in the United States.[88] Studying the period from 1789 to 2011, Kuo (2018) finds that clientelism skyrocketed in the second half of the nineteenth century, peaked around the turn of the century, fell in the first half of the twentieth century, and has remained low since then.[89] The pattern is similar in looking at contested elections as a percentage of all seats from 1789 to 2000.[90] In sum, the apex of machine prevalence corresponds roughly to a peak in contested elections in Congress in the late nineteenth century.

Kuo (2018) also estimates clientelism in policymaking by examining the number of public versus private acts of Congress over time. While many public acts during this period were distributive—used, for example, to build post offices and railroad lines—they were targeted to areas rather than individuals. In contrast, "Private legislation in Congress aids specific individuals on issues like naturalization, pensions, and patents."[91] Kuo shows that private legislation grew from roughly half of all legislation in Congress in 1870 to a stunning peak of more than 80 percent around the turn of the century. It began to plummet in the late aughts, reaching a low just over zero around 1920 before climbing back to just under 40 percent in 1930. Data from the Congressional Bills Project show that private bills remained at a moderate level, between roughly 25 and 45 percent between the 80th Congress (1947–49) and the 90th (1967–69), before falling dramatically. They remain very low as a percentage of congressional legislation today.[92]

A few important points emerge from this analysis. First, multiple measures suggest that the pinnacle of clientelism was around the late nineteenth century; and, notably, my measure of programmaticism began its first significant upward trend shortly after the turn of the twentieth century. Kuo (2018) presents qualitative evidence that lends additional credence to the notion that programmaticism rose around this time, which in turn supports the theory that clientelism and programmaticism have an inverse relationship in the United States. By the end of the nineteenth century, Kuo argues, Republicans and Democrats fundamentally reconstructed their approaches: "They established party organizations that campaigned using ideological appeals, and touted policy victories in election campaigns. Rather than creating policy through incremental and ad hoc distribution of resources, parties established institutions to regulate the national economy and provide public goods."[93] Around the same time, "national party organizations became more attuned to national issues such as currency policy, tariffs, and railway regulation as they crafted party platforms and developed policy agendas" and "developed issue-oriented campaigns with which to attract voters."[94]

Nevertheless, clientelism remained a major force in the mid-twentieth century. Machines were still present in approximately half of American cities in 1945, and private legislation was a significant proportion of all congressional legislation between the mid-1920s and the late 1960s. Contested elections for the U.S. Congress had fallen, but clientelism was still common in local elections.[95] It is not surprising, then, that the first rise of programmaticism was modest and unsustained—the trend flattens from the early 1940s through the late 1960s (see figure 1.1). Underscoring the relatively small slope of this rise, scholars have noted that Democrats and Republicans took very similar positions on the major issues of the day in the nineteenth century.[96]

One might wonder how clientelism endured in the face of reforms and the rise of multiple factors associated with its decline, like economic growth, urbanization, and welfare state development. The answer, at least in part, is that the New Deal had a complex relationship with clientelism.

The New Deal: Friend and Foe to American Clientelism

Clientelism became embroiled in the politics of state building during the New Deal era. If we shift our institutional focus to the federal government, clientelism becomes a good example of what Greif and Laitin (2004) call a *quasi-parameter*, something that is parametric for people working within an institution at a particular moment, but that can ultimately be changed by that institution. In other words, it is exogenous to individuals in the short term but endogenous to the collective in the long term. The New Deal, which built the modern American state after the Great Depression undermined the nation's historically laissez-faire approach to governance, temporarily propped up machines while planting seeds for their ultimate dissolution.

Thinking about clientelism as a quasi-parameter for national state builders is useful for two reasons: (1) it helps explain both stability and change in the party system; and (2) it shows how the New Deal contributed to the sharp rise of programmaticism—and, by extension, polarization—in the contemporary era, even though the latter happened decades after the former. Typically, studies of the origins of contemporary polarization focus on the late 1960s to the present. Considering clientelism as a quasi-parameter for national state builders encourages us to take a longer view, revealing critical foundations for these contemporary changes that we would otherwise miss. "The fate of courts and parties in the new American state," argues Skowronek (1982, 288), "was sealed during the New Deal" as new bureaucratic institutions pushed these older institutions away from the center of the American political system.

In crafting New Deal policies, federal lawmakers had to contend with machines, whose power was parametric for them at the time.[97] This was not new—presidents and members of Congress had long worked and wrestled with clientelistic subnational parties. "Presidents who shunned machines and patronage, like Rutherford Hayes, risked isolation and defections from within their party," note Stokes et al.[98] Even reform-minded presidents could not evade this dynamic. Woodrow Wilson, whose early vision for programmaticism provided a foundation for the work of Schattschneider and APSA's Committee on Political Parties and whose advocacy for civil service reform intensified over time, was not able to shift the nation away from clientelism. "The spoils remained an embarrassment to the former professor," but he struggled to come up with a viable way to displace them while the administrative system remained weak.[99]

Even Franklin Delano Roosevelt, whose power during an era of international crisis was so great that mainstream journalists and intellectuals pondered whether he was or should become a dictator, accommodated the party system to a significant degree.[100] Famously pragmatic, FDR allowed machines to use some of the public jobs created by the New Deal as patronage so long as they supported the administration's goals. For example, the Works Progress Administration (WPA), a public employment program established in 1935 to reduce unemployment and build public works infrastructure, fed many jobs to party machines.[101] The Roosevelt administration initially tried to keep the program from becoming entangled with clientelism but relented after the

1936 election. A windfall ensued for machines, as "WPA projects doubled the number of public-sector jobs available in Depression-ravaged cities like New York, Jersey City, and Chicago."[102] To be clear, machines did not control the WPA—distribution of funds across states was based in part on transparent formulas (a key criterion for programmatic spending according to Stokes et al.), need, and the administration's own electoral considerations.[103] Nonetheless, many machines benefited from the WPA and other public jobs created by New Deal programs and its expansion of the administrative state. The percentage of total federal employment that was competitive dipped in the first half of the 1930s after rising between the 1880s and the 1920s. It went back up by 1940 (the end of Kuo's period of analysis), though not quite to 1920s levels.[104] The era was, in this sense, a boon for clientelism.

Welfare state programs had a nuanced relationship with machine politics. The New Deal is often credited with weakening machines because laws like the Social Security Act of 1935 provided benefits that machines had traditionally offered.[105] Government, not the machine, became people's primary safety net from the vagaries of capitalism and inevitable poverty that had long attended old age for millions of Americans, for example. Labor unions, strengthened by collective bargaining rights established by the New Deal's Wagner Act, also fulfilled needs that machines had once served. Ultimately, this argument is compelling. For a while, however, the expanded welfare state counterintuitively provided opportunities for machines to offer new services to their constituents. The system appeared labyrinthine to many people unaccustomed to accessing government programs, and machines offered navigational assistance. They also used less benign tactics, providing preferential access to programs for political supporters. Erie (1988) points to an example from Chicago's Kelly-Nash machine: "To expedite Social Security and [Aid to Families with Dependent Children] eligibility . . . precinct captains initiated client contacts with social service agencies." Indeed, the New Deal actually increased rather than crowding out machines' involvement in social services in some places for a while—Erie notes that "by 1936 two-thirds of the [Kelly-Nash] machine's lieutenants reported serving as employment and welfare brokers, up from one-third in 1928."[106]

At the same time, the New Deal's boldness generated constituencies for and against its goals in a manner that ultimately facilitated programmaticism.[107] It also ignited power struggles between those wanting a national approach to politics and state and local incumbents, which ended with a rise in party competition based on national issues in many places. Variation in the outcome of these struggles was largely a function of state and local incumbents' responses to the New Deal and the nature of their organizations.[108] While the Roosevelt administration largely accommodated those supporting its ambitious goals, recalcitrant machines faced challenges by New Deal liberals. In cities with strong mass-based organizations (e.g., New York), New Deal liberals established organizations (e.g., third parties, reform clubs) to challenge the machines. These clashes between "professional" and "amateur" politicians echoed earlier conflicts between machines and Progressives.[109] In places without a strong machine (e.g., Michigan, Minnesota), New Deal liberals did not need to go through such protracted battles with uncooperative state and local incumbents. Rather, "the liberals were able with little difficulty to take over the Democratic caucus structure by allying with labor unions and farm organizations that had benefited from New Deal programs." Notably, those assuming control of subnational parties in this manner "became advocates of party government, by 'responsible,' issue-oriented parties."[110] On the whole, variation in responses to the New Deal's centripetal force lends credence to the notion that clientelism constrained the growth of programmaticism—it was in cities without strong machines that issue-oriented parties arose.

Advocacy for programmatic partisanship was driven by short- and long-term considerations. New Deal liberals wanted to gain power locally, especially in places where the incumbent leadership did not support them. Their long-term interests were also served more by programmatic partisanship than clientelism. They wanted government to do a lot, which requires bureaucratic capacity and professionalism. In this sense, they were much like managerial capitalists frustrated with clientelism half a century earlier. Issue-based competition was also in the self-interest of these middle-class liberals, as it would increase "need for the advice of professionals, technocrats, and administrators who are the most fertile source of ideas for new public policies."[111] In any event, these liberals were stronger advocates for increasing programmaticism—rather than just reducing clientelism—than reformers who came before them, like Progressives and Mugwumps.

This era also brought trouble for machines in the shape of civil service reforms at the federal level and—finally—in the states as well. The Hatch Act of 1939, largely a conservative coalition win, limited the political activities of federal employees. This law, "widely perceived to have limited the ability of politicians to exploit patronage appointments for electoral gains," extended its reach through a 1940 amendment to "any state and local government employees who work in areas financed by federal government loans and grants."[112] State-level civil service reform, elusive for Progressives, would also become more common during the New Deal era, accelerating between the 1930s and 1960s.[113] By the end of this period, civil service reforms were present in forty-three states, and they were generally lasting. This sea change, induced largely by pressure from the federal government, presented difficulties for machines relying on patronage.[114]

Along with challenging clientelism, the New Deal provided an important foundation for programmaticism by extending the work of late nineteenth-century bureaucratic state builders. The Roosevelt administration established new agencies and executive institutions (e.g., the Securities and Exchange Commission, the Federal Housing Administration, the National Labor Relations Board), as well as pushing for the Executive Reorganization Act of 1939, which increased the White House staff and improved bureaucratic efficiency. These reforms had important implications for programmaticism, as they "would endow the administration with the institutional capacity to control the initiation, coordination, and implementation of public policy—a capacity whose only precedent in the political experience of the United States ... was the control exercised by the party apparatus in cities ruled by centralized machines."[115]

The New Deal's broader expansion of executive power also affected machines. Noting "an inherent tension between executive power and party politics," Sidney Milkis (1993, 5) argues that Roosevelt shifted the balance of power toward the former. Milkis states the case quite strongly, arguing that "the reconstruction of the executive during the New Deal caused the decline of the traditional party system by displacing parties as the principal instrument of popular rule."[116]

In sum, the New Deal had a complex relationship with clientelism and programmaticism. It set off processes that would ultimately reduce clientelism, but machines were nowhere near elimination at the end of the New Deal era or even soon thereafter. In a sweeping history of American parties, David Mayhew (1986) assigns each state a score between 1 and 5, indicating the level of traditional party organization (TPO) present in that state in the late 1960s.[117] States with a score of 1 (e.g., Minnesota, North Carolina) had no TPOs at this time, while states with a score of 5 (e.g., Illinois, Pennsylvania) had strong TPOs. Figure 3.5 displays these scores.

On the whole, twenty states had at least some degree of TPO in the late 1960s (TPO score >1). The level of strong TPOs was lower, but still notable, with eight states receiving the maximum score of 5, and another five states

Prevalence of traditional party organizations, late 1960s

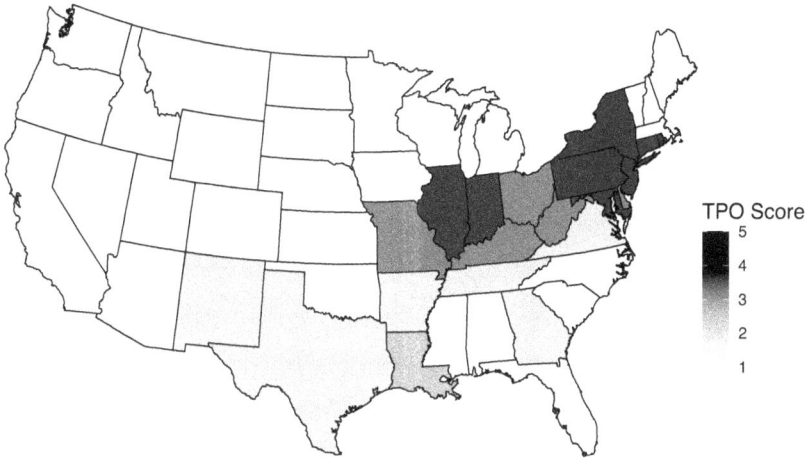

FIGURE 3.5. Map of TPO scores.
This map displays Mayhew's (1986) measure of traditional party organization in the late 1960s. The scale runs from 1 (no TPO) to 5 (strong TPO).

receiving a score of 4. Simple tallying understates the power of machines at this time, given that the highest scores tend to be in states with relatively large populations. Fifty-six percent of the country's population lived in states with some degree of TPO, and 40 percent lived in a state with a high score (4 or 5). But this would not last. Mayhew (1986) chose to measure TPO strength in the late 1960s because they declined sharply after this time.

The Decline of American Clientelism

Machines atrophied after the late 1960s for numerous reasons, many of which involved the maturation of factors already discussed. While industrialization initially increased poverty along with economic growth in the United States, modernization would ultimately render the political environment less amenable to clientelism. Stokes et al. (2013, 237) argue, "Only with some equalization of the distribution of income, between the 1930s and the 1970s, as well as rapid post-World War II economic expansion, did the center of gravity of the electorate shift from working- to middle-class voters." They call this "a key factor lying behind the belated demise of American clientelism." On top of these forces, the children of immigrants gradually shrank machines' constituencies by moving en masse to the suburbs after World War II.[118]

Institutions, programs, and processes established during the New Deal also began to bear fruit from a programmatic standpoint. State-level civil service reforms reduced the electoral advantage that patronage had long provided, especially for strongly entrenched parties.[119] Combined with the expansion of federal civil service reform's reach, this depleted one of machines' most important forms of currency.[120] Collective bargaining, protected by the Wagner Act of 1935 and credited with the steep rise of union membership between the mid-1930s and late 1940s, further undermined patronage practices by making rules for firing employees more explicit. Though the Taft-Hartley Act of 1947 weakened existing labor strongholds, many states introduced collective bargaining provisions in the second half of the twentieth century, even as union membership overall was declining, and public sector organizing increased. By the 1960s and 1970s, public sector collective bargaining strained clientelism as well.[121]

Embattled machines also faced a new set of determined reformers. The New Politics movement arose after the 1960 election and was invigorated by the infamous 1968 Democratic National Convention, which crowned a nominee who had not won a single primary election. The movement's rise and legacy "occurred within and was conditioned by the breakdown of the New Deal order," which had "rested on a tripartite coalition of northern liberals and labor unions, urban machines, and the authoritarian enclaves of the Jim Crow South."[122] The movement's ambitions and accomplishments reflected changing power dynamics among these groups.

In some ways, the New Politics movement echoed themes of its predecessors. It was composed of groups seeking more influence and wary of the clientelistic style that had long dominated party politics. Repeating what had become a refrain for reformers, the movement argued that machines were incapable of handling key tasks required by modern governance, and its adherents disdained the power that local party leaders in "smoke filled rooms" wielded over presidential nominations. But this movement was born in a different political context than its predecessors had faced, one in which other forces had loosened clientelism's grip on the party system. It was better positioned than earlier movements to slay patronage-hungry "tigers" in the manner so often depicted by Mugwumps, for whom this image was more of an aspiration than a reflection of reality. In other words, friction between *multiple orders* created an opportunity for the New Politics movement to facilitate change in the party system.

In contrast to prior challengers, the movement aimed to improve rather than weaken party organizations, working to steer party politics toward pro-grammaticism, not just away from clientelism.[123] They had strong views on various matters (e.g., full employment, the Vietnam War, African American rights) and wanted issues to play a key role in party competition.[124] In other words, they were more powerful and direct political entrepreneurs for programmaticism. While they were primarily involved with the Democratic Party, their actions also affected Republicans, as their rise on the left "was a focal event in the formation of neoconservatism before its migration to the Republican Party in the 1980s."[125]

Like previous reformers, the New Politics movement achieved influence more easily on the federal level than on the state level. Shefter (1994, 87) argues, "If for no other reason than to retain the loyalty of this element of their constituency, Presidents Kennedy and Johnson were constantly in the market for 'program material', proposals for new programs and policies." This is notable because it shows that the movement commanded attention from the executive branch and exposes the dearth of party positions on issues at this time. The Kennedy and Johnson administrations responded to this supply-side problem by creating task forces, which devised key New Frontier and Great Society programs. These policies were a product of programmatic pressure from the New Politics movement more than demand from the programs' beneficiaries.[126]

Though it faced familiar resistance at the local level, the New Politics movement was working in an environment with a far more robust federal government than had existed during the Progressive era. Movement members used this development to their advantage, responding to local opposition by arguing that municipalities were incapable of accomplishing the president's goals, and pushing for grant-in-aid programs that would allow the federal government to exert more control at the subnational level. Members of the administration concurred.[127] Federal grant-in-aid programs established under the Kennedy and Johnson administrations pushed cities to "either establish independent agencies under the control of the local counterparts of the officials in Washington who dispensed this money or to have existing municipal departments contract with consulting forms or hire administrators who shared the outlook and knew the vocabulary of dispensers of federal grants."[128]

One could strain to identify a critical moment at which change from path dependence was possible, when party leaders stopped continuing down the

branch of the tree that people generations before them had chosen, to borrow an analogy developed by Margaret Levi (1999) and highlighted by Paul
Pierson (2000a) in his influential work on this concept; but it is probably
more correct to say that the system slowly outgrew its path before reaching
its breaking point. A largely clientelistic party system could no longer meet
the demands of modern governance; the proverbial "branch" buckled under
the weight of changing expectations regarding what government ought to do.
And while pressure from groups like the New Politics movement and forces
like modernization facilitated this evolution, endogenous dynamics were also
important. Federal state builders, once constrained by a seemingly immov-
able clientelistic tradition, played a critical role in changing this system over
the long term.

The New Politics movement was also a key driving force behind Democratic reforms that followed the party's tumultuous 1968 convention.[129] The
uproar sparked by Hubert Humphrey's nomination led to the establishment
of the McGovern-Fraser Commission (formally, the Commission on Party
Structure and Delegate Selection), which recommended, among other things,
that the party's nomination process be made more accessible to the general
public, and that the party's convention be more representative of a wider range
of groups.[130] The Democratic Party proceeded to enact major reforms, and
state legislatures—generally controlled by Democrats at this time—extended
many of these changes to the Republican Party. The 1972 Democratic Convention exhibited significant differences from the previous one, not only in
the method by which the candidate was selected but also in terms of party
positions. The platform supported withdrawal of troops from Vietnam, the
Equal Rights Amendment, more racially liberal policies, and guaranteed jobs.
Moreover, as Adam Hilton (2016) notes, "Perhaps the most important sym-
bol of the new direction of the party was the unseating of Chicago mayor
[and machine leader] Richard Daley and his handpicked Illinois delegation
and its replacement with one meeting the racial, gender, and age requirements
codified in the new reforms."[131]

These reforms had long-lasting impacts on the party system, key among
which was contributing to the rise of modern polarization.[132] This effect
occurred, at least in part, through the mechanisms of reducing machine
power and generating opportunity and pressure for programmaticism. While
these reforms may not have reduced the power of parties on the whole—an
important insight offered by Cohen et al. (2008) and others associated with
the group-centered theory of parties—they did affect intraparty dynamics,

diffusing power and amplifying the voices of previously underrepresented groups. This put more influence in the hands of party actors desiring a shift toward issue-oriented party competition centered more on national than on state or local issues, even after the New Politics movement faded.

In sum, the accretion of New Politics efforts with those of other reformers ultimately weakened American clientelism. At the same time, Stokes et al. (2013, 242) argue, the forces of modernization made clientelism's brokers less reliable and the system as a whole less efficient, leading party leaders at all levels of the federal system to desire reform. Stokes and colleagues acknowledge the influence of movements to some extent but argue, "it was party leaders, in the state legislatures and in Congress, who distrusted the machines that they had relied on, who were the driving forces behind reforms."

Although different scholars emphasize different factors undermining American clientelism and put forth timelines that vary on the margins, it is generally thought to have declined by the late 1960s—the very point at which programmaticism began its steep and steady rise.[133] Stokes et al. (2013) remark that Banfield and Wilson (1965), in their canonical work, "were writing about a vanishing phenomenon," noting that the "classical" machine no longer existed in any large city. Mayhew (1986) argues that machines were mostly gone after the late 1960s.[134] Other measures of clientelism also indicate decline over this period. The number of private bills in Congress dropped significantly after the late 1960s, and contested elections continued to decline as well (though that trend started earlier, around 1940).

Other forms of clientelism also faded. The New Politics movement achieved bureaucratic reforms offering more representation for consumers and the public interest, pushing back against "administrative clientelism—the 'capture' of regulatory and administrative agencies by producer interests."[135] This variation of clientelism, another example of its ability to evolve over time in a way that facilitated its durability, stemmed from the fact that businesses were strongly involved in administrative development in the late nineteenth century.[136]

Distributive spending became mostly programmatic as well. While machines long offered their supporters privileged access to public benefits, "the welfare state in twenty-first-century America is, generally speaking, thoroughly rule-bound, bureaucratized, and insulated from partisan manipulation."[137] Politicians can, of course, influence welfare spending, just not in a way that targets individual voters. In fact, it's common for spending dynamics to change along with party control of institutions, "but the resulting patterns of distribution are usually predictable from public debates and from the formalized rules of distribution; that is, they are programmatic."[138]

State-Level Analysis

It is simple enough to see that programmaticism and standard measures of party polarization began rising dramatically in the late 1960s to early 1970s, soon after machines dissipated. This is consistent with the clientelism constraint hypothesis but could, of course, be a coincidence. To test the relationship in another way, we can exploit state-level variation on these variables.

Some state platform data are available thanks to significant efforts by a group of scholars; but given the difficulty involved in collecting state platforms, coverage remains spotty, especially for earlier years.[139] I use data from 2012, a year for which a relatively high number of platforms is available. Daniel Coffey calculated ideology scores (ranging from −1 to 1) for these platforms.[140] The observed range for 2012 is 0.28 to 0.76 for Democrats (mean = 0.51, standard deviation = 0.13) and −0.73 to −0.09 for Republicans (mean = −0.51, standard deviation = 0.14). I take the absolute difference between the two parties' scores as a measure of programmaticism (mean = 1.03, standard deviation = 0.22). This results in a sample size of thirty-one states, as platforms need to be available for both parties in order to calculate the difference. To measure the strength of patronage organizations, I use Mayhew's TPO scores.

While the temporal gap between platform data availability and machines' decline may not be ideal, these data are still worth examining. If the clientelism constraint hypothesis is correct, we might expect states with a strong history of patronage organization in the 1960s to lag behind states without such legacies in the development of distinct party positions. Presumably, in states without strong patronage organizations, parties always needed to rely on other types of incentives to appeal to voters. While parties in former machine states eventually needed to transition from material to purposive incentives, they would have started this process later. With less time for parties to develop strong, alternative positions, we should see lower levels of differentiation.

I begin with a simple bivariate analysis, results of which are displayed in figure 3.6. The dotted line shows the linear relationship with a 95 percent confidence interval shaded in gray. We observe less platform differentiation, on average, in states that had stronger patronage organizations in the late 1960s. This negative relationship is both substantively and statistically significant.

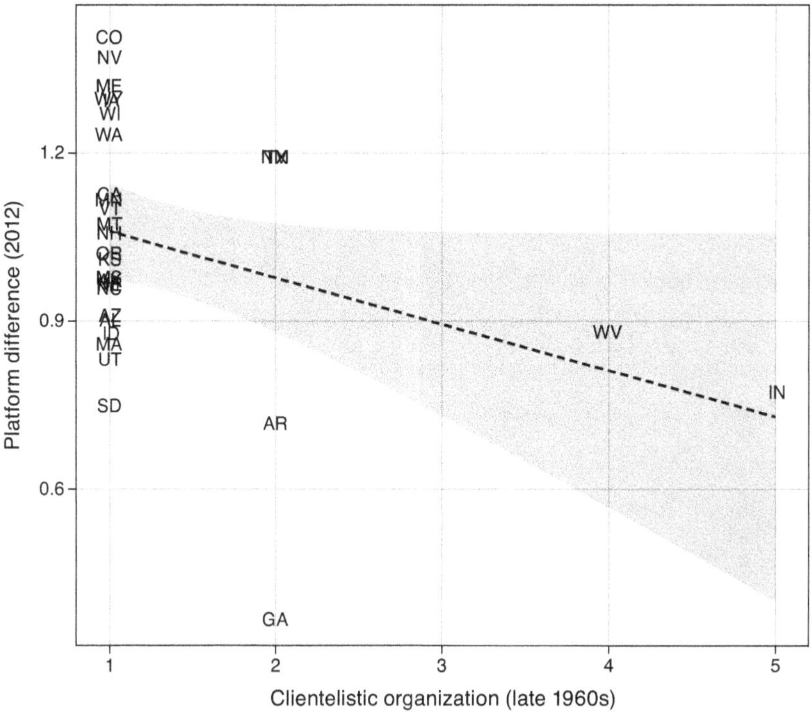

FIGURE 3.6. Patronage legacies and differences in state platforms. Clientelistic organization reflects Mayhew's (1986) TPO scores, and the measure of state platform differentiation comes from Daniel Coffey. The dashed line shows the linear relationship with a 95% confidence interval shaded in gray.

For each additional point on the TPO scale, platform differentiation goes down by 0.08, on average. This means that moving from the minimum to the maximum TPO score reduces differentiation by more than a standard deviation. This is remarkable, given that nearly half a century elapsed between the fall of traditional party organizations and this measure of programmaticism. Patronage organizations had powerful legacies.

To consider the effects of other factors, I ran a set of four ordinary least squares (OLS) models. The main independent variable of interest is the state TPO score. Model 1 includes only these scores (i.e., the analysis shown in figure 3.6). Model 2 adds two control variables known to be associated with polarization: income inequality, measured by the Gini index for each state; and immigration, measured by the percentage of each state's population that is foreign born.[141] Model 3 adds covariates known to be associated with

TABLE 3.1. Patronage legacies and contemporary state platform differentiation (ordinary least squares models with robust standard errors)

	Model 1	Model 2	Model 3	Model 4
TPO	−0.08*	−0.07*	−0.07*	−0.07*
	(0.03)	(0.03)	(0.03)	(0.03)
Gini index		−2.15	−4.26	−2.83
		(2.33)	(3.94)	(4.55)
% Foreign born		0.01	0.02	0.01
		(0.01)	(0.02)	(0.02)
Median income (HH)			−0.00	−0.00
			(0.00)	(0.00)
% Urban			−0.00	−0.00
			(0.01)	(0.01)
Population			0.03	0.06
			(0.08)	(0.11)
% Black				−0.05
				(0.07)
N	31	31	31	31
R^2	0.11	0.16	0.19	0.23
adj. R^2	0.08	0.06	−0.01	−0.01
Resid. sd	0.21	0.22	0.23	0.23

Robust standard errors in parentheses.
Intercepts not shown.
Population and percentage Black are logged.
[†] significant at $p < .10$; *$p < .05$; **$p < .01$; ***$p < .001$.

programmaticism, either positively or negatively: income, urbanization, and total population (logged). Model 4 adds the percentage of each population that is Black (logged) to account, albeit coarsely, for variation in programmaticism stemming from racial politics. Data for all these covariates come from the U.S. Census Bureau.

Results are shown in table 3.1. The coefficient on TPO scores is not simply robust to the inclusion of additional variables; it is virtually unchanged by them. TPO scores have a statistically and substantively significant negative association with party differentiation across all model specifications.

Given that platforms were available for only thirty-one states, I reran this analysis using state polarization scores in lieu of the difference between platforms.[142] While polarization and programmaticism are not the same, they are related, and though polarization can be caused by forces other than policy differences, policy differences will tend to contribute to polarization.

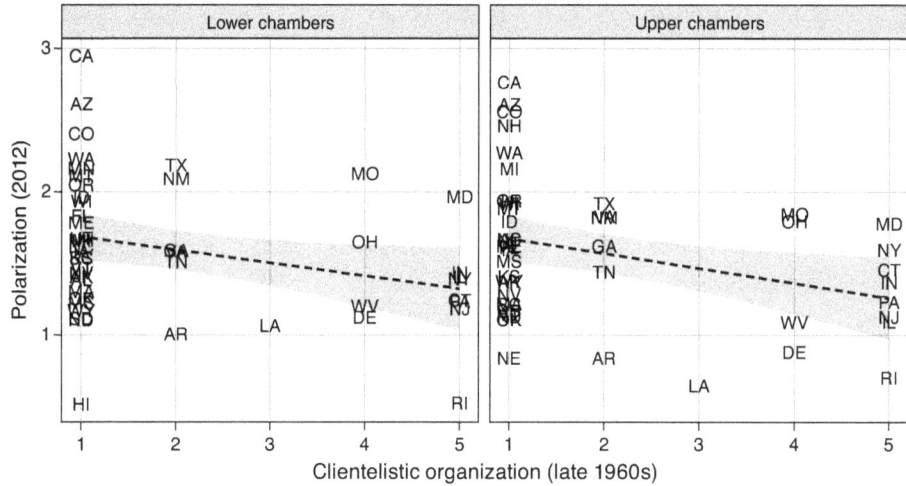

FIGURE 3.7. Patronage legacies and contemporary polarization
in state legislatures.
Clientelistic organization reflects Mayhew's (1986) TPO scores, and state polarization measures come from Shor and McCarty (2011). The dashed line shows the
linear relationship with a 95% confidence interval shaded in gray. Similar figures
appear in McCarty (2016) for bivariate models that pool data from all years for
which polarization data were available at the time (1996–2008).

To measure state polarization, I use Shor and McCarty's (2012) data.[143]
They estimate ideal points for state legislators that are comparable across
chambers, states, levels of government, and time, using roll-call data (the traditional source for ideal point estimation at the national level) and surveys of
state and federal legislators. To calculate polarization for each chamber in each
state, they measure the distance between the ideal points of the median member of each party. In 2012, this measure ranges from 0.51 to 2.95 in state lower
chambers (mean = 1.57, standard deviation = 0.49), and 0.64 to 2.76 (mean
= 1.56, standard deviation = 0.49) in upper chambers.

As evident in figure 3.7, the results were very similar to the results for platforms (see also table 3.2 for polarization in lower chambers and table 3.3 for
polarization in upper chambers).

Discussion

There is no "smoking gun" for the clientelism constraint hypothesis, but the
combination of different types of evidence analyzed from different angles

TABLE 3.2. Patronage legacies and contemporary state-level polarization, lower chambers (ordinary least squares models with robust standard errors)

	Model 1	Model 2	Model 3	Model 4
TPO	−0.09*	−0.11*	−0.11*	−0.08[†]
	(0.04)	(0.05)	(0.04)	(0.05)
Gini index		1.86	−7.60	−1.97
		(4.89)	(4.71)	(5.91)
% Foreign born		0.02	0.01	−0.01
		(0.02)	(0.02)	(0.02)
Median income (HH)			−0.00	0.00
			(0.00)	(0.00)
% Urban			−0.00	−0.00
			(0.01)	(0.01)
Population			0.33**	0.43***
			(0.10)	(0.11)
% Black				−0.22*
				(0.09)
N	48	48	48	48
R^2	0.09	0.16	0.39	0.51
adj. R^2	0.07	0.10	0.30	0.43
Resid. sd	0.47	0.46	0.41	0.37

Robust standard errors in parentheses.
Intercepts not shown.
Population and percentage Black are logged.
[†] significant at $p < .10$; *$p < .05$; **$p < .01$; ***$p < .001$.

strongly suggests that clientelism and programmaticism have been inversely related in the United States, and more specifically, that clientelism long constrained the growth of programmaticism. We can see this first by simply comparing their trajectories, as clientelism's weakening in the late nineteenth to early twentieth century was followed by a modest rise in programmaticism, and its ultimate demise in the late 1960s opened a window for programmaticism to skyrocket.

Looking more closely at the history of the American party system gives us a sense of why these two types of party appeals have an inverse association, and why clientelism endured for such a long time. This strategy emerged early and conferred increasing returns to politicians and voters, making it difficult to dislodge. State builders could not simply extend existing institutions to adapt to new developments like industrialization but had to challenge an entrenched institutional order. The clientelistic party system's decentralized

TABLE 3.3. Patronage legacies and contemporary state-level polarization, upper chambers (ordinary least squares models with robust standard errors)

	Model 1	Model 2	Model 3	Model 4
TPO	−0.10**	−0.12*	−0.14**	−0.11*
	(0.04)	(0.05)	(0.05)	(0.05)
Gini index		−0.71	−6.75	−1.64
		(3.16)	(5.37)	(6.16)
% Foreign born		0.03*	0.01	−0.01
		(0.01)	(0.02)	(0.02)
Median income (HH)			0.00	0.00
			(0.00)	(0.00)
% Urban			−0.00	−0.00
			(0.01)	(0.01)
Population			0.31***	0.41***
			(0.08)	(0.07)
% Black				−0.20**
				(0.07)
N	48	48	48	48
R^2	0.11	0.23	0.42	0.53
adj. R^2	0.09	0.17	0.33	0.44
Resid. sd	0.47	0.45	0.40	0.36

Robust standard errors in parentheses.
Intercepts not shown.
Population and percentage Black are logged.
[†] significant at $p < .10$; *$p < .05$; **$p < .01$; ***$p < .001$.

power structure also dampened its response to the rise of more national-level issues.[144] Consequently, the growth of programmaticism and factors that would facilitate it, like administrative institutions and a welfare state, were delayed and piecemeal relative to other advanced industrialized nations. In a state with a weak bureaucracy entangled in patronage politics, programmatic partisanship had limited space to develop. Perhaps realizing this, early movements against clientelism were not pushing strongly and directly for programmaticism.

These dynamics changed in the mid- to late twentieth century. New Dealers had to contend with the clientelistic subnational party system that remained robust at the time, and they cooperated with machines to some extent. Their state-building efforts also provided an unprecedented level of public resources that could be used for patronage. Nonetheless, the New Deal's expansion of federal power and benefits ultimately undermined machines. Of course, this was not the only challenge to machines—they also faced a highly developed economy with a larger middle class, owing partly to economic growth and partly to the GI Bill, a more urbanized population, and challenges by groups left out of machine politics. In the New Politics movement, programmaticism had much stronger political entrepreneurs than it had in earlier movements challenging clientelism. The political environment was also more auspicious for New Politics leaders, who faced a foe that had been weakened by earlier movements like Mugwumps and forces like modernization. While clientelism's overall decline was gradual, the final descent—from the moderate level Mayhew described in the late 1960s to near extinction with exceptions—occurred quite quickly, much like a cracked branch can fall off a tree in a storm. At this point, there was pent-up demand for programmaticism and a bureaucracy ready to support this type of party system. This helps explain why, after a long period in which programmaticism was far lower than one would expect based on the nation's level of development, it soared in the contemporary era.

In examining tools for appealing to voters, it is important to recognize the realities of party systems: they are complex and messy, like all other facets of politics, and no system relies entirely on one tool at any given time. The argument here is not that the system went from being entirely clientelistic to entirely programmatic. Indeed, Gerring (1998) has argued that American parties have always stood for something, and scholars have argued that some differences in party programs emerged in the late nineteenth century.[145] This shows up in my measure of programmaticism, which is always above zero and rises modestly around the turn of the twentieth century. Moreover, even at clientelism's apex during the Gilded Age, parties also appealed to voters along "economic, sectional, ethnic, and religious" lines.[146] They could and did use multiple strategies. And though the general consensus is that machines declined significantly after the 1960s, clientelistic practices still pepper the nation's politics. Some cities (e.g., Newark, NJ) maintained machines well beyond that time, local governments used machine-like tactics (e.g., through their power over contracts and zoning) in cities long after the period of their technical machine rule, parties still use "walking around money" for voter mobilization in certain places, and nonprogrammatic distributive policies have endured to some degree, even though most distributive spending is programmatic.[147] For all of these reasons, it's important to avoid oversimplification. Nevertheless, the U.S. party system clearly evolved from a more clientelistic to a more programmatic style.

4

National Party Institutions and Programmaticism, 1856–1950

There have been occasions when political organizations were afraid or unwilling to speak plainly or intelligently on problems of transcendent importance to the American Republic; when language was employed not to convey but to conceal ideas; when each pronouncement made a frontal attack on all others, and the whole appeared to have been written in mud by the migratory feet of a weasel.

—ALBEN BARKLEY, PERMANENT CHAIRMAN OF THE 1940
DEMOCRATIC NATIONAL CONVENTION

THE 1860 DEMOCRATIC platform contained 374 words, briefer than many courtship letters and other personal correspondence. In 2020, at more than 42,000 words, the party's platform length surpassed most academic journal articles on politics. Republicans exhibit a similar trajectory. Figure 4.1 shows a striking, if not simple, lengthening of manifestos over time for both parties.[1] Platforms have transformed from short statements to rhapsodies in red and blue.

The process for writing party manifestos has also changed—no longer are they created in the kind of ad hoc manner illustrated by Alben Barkley's witticism. In 2016, for example, Republican Platform Committee chairman Sen. John Barrasso of Wyoming and co-chairs Gov. Mary Fallin of Oklahoma and Rep. Virginia Foxx of North Carolina had a robust team working under them: chairs and staff for each policy subcommittee, along with an executive director, policy director, editors, counsel, clerks, a graphic designer, and many others. Democrats, under the leadership of Platform Committee

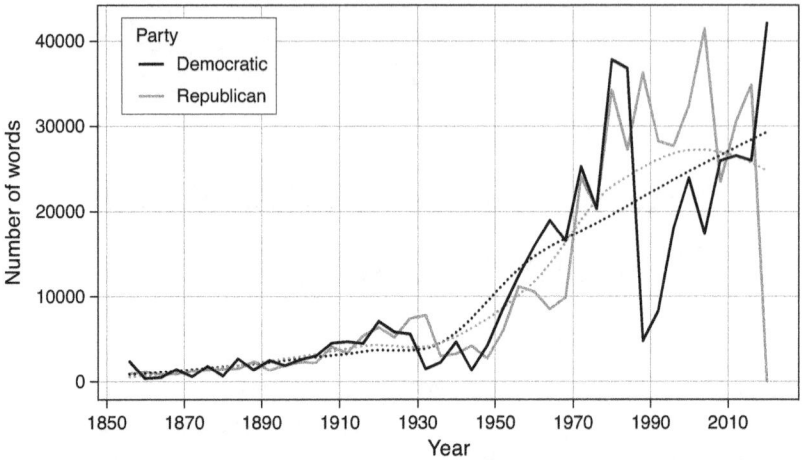

FIGURE 4.1. Party platform length, 1856–2020.
This graph shows the number of words in the Republican and Democratic party platforms over time. The solid lines reflect the raw data, and the dotted lines are loess curves. Platforms were obtained from the American Presidency Project (Woolley and Peters, n.d.).

chairs Gov. Dannel Malloy of Connecticut and former Atlanta mayor Shirley Franklin, also engaged in a complex process involving many people. The party held hearings across the nation in which people could testify in person or through video or writing. Four two-day meetings were dedicated to this process, involving people who supported the eventual nominee, Hillary Clinton, and her main challenger, Bernie Sanders.[2]

It takes a village of many people with different skillsets to construct the kind of encyclopedic platform offered by the nation's two major parties in an era of high programmaticism. Parties did not always have the institutional capacity for this kind of project. Indeed, for a long stretch of American history, they did not have the capacity to do very much at all. Nor did they always place significant value on the notion of developing issue positions. In addition to changes in organizational strength, there was also a shift over time in perspectives on the role of issues in party politics—whether developing positions was considered an important or even legitimate part of parties' work internally and whether these positions played an important role in party competition.

This chapter, along with the next, details the evolution of national party organizations from the time they began competing with each other through the modern era, with an eye toward this book's central questions about the shift toward programmaticism in America. This is a history of institutions and ideas, with descriptive and analytical components. I examine indicators of programmaticism beyond the measure presented in chapter 2, different ways we can gauge the extent to which parties directed attention toward issues. Some, like the length of party platforms, are quantitative. Others are qualitative, most notably the degree to which party officers focus on issue positions, particularly as a means of competition, in speeches and other public and private communications; the extent to which the party platform-writing process indicates that position development is considered important; and the volume and nature of party organization resources devoted to issue position development between elections (i.e., outside the context of an active platform-writing process). While each indicator might have limitations, together they are instructive. In addition to offering alternative ways to estimate programmaticism, these chapters investigate factors facilitating and impeding its growth.

This chapter focuses on the period from 1856 until 1950, when APSA released its report indicating that the national parties still had meager infrastructure and exhibited excessive programmatic similarity. It therefore faces the unenviable challenge of discussing a "non-event": the absence of major programmatic growth. There is plenty to be learned from this period if we investigate the right questions, however. For example, at what points (if any) in the first century of competition between Democrats and Republicans did they move or even consider moving in a programmatic direction? If and when this happened, can we get a sense of why it was supported (i.e., expected benefits), what facilitated it (i.e., organizational support), and why it did not lead to significant, sustained programmaticism (i.e., costs or other constraints encountered or expected)? During periods in which parties were not even attempting to move in a programmatic direction, can we tell why? What was occupying their attention, and why didn't they have the will or ability to become more programmatic?

I turn to various primary and secondary sources to address these questions. Studying party organizations can be difficult because they keep less comprehensive and accessible records than institutions like Congress; but there are a few ways in which we can gain insight into their development over the periods covered in this chapter (1856–1950) and in chapter 5 (1950–2020). One valuable source is transcripts of party conventions, which for much of American history were forums for discussing party business more than public-facing extravaganzas, as they are today. I examine speeches made by party officers, defined as anyone with formal party responsibilities, including the convention and national committee chairs. This amounted to 104 speeches on the Democratic side and 92 on the Republican side between 1856 and 1988, the last year for which transcripts are available through the Library of Congress.[3] I look at the parts of the transcripts relating to party platforms as well, from the creation of the platform committee in each convention to restlessness on the floor as delegates waited for the committee to complete its work, to the presentation of the platform itself and ensuing discussion. I also examined all available oral histories of DNC and RNC chairs and staff members (20 on the Democratic side, 13 on the Republican side), national party committee meeting transcripts, and other primary source documents collected from various archives.[4]

A benefit of qualitative materials like oral histories is that they can offer insight into not only what people did but also how and why they did it. This can help us evaluate the plausibility of the national party strength hypothesis, introduced in chapter 2, by illuminating the extent to which national party organizations aided programmatic entrepreneurs. Considering who aided and who resisted programmatic developments, we can also evaluate the plausibility of the clientelism constraint hypothesis (that political machines and other clientelistic institutions and agents long constrained the growth of programmaticism in the United States) and the racial oppression hypothesis (that institutions and agents committed to racial oppression delayed programmatic development in the United States, particularly as racial orders cross-cut parties, and fundamental barriers to political equality like franchise restrictions were the status quo). By engaging in an analytical history, we can also get a sense of the extent to which these factors, articulated formally in different hypotheses, relate to each other.

It turns out we can learn quite a bit from what appears in figure 4.1 to be a rather dull century for issue competition. At the start of competition between Democrats and Republicans, the process for creating party platforms was rudimentary. It's no wonder early platforms were short and not very programmatic. This period's barebones national party organizations offered little help in creating positions. Moreover, political context was not conducive to programmaticism in the nineteenth century. The nation faced a brewing crisis, the potential dissolution of the union itself due to intractable conflict over slavery, and the parties struggled with internal coherence. In this light, it's not particularly surprising that interparty competition on issues was not strong at this time. Programmaticism did not draw parties' focus, nor was it something they had the organizational capacity to carry out.

Over time, however, party organizations evolved in their goals, processes, and infrastructural capacities. This history warrants patient examination. It shows that the simple processes and organizations of the parties' early history could not support even the modest increase in attention to national issues and policy positions that occurred during this period, and they required innovation. By examining such changes, this chapter reveals the foundation on which modern programmaticism was built, how ideas and processes evolved to be able to support the system we see today. It also underscores the point that building party positions is difficult, requiring significant work and conflict resolution. Evidence for this point shows up in the way party leaders and officers talk about position development, and in the complex, laborious nature of the processes parties end up developing for this purpose. This supports my hypothesis that stronger national party organizations can help facilitate programmaticism.

This chapter also lends credence to the notion that the nation's fraught history of race-based oppression delayed programmaticism. Efforts to maintain slavery led to a civil war, which crowded out careful consideration of party positions on other issues and created significant intraparty division. Even after the war was over, conflict over white supremacy—codified by Jim Crow laws and interwoven in the nation's political and social fabric through other rules and norms—continued to occupy attention, stoke sectionalism undermining party coherence, and keep the perceived stakes of position taking on national issues high.

The analytical history in this chapter proceeds in two parts, the first covering nineteenth-century competition between Democrats and Republicans, and the second covering the first half of the twentieth century, leading up to APSA's publication of *Toward a More Responsible Two-Party System*. Chapter 5 then takes us from APSA's critical assessment of parties' lack of distinction on issues in 1950 to the present era, with programmaticism at historic and global highs.

The Early Years: Democratic and Republican Parties' Orientation toward Issues in the Nineteenth Century

In the early years of competition between Democrats and Republicans, there was little indication of programmaticism in discussions at national committee meetings or quadrennial conventions. This is not to say that they ignored policy issues. Republicans had impassioned discussions of slavery from their first convention in 1856. These speeches, however, did not indicate a desire for movement toward programmatic competition; rather, they reflected the view that slavery was a critical issue.[5] This was consistent with a broader pattern in speeches by party officers at early Republican conventions. Leaders were responding to major crises before them, particularly conflict over slavery and the union's survival. After the Civil War, speeches continued to be entangled in its legacies.

Toward the end of the century, Republicans inched toward programmaticism. At the 1888 Republican Convention, leaders criticized the Democratic Party's record, reviewed the Republican Party's accomplishments, and listed valued ideals and policies.[6] They discussed party conflict over trade and white southerners' continued race-based oppression, as well as the economic advantages it bestowed on these Democrats and their constituencies. In 1892, temporary chairman J. Sloane Fassett spoke more explicitly about disagreement between the parties on significant issues of the day (e.g., tariffs, voting rights). This continued in the next convention, as temporary convention chairman Charles Fairbanks and Chairman John Thurston made programmatic distinctions between the parties on issues including tariffs and fiscal policy.

This was quite mild compared to the contemporary era, however. Even when Republican party officers distinguished between the parties on certain issues, they fell short of offering a full-throated case for programmaticm. They were not talking explicitly about the notion of issue-based competition. Even in 1896, the most programmatic year to date, Chairman Thurston's speech was brief and focused more on issues themselves than the party's responsibilities regarding position development, putting forth a long list of policies that he said would motivate the American people to elect a Republican president. This is better characterized as programmatic *spirit* than systemic programmaticism.

Democrats were not strongly programmatic over this period by today's standards either. The degree to which they focused on policy waxed and waned between 1856 and the turn of the century. Party officers spoke—sometimes in an impassioned manner—about major issues of the day, like currency and tax policy. At times, they even distinguished their own party's position and behavior from that of their opposition. The tone of these discussions, however, reflects a sense of problem solving major issues of the day from a national standpoint more than a partisan one. These leaders don't appear to be turning to issues as a means of competing with Republicans, or strategizing around this notion.

This largely reflects political context. The inchoate nation needed both hands, so to speak, to grapple with conflict over slavery, an issue paradoxically central to the notion of liberal democracy but deferred at the founding because of its explosiveness. Put differently, a lot of concern and effort during this period was devoted to problems bigger than interparty competition. Concern about impending dissolution of the union preoccupied party officers. This is evident, for example, in Democratic Convention president Caleb Cushing's 1860 speech pleading with delegates to remember how the former colonies weathered the American Revolution, and how the new nation emerging from that conflict survived its rocky infancy. President pro tempore Francis Flournoy begged for unity as well, clearly seeing potential civil war as the most urgent problem of the day. Sectionalism, which "obliterates the kindest feelings from our hearts," was seen as an existential threat to the party and nation. Said Flournoy to the floor:

> You should regard each other … as brothers, and not as hostile armies engaged and encamped upon the same hostile field, marching under different martial music, and under opposing flags. The Democratic Party has but one flag. It is the flag of my country—the star spangled banner [Applause.] When you look upon that emblem, recollect it teaches you fraternity. Then let us talk no more about sections. No, we know no North, no South, no East, no West, where Democrats are concerned.[7]

Hand-wringing over sectionalism, particularly conflict between the South and other regions over African American rights, continued through and after the war. Sectionalism on the Democratic side can be seen clearly in votes on platform amendments, shown in figure 4.2.

Intraparty conflict on both sides of the aisle appears to have constrained the notion of interparty competition over programmatic agendas. The cavernous cleavage over slavery and Reconstruction consumed most of the Democratic Party's energy for issue conflict. And on the Republican side, as discussed in chapter 3, reformers challenged the party's establishment in the second half of the nineteenth century. This conflict would grow strong enough that a faction of Republicans would reject their own party's candidate in favor of Democrat Grover Cleveland in 1884.

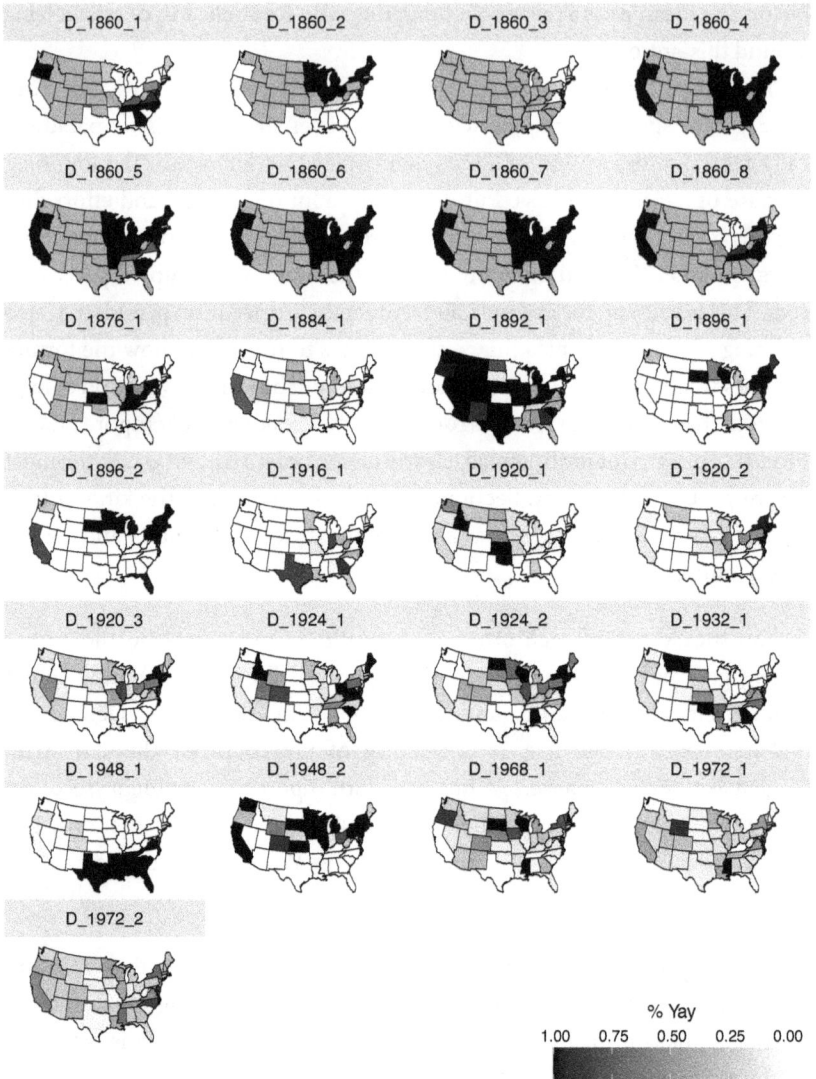

FIGURE 4.2. Democratic platform amendment votes.
This graph shows the percentage of delegates in each state who voted in favor of proposed amendments to Democratic Party platforms over time.

Interestingly, Democratic party officers saw discord across the aisle as an opportunity for cross-party coalition building. In 1872, Democratic Convention president James R. Doolittle—who hailed from Wisconsin, a bastion of party reform—encouraged support for the liberal Republicans, and the convention floor was clearly receptive to this. He indicated interest in issues over patronage ("It means no union for the spoils of office [applause], but it means a union of men with the same faith, upon the great and paramount issue of the present hour"), but this preference had or at least could accommodate a cross-partisan dimension. He envisioned joining with like-minded people to work toward important goals, even if this meant crossing party lines. This notion stands in striking contrast to what we observe today, when policy accomplishments are so entwined with partisanship that governance often suffers at the hands of a minority party determined to deprive the majority party of any perceived success.[8]

Nineteenth-Century Platform Writing

Looking more specifically at the process for writing platforms, we also see a low level of emphasis on issue position development in the early years of competition between the two major parties, relative to the contemporary era. This process evolved somewhat over time, as people became frustrated with the limitations of existing methods for platform construction and resolution of conflict thereon. Parties adjusted as their needs with respect to issues outgrew existing processes. Over time, these adjustments created a foundation on which complex modern processes were built.

REPUBLICAN PARTY

At the beginning of each quadrennial national convention, Republican party leaders would typically nominate delegates to serve on a platform committee, called the Committee on the Platform, Committee on Resolutions (reflecting the fact that platform planks were often called "resolutions"), or something similar. The committee was usually composed of one delegate—more specifically, one "gentleman"—from each state in early conventions, expanding over time to one man and one woman from each state. In the nineteenth century, it was typical for the committee to convene in a separate space to draft the platform and then present it to the floor of the convention. Ultimately, the convention body had power of approval over the platform; but, while there was sometimes debate and dissent, the body as a whole tended to accept the committee's final majority report.

The second Republican convention, held in 1860, evinced contradictions in early thinking about platforms while also demonstrating the degree to which conflict existed within a narrow range of considered processes and outcomes. Kansas governor Andrew Horatio Reeder questioned whether a committee dedicated to the platform should be appointed early in the convention. The platform "is not at all necessary to our organization" and should wait for consideration until later in the convention, he argued.[9] Another delegate, Hon. D. K. Cartter of Ohio, claimed a committee for platform should be appointed early given the demands of creating such a document. "It is laborious work and ought to be performed while the Convention is in its vigor," he remarked to his peers.[10] Eli Thayer of Oregon seconded these sentiments, arguing that the platform was important and that creating it "is the great burden of the work of this Convention." Horace Greeley, also representing Oregon, agreed. "It will take thirty-six hours for the committee to prepare their report," he noted, "and the committee should be appointed now so they can have full opportunity."[11] Thayer and Greeley's comments reflect a reality of platform creation discussed in chapter 2, that articulating a party manifesto is arduous work. This was thought to be true even at this point of relatively low programmaticism. Indeed, proponents of this position won the argument—a platform committee was appointed at the beginning of the convention. But even those acknowledging the labor involved expected the platform to be written while the convention was in session. Thirty-six hours, considered by Greeley at this time to be a long stretch, is a blink compared to the amount of work that goes into platforms today.

Responses to the committee's proposed platform varied widely. At times, the platform committee's work received little attention, much less pushback, from the floor. Right after the platform was read into the record at the 1864 National Union Convention, for example, C. S. Bushnell of Connecticut stated, "Those resolutions are their own argument. I move their adoption by acclamation." Without pause, "The motion was agreed to amid enthusiastic applause."[12] The 1872 platform was adopted in a similarly unceremonious manner, receiving unanimous approval after being read into the record. This was also true at the 1884 and 1888 conventions, the former being particularly notable because it was the forum in which James Blaine's nomination provoked Mugwumps' defection to Democratic candidate Grover Cleveland. This suggests that the platform was not considered especially important at the time.

The process was not always so simple and insular. People, organizations, and state delegations tried a few methods to make their voices heard in the platform creation process, even if they were not on the committee responsible for drafting it. Sometimes they would compose a set of resolutions beforehand, which would be referred to the platform committee for consideration.[13] This was a mechanism through which reformers could express their vision for the party. For example, the Union League of America offered sets of resolutions to conventions in the 1860s criticizing the spoils system and advocating for civil service reform. In 1876, in addition to antispoils statements from the Reform Club of New York, there were speeches and requests for platform planks on African American and women's rights by Frederick Douglass and the National Woman Suffrage Association, respectively. The rules often specified that referral would occur without debate, but this was not always enforced—when it was announced to the floor that a group had a statement of this nature, discussions and even heated arguments sometimes followed.[14]

At some conventions, dissent arose within the platform committee itself. As noted earlier, when the committee finished its work, it would report back to the floor. Often, they presented just one platform, but sometimes they offered a majority platform along with one or more minority reports. A minority report could be focused on one particular resolution or depart from the majority in a more significant way. Even if the platform committee presented only one manifesto, the floor (i.e., delegates who were not on the committee) would frequently want to discuss it and sometimes—with varying success—attempt to amend it. There were often debates and votes on these amendments, and sometimes even arguments about whether amendments or debates thereon were allowed (e.g., 1868). Civil service reform and currency (relative merits of the gold standard, silver, bimetallism, and paper money) were common subjects of contention.

Disagreements, even when strong, proved manageable in this forum. While there was a fair amount of squabbling over amendments and platforms on the whole, delegates were generally able to settle disputes on the floor. This reflects some interest in the platform, but not so much that it required a great deal of time, energy, or conflict resolution. The final disposition of amendments was usually determined by voice vote, but roll calls were sometimes held. Four such votes were held between 1856 and the turn of the century, none of which were close—the winning side got between 88 and 97 percent

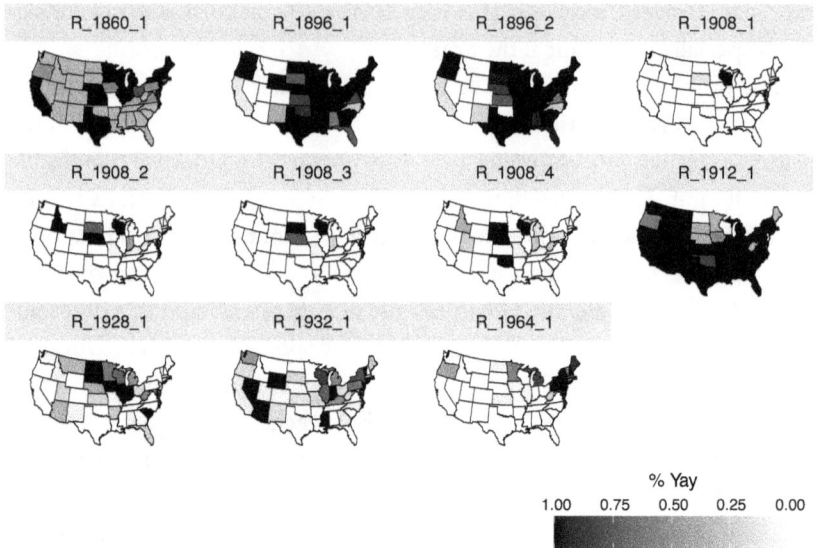

FIGURE 4.3. Republican platform amendment votes.
This graph shows the percentage of delegates in each state who voted in favor of
proposed amendments to Republican Party platforms over time.

of delegates' votes (see figure 4.3, which shows the percentage of delegates in
each state who voted in favor of each amendment).

Conflict grew more serious in 1896. At first, it seemed like the party would
be able to resolve the problem using standard procedures of the time. After
the chair presented the platform, Senator Henry Teller of Colorado presented
a minority report regarding currency, intended as a substitute for the financial
plan laid out in the platform, which supported the gold standard.[15] Delegates
voted (overwhelmingly) to table the minority report. Given disagreement
within the party, Senator Fred Dubois of Idaho moved for the financial plan
to be voted on separately from the platform. This was approved, and the
platform committee's financial plan and the platform as a whole were then
adopted. At this, a group of six mostly western delegates withdrew, offering
a statement for the record expressing their protest upon their departure.[16]
The silver-supporting delegates then withdrew as well, "amid great excitement
and a magnificent demonstration upon the part of the remaining delegates
who tried to outvie each other in demonstrations of loyalty to the party and
her principles."[17] Alternate delegates were brought in. This was a significant
escalation from previous years, when there were amendments and minority

reports, but disagreements were resolved more smoothly. This conflict did not last, however. In the following two conventions, the process was quick—the platforms of 1900 and 1904 were adopted unanimously right after being read into the record.

DEMOCRATIC PARTY

While the Republican Party's platform creation process was relatively straight-forward in the mid-nineteenth century, Democrats' process was more conflict-ual. This is unsurprising, given that the Democratic camp in 1860 included what would become the states of the Confederacy during the Civil War. Indeed, a sense of impending existential crisis loomed over early Democratic conventions. Disagreement erupted on the floor in 1856 after the platform was read into the record. A delegate from the South wanted to divide the resolutions, as he and others were not prepared to approve them in toto. A delegate from Massachusetts responded disapprovingly, noting that "this report is the unanimous result of the labors of a committee composed of delegates from all the States," implying that the party was not trying to strong-arm its southern contingent. Some resolutions were adopted after a bout of bickering, but conflict reignited over the question of whether they could have time before voting on the rest of the resolutions. They ended up taking a recess and then voting on the remaining resolutions one by one. While perhaps a creative solution for managing intraparty disagreement in the moment, this strategy would become untenable as the number of planks grew over time.

As early as 1860, party members realized they needed a better process for handling resolutions. The effort to create one did not go smoothly, but an attempt was made nonetheless. Delegates discussed potential strategies for managing resolutions—whether delegates should be able to offer resolutions or even a whole platform to the floor of the convention or whether they would need to be first referred to the Committee on Resolutions, and what the rules should be for discussing the resolutions, for example. With the for-mer issue remaining unsettled, several resolutions were offered to the floor, generally having to do with fugitive slaves. Finally, the leadership stopped this practice, noting that if two hundred resolutions were referred to the Committee on Resolutions, they would never be able to finish their work. A delegate moved that from that point, resolutions should go to committee without reading.

It was clear from these proceedings that the issue of slavery was both powerful and irreconcilable through processes such as platform writing at this time. A short majority platform from fifteen slaveholding states plus California and Oregon was offered, along with a minority report from fifteen nonslaveholding states. A great deal of convention time was dedicated to speeches about slavery. The floor voted down the majority platform, infuriating southern delegates, who started withdrawing from the convention. The whole event was a fiasco, painfully revealing that the party could not agree on a platform and was generally dysfunctional. The convention then split, two different platforms were released, and two different candidates, both of whom would ultimately lose the general election to Abraham Lincoln, were nominated.

With the Civil War ongoing, the next Democratic National Convention did not include delegates from Confederate states, simplifying the process of platform writing, at least temporarily. After meeting for approximately two days—roughly the same amount of time that the committee met to draft the platform in 1860 but with less rancor—the Committee on Resolutions reported a short platform to the floor. Though two delegates attempted to add amendments, the platform was adopted quickly. Even though things went more smoothly without the party's southern delegation in attendance, the party was clearly still not in a strong programmatic mindset. They did not intend to develop positions on a wide range of issues. Indeed, in response to the question of whether the convention should adjourn to the afternoon and ask the Committee on Resolutions to report then or adjourn to the next day, a delegate from New York quipped, "If the platform is so long that it requires such a clerical force as intimated to copy it out, it ought not to be adopted," evoking laughter and applause.[18]

In 1868, the states of the former Confederacy rejoined the main Democratic National Convention. Toward the beginning of the convention, in designating who would compose the Committee on Resolutions—a part of the convention that was perfunctory on the Republican side for the entire history examined—a delegate put forth a long resolution that set off a discussion. While it did not take up a great deal of time, it's worth noting that there was more contention here than at the Republican National Convention on this procedural matter. Questions were also raised about whether individuals and states (e.g, resolutions of the Pennsylvania and Michigan state conventions) could refer resolutions to the Committee on Resolutions or present them to the floor. Ultimately, though—in contrast to 1860—a platform was adopted (unanimously, by voice vote).

There was an attempt to streamline the process four years later. At the beginning of the 1872 convention, rules were adopted stating that all platform resolutions should be referred to the Committee on Resolutions without debate and without being read into the record. Platform proceedings remained contentious, however. During a debate on whether a set of resolutions adopted at an earlier Cincinnati convention of liberal Republicans should be adopted by this convention and whether debate should even be allowed thereon, a delegate made a set of remarks reflecting the challenges of programmaticism at this time. Speaking briefly about the purpose of parties, he argued that they "have no justification except that they are a means to an honest end," reflecting skepticism about parties dating back to the nation's founding and the fact that their purpose was unsettled. He proceeded: "I think it becoming the dignity of this grand National organization of nearly three millions of freemen, or those who deem themselves freemen, that we should at least be permitted to have an unrestrained moderate, straightforward expression of our own opinions, without having the words of other men, unchosen by us, forced down our throats (Cheers and hisses)."[19]

Creating a platform in a diverse nation with only two major parties is difficult. Indeed, the Democratic Party's struggles with sectionalism were on full display during these 1872 proceedings. Once the time allotted for debate was over, after speeches from delegates of South Carolina and Texas, a delegate from Mississippi asked that the convention be able to vote on each resolution separately, as in 1856. This request was unsurprising coming from a region in which one issue, white supremacy, mattered far more than any other. It was not heeded, however. A vote on the platform's adoption occurred, and the platform was approved, with most of the dissenting votes coming from southern and border states.

Disagreement continued to be expressed on the floor of the convention in 1876. Resolutions were offered by a group of suffragists and also by delegates from various states (e.g., Illinois, Nebraska, New York, Georgia). These resolutions were referred to the Committee on Resolutions. When this Committee finally reported to the floor, the introductory speech made clear that it was difficult for them to agree on a platform. A majority and minority platform were presented, and discussion ensued on various issues, some that directly involved matters of race and some that did not (e.g., debate on currency). Finally, they held a series of votes.

Over the next few conventions, existing procedures for platform construction were strained even further. Conflict over party machines and civil service reform, which rose along with growing national attention to this subject, was reasonably contained in 1880 but burst open on the floor in 1884. People and groups (e.g., the Woman's Christian Temperance Union) began offering resolutions early in the convention, occupying considerable floor time. This was not an efficient way to manage disagreement over the platform. Unsurprisingly, the Committee on Resolutions was not ready to present a platform when the floor was ready to receive one. This was a theme of early conventions, and a likely reason that the party committees moved away from drafting platforms at conventions. There was simply not enough time, even when the economy was less complex and the government had fewer responsibilities.

What's more, delegates' patience did not pay off in terms of conflict resolution. Even after the committee finally drafted its platform, and copies were printed and distributed in 1884, people ventured to offer resolutions, leading to some quibbling about whether that should be allowed. A majority and a minority report were read into the record, and a fixed set of time was given to particular people to discuss them. Once these speeches were concluded, a roll call was held. But even that did not settle the matter, as delegates continued to attempt to make motions relating to the platform after the vote. The party, and the nation more broadly, had clearly outgrown existing methods of managing the platform-writing process, and the growing pains were felt by all.

In 1892, after struggling with language about trade, delegates bemoaned the fact that the party might need to give up attempted revisions and revert to the language from the 1884 platform. Amid unruly arguments about the tariff, the chair had to suspend proceedings. "When order is restored," he announced, "the Chairman will state the question. He will recognize no one until there is order in the Convention." At this, Rep. W. Bourke Cockran of New York retorted, "Then I think you will have to wait a week."[20]

Party leaders knew that conflict over currency would dog the next convention, as evidenced in discussions in an executive Democratic National Committee meeting in January, and devised a more structured process for managing intraparty disagreement regarding the 1896 platform.[21] All things considered, the process was reasonably successful. After someone explained the contents of the platform to the floor, it was announced that one amendment would be offered by a minority of the committee, and two additional amendments would be offered by New York governor David B. Hill. Following this, Committee on Resolutions and Platform chairman Hon. James K. Jones of Arkansas said, "by agreement, there are to be two hours and forty minutes' debate, one hour and twenty minutes on each side. I hope the Convention will listen patiently to what is to be said."[22] This happened, roll-call votes were taken, and the platform was adopted. It is worth noting, however, that this orderly process followed arguments over currency at the beginning of the convention, which erupted during the process of picking a temporary chairman. Greater efficiency and comity would require further change.

Support was unlikely to come at this time from the Democratic and Republican National Committees, which were meager organizations in the nineteenth century, with little in the way of stable leadership, infrastructure, or operations. The center of party power at this time was at the subnational level, mirroring the dynamics of American federalism during this period.[23] The RNC and DNC met periodically, but primarily to handle procedural matters like choosing a city for the next convention. There was not much consideration of substance or strategy for party competition—programmatic or otherwise—in nineteenth-century national committee meetings. But the situation would not stay this way.

Building a Foundation for Modern Programmaticism in the Early Twentieth Century

Party officers' convention addresses reflected a significant turn toward programmaticism at the beginning of the twentieth century, consistent with the measure presented in chapter 1. In 1900, permanent chairman of the Democratic Convention James Richardson noted that a key authority of the convention was "to lay down a platform of principles upon which the battle is to be fought and the victory won." He then proceeded to discuss sixteen issues—numbered, indicating thought and formality—including key issues of the day, like currency and tariffs. There was a similar increase in programmatic ethos on the Republican side. Permanent chair of the convention Henry Cabot Lodge offered a substantial list of Republican positions, highlighting party differences on tariff policy. Democrats and Republicans continued to discuss party positions and differences between parties on policy over the next few years on questions of domestic policy (e.g., responding to monopolies) and foreign policy (e.g., whether the United States should join the League of Nations). It would take some time for parties to have the institutional capacity to undergird strong programmaticism, but changes were afoot.

For one thing, the parties established permanent headquarters. The RNC made this move around 1918, though its operations still declined significantly between presidential elections.[24] On the Democratic side, Chairman John J. Raskob announced in 1929 that the party would establish a permanent headquarters in Washington, DC, with a permanent executive committee and a full-time director of publicity to facilitate continuous operations between elections. This, he thought, would "build up our Party into a real live national force."[25] While the DNC was still running a deficit, it was substantially smaller than it had been, and the party could afford to make what he viewed as a critical change.

Democratic Executive Committee chairman Jouett Shouse called this a "noble experiment."[26] In addition to providing a place for Democrats to hold meetings, the office was also to have publicity and research capabilities. Raskob hoped that a more active DNC could help coordinate different parts of the party. The party organization could provide stable leadership, which was especially needed when they did not have a co-partisan president, Raskob argued.

Not everyone agreed that a stronger, more centralized DNC was a good idea. In response to speeches by Raskob and others extolling the virtues of a stronger national organization's potential ability to develop positions, a few southern senators gave speeches raising objections to this notion. It was unrealistic, argued Senator Cordell Hull (TN), to expect the DNC to be able to reconcile dramatically different views among party members. Nor did he, or some of his colleagues, think the party should even try to do this.

> Every Democrat should have the utmost freedom in any party gathering or outside of any party gathering, to express his individual views *ad libitum*, but to express official views pertaining not to one individual opinion, but to articles of public faith is calculated, in my judgment, to contravene the well-defined authority and prerogatives and jurisdiction of the party organization. It is never safe, my friends, when an organization is one of limited powers, which must be strictly construed—in fact, it is always dangerous to exercise the doubtful power, and when no power at all exists it is all the more dangerous to undertake to exercise prerogatives in that direction.[27]

Rather than stepping outside the scope of its authority by trying to come up with party positions on controversial issues, Hull argued, they should focus on the many matters on which they agreed. If the party ignored this appeal for "unity," he warned that the country could follow in the footsteps of other nations that were sliding into autocracy. Senators Joseph T. Robinson of

Arkansas and Cameron Morrison of North Carolina also made fiery speeches to this effect, warning against stoking division within the party by attempting to take issue positions. "Why should this organization depart from the precedents and practices which have prevailed throughout its history?" queried Robinson. "Why should this organization, either at this meeting or any subsequent meetings, undertake to determine party principles and party policies? Why should it not perform the functions for which it was created?" This remark, challenging core principles of programmaticism, arose in the context of a discussion about the 18th Amendment, but speaks to broader intraparty tensions. Comments by Hon. Watt T. Brown, National Committee member from Alabama, underscore this impression. "We want harmony in the Democratic Party. You know the South is purely Democratic on principle. It is not money with the South, it is principles with them, and if you do not disturb us, we will stand for the Party and help you finance other states that are somewhat doubtful; but do not disturb us."[28] While the 18th Amendment was no small issue, it is well documented that white supremacy was by far the most important concern among southern Democrats at this time.[29] One can read between the lines to infer that these southern Democrats opposed hypothetical party mandates that could potentially extend to racial issues in the future.

Along with changes in facilities (i.e., permanent headquarters), the chairmanship position also evolved in the first half of the twentieth century. After the 1936 election, the RNC made its chairmanship a full-time salaried position.[30] The DNC followed eight years later, in 1944. These "full-time" chairmen could still hold other positions, however. Several DNC and RNC chairmen held federal executive positions during their tenure with the party committees. DNC chairman Robert Hannegan, for example, simultaneously served as United States postmaster general under Harry Truman. The fact that the postmaster general controlled a great deal of patronage underscores the largely clientelistic nature of parties at this time.[31] Before Hannegan, James Farley and Frank C. Walker both served this particular dual role, from 1933 to 1940 and 1943 to 1944. In fact, Farley also served as state party chairman. "I handled it without any difficulty at all," he remarked in a 1957 oral history interview. "I was known as 'Three-Job Jim' in those days."[32] Dwight Eisenhower would eventually stop this trend during his presidency, "adamant that neither the party chairman nor any member of the national committee would simultaneously hold a federal executive position."[33] By mid century, the position was more significant than it had been earlier, but it was still somewhat limited. Reflecting on the period from 1947 to 1949, former DNC assistant director of publicity Samuel Brightman remarked, "We hadn't reached the development when a chairman really needs to be a full-time, full day, three hundred sixty five days a year chairman."[34]

Both parties attempted to increase their between-election activities over this period, but this effort moved in fits and starts. As noted earlier, the Democratic and Republican National Committees had traditionally been relatively dormant between elections. The APSA report quotes a DNC member's remarks to this effect in 1919: "It was the custom of this body immediately after the Presidential election had passed . . . of going out of business in a week or two, just as soon as we could pay up the bills, and indeed sometimes we went out of business before we did that."[35] DNC chairman James Farley actually distributed termination notices at the 1932 convention in Chicago, telling staff they would need to "return to [their] place of origin under [their] own steam, and [they] would be reimbursed later."[36] With a six dollar per week salary, staff member Neale Roach recalled, "I had to borrow enough money for an upper berth on the B & O railroad from Chicago to Washington, it took me eight months to pay it off."[37] When he was asked to come back to the DNC, though, he did so with "pleasure," working as a writer for the party organization from 1936 to 1940 and eventually taking on some other roles as well. He believed the party could do more.[38] And, indeed, it would. Both national committees maintained operations after the 1936 contest, despite their post-election indebtedness.[39] While there was less activity after the 1940 election, this period was nonetheless significant in the degree to which continuous operation gained favor.[40]

The parties even took some modest steps toward enhancing their research capabilities in the first few decades of the nineteenth century. After the First World War, the RNC established an Advisory Committee on Policies and Platform (ACPP). Largely through the work of eighteen subcommittees devoted to different issues, the committee was meant "to investigate the existing needs and conditions affecting specific problems that would have to be considered by the National Convention; to gather facts and data; to invite a full expression of leading Republicans; and to submit its recommendations and the material it collected, in convenient form, to the Resolutions Committee of the National Convention of that Committee and also of the Convention." The ACPP had a "distinguished staff" and surveyed 100,000 people on a range of topics. This information was given to the Republican National Convention's Resolutions Committee, and the ACPP's recommendations were "quite effective in shaping form and substance, if not orientation, of [the platform committee's] decisions."[41]

The shift toward programmaticism was not linear or straightforward, however. The ACPP disbanded in 1920, though one person tried to continue some of the group's activities. This was a theme of early moves toward programmmaticism—the kind of research necessary for this mode of competition was often performed by one or a very small number of people. While it coaxed the needle toward programmaticism, the movement was modest. Only so much could be accomplished under these conditions.

Programmaticism was also unlikely to skyrocket during this period because differentiation on issues was not always seen as a goal or even a good thing. At the 1908 Democratic National Convention, for example, permanent chairman Henry Clayton talked about how Republicans had gotten closer to Democrats in some of their issues, and viewed this as something to be celebrated—a sentiment met with applause from the floor. There were also signs that they valued forbearance in partisan conflict under some conditions. On the Bill of Rights, for example, permanent chairman of the Democratic Convention Joseph Robinson argued in 1936, "there can be no partisan division." It was also thought, to echo an old adage, that partisan politics should "stop at the water's edge." Robinson articulated this principle at the 1920 Democratic Convention, stating: "Within the confines of our own country, we may indulge in reasonable partisanship, but when we come to deal with foreign powers, all men who are patriotic, without regard to politics, stand together united under our flag and support our government. (Applause.)"[42]

Many party leaders called for restraint in party competition more broadly when faced with the twin crises of the Great Depression and dissolution of democracies worldwide—"a convulsion of history" with "inconceivable influence upon the destiny of mankind," in the words of Massachusetts Rep. Joe Martin at the 1940 Republican National Convention. "An election must be held," temporary Democratic Convention chairman William Bankhead declared in 1940, "but aside from legitimate discussions of records of the two parties and of their candidates and platforms, the major objective of both parties must be unity and solidarity of purpose in preserving inviolate the structure of our government and the perpetual freedom of its people." Similar sentiments were echoed at the 1944 Democratic and Republican conventions, as the nation's involvement in World War II added gravity to the period. This isn't to say they did not jab at each other on issues—they did, to some extent. But it was clear that once again, the nation and its parties were facing a crisis larger than interparty competition. The greatest imperative was "maintaining our Constitutional Republic" and coming out of the war victorious, with as few American lives lost as possible.[43]

Internal coherence was a major constraint as well, especially on the Democratic side. As the 1932 Republican National Convention's permanent chairman, Hon. Bertrand H. Snell, remarked, "The Democratic Party has as many wings as it has candidates, and . . . [t]hese wings do not flap together, they flap against each other." With more biting conciseness, Gov. Dwight H. Green of Illinois jeered at the 1948 Republican National Convention that the Democrats' "strange alliance was held together by bosses, boodle, buncombe, and blarney."[44] Of course, one must always be responsibly suspicious of statements made by an opposing party, but in this case, they were not far off the mark. Ire arose from the mere suggestion at a 1919 Democratic National Committee meeting that the party discuss issues and positions they could support, particularly women's suffrage. "It would be dynamite to throw that in," warned W. B. Haldeman of Kentucky. "You are going to take a harmonious committee and disorganize it by introducing into it this resolution of Senator Jones [regarding women's suffrage]."[45] He notes that there are many things he could express a position on, but that any such action would be "dynamite" and that states' rights needed to be respected. So many people wanted to enter the debate, the chair eventually suggested that everyone could have two minutes to talk. One of the committee members complained that this would add up to three hours of debate. This discord and inefficient use of convention time exemplified the need for better procedures for managing conflict over issue positions.

Not everyone wanted to hold back issue competition completely. There were some concerted efforts to build party positions in the late thirties and forties. In 1936, Republicans worked to establish a Research Division, headed by Yale economics professor Glenn Saxon, to help "lay the factual foundation for the propaganda activities of the 1936 battle."[46] Leaders decided to make the Research Division a permanent part of the RNC and acquired office space, staff, and some facilities (e.g., books), so they could help candidates and officeholders with substantive and political information about different issues. They also held a few weekend conferences for members of Congress on different issues. These conferences were impactful, according to contemporaneous scholar C.A.H. Thomson: "The substance of the bills, speeches on the floor of both Houses, public statements issued by individual Senators and Congressmen or the Committee, and the Minority Reports of the committee on individual measures, followed the line, by and large, determined by the consensus achieved through the conferences."[47] The division also created a series of booklets, which were circulated mostly to party officials and officeholders, called the *Reporter*, which provided information, including where prominent Republicans stood on particular issues.

The addition and centralization of party policy research capacities was a step forward in terms of programmaticism, even if it did have limitations. The Research Division started to normalize the idea of party research, but it was not working toward creating party *positions*. As Thomson (1939) notes, "Personnel of the Research Division did not conceive of their role as in any way one of formulating policy, and certainly not policy purporting to be a statement of an authoritative Republican Position."[48] Indeed, when they wrote about Republican positions, they often had to include conflicting viewpoints.

After the party experienced a "terrific licking" in 1936 with the resounding reelection of Democrat Franklin Delano Roosevelt, leaders took further steps toward programmaticism. Republican chairman John Hamilton traveled to England, where he spent some time in the headquarters of the British Conservative Party, which had gone through a similar experience of electoral defeat. He found himself intrigued by the nature of British parties, particularly how different they were from U.S. parties from a programmatic standpoint. He was "impressed" by "the fact that all of the British parties did then, as they do today, have their annual meetings in which the Prime Minister, if the party is in power, justifies his policies and makes a statement of policy, and the opposition party also meets … and makes its policy of opposition."[49] This was novel to the American in 1937, but he thought the idea could be applied back home. He found that several high-profile people agreed, most notably former president Herbert Hoover.

There was considerable disagreement about how this should be accomplished. Hoover wanted to recall delegates from the 1936 Republican National Convention to meet and, in Hamilton's words, "issue—well, we'll call it a platform if you want to, or a policy statement."[50] This idea "met with immediate and violent opposition" from Congressional Committee chairman Joe Martin and 1936 Republican presidential nominee Alf M. Landon, along with other members of Congress. They did not want the party to go down that road. Hamilton recalls that they "didn't want anything done"; they "all wanted to go home in their own district and run in '38; run their own campaigns; and they didn't want any general policy statement." But Hamilton felt strongly that there needed to be at least some compromise with what Hoover and the others were asking. "I had to take a realistic approach," he remarked later in an oral history. "I was out in the field trying to raise money to keep the party alive and I was being asked time after time 'What does the party stand for?'" Conflicting messages were coming from different parts of the party, and between what some of them were saying and "what people were thinking in '37 and '38," and he "had to have something to go out and raise money on."[51] There was more demand for progammaticism than there had been before, and the party needed to adjust. By the time the Republican National Executive Committee met to figure out what to do, "popular demand for action was so insistent that opponents of the plan saw fit to compromise."[52]

While Hamilton was on the same page as Hoover in terms of generating a statement of policy positions, he found the convention idea implausible. It would be far too expensive for the financially embattled party; he estimated that "it would cost two or three hundred thousand—and we didn't have enough money from month to month to keep the headquarters open."[53] Even if cost were not an issue, he thought it would be too hard to work out intraparty differences on policy with a large group at a convention. Indeed, he said, "It seemed to me that with the differences of opinion in the party as to what the party should stand for on certain issues—and there were a great many differences in those days—that we would just have a big ruckus of a thousand shouting delegates with no one with the power to lead them." He did not think Landon or Hoover was suited to the job but "did want the policy statement." He thought this could be better accomplished by a smaller committee.

The RNC's compromise solution was to set up what would become known as the Glenn Frank Committee (officially the Republican Committee on Program), named after the former University of Wisconsin president who would be chosen by the Republican Executive Committee to lead it, and who was reportedly acceptable to both Hoover and Landon.[54] Underscoring its novelty, contemporaneous scholar Ronald Bridges noted in a 1939 edition of *Public Opinion Quarterly* that this was "the most unusual experiment to be conducted by a major party in the United States."[55] The committee's work was widely covered by news outlets. Initially, they were planning to have only 100 members, but it became clear as they began their work that a larger body would be needed to have the "real cross-section committee" they wanted.[56] The committee grew to approximately 280 members from forty-four states (along with Washington, DC, and Alaska) who came from a wide range of backgrounds, including farmers, educators, bankers, doctors, clergymen, and homemakers.

The Glenn Frank Committee set up a central headquarters in Chicago and had ten subdivisions, eight of them regional and two operational, with paid technical and stenographic staff. There were also regional subcommittees on different issues (e.g., taxation, labor). "Regional groups," Frank reported to the *Los Angeles Times*, "will make their reports to the parent organization. As problems arise, such as the co-ordination of diverse opinion, they will be met as the need comes."[57] Chairmen of the regional committees would serve as liaisons between the subcommittees and the central headquarters, which had two vice-chairmen along with Frank.

They had a complex relationship with the RNC, set up by the organization's Executive Committee but not directly funded by the party. The Glenn Frank Committee had its own finance committee, which operated on a strategy of recruiting a large pool of small donors "so that interest in its activities will be widespread."[58] In reality, members of the committee ended up relying a lot on their own networks to recruit small donors, covering a lot of their own expenses (e.g., travel) and donating a great deal of their time. They were to operate independently of the RNC but report their findings to the party organization. RNC chairman Hamilton stated, more specifically, "You are charged with the consideration of pertinent policies and issues of government. The scope of that consideration is for your sole determination. The method by which you will approach that duty is also for your sole determination. There is no political restriction upon your specified activities."[59] They would research party positions and make their findings available to the RNC and the convention's platform committee, but Frank made clear that they were not responsible for writing the 1940 platform. It was ultimately the RNC's decision regarding what to do with the Frank Committee's report.

From the beginning, Frank argued that they needed to move away from "government by hunch." A rigorous evaluation of the New Deal was needed, and policy areas had to be thoroughly researched. This was not to be an exercise in gathering ammunition to throw bombs from the sideline or engage in "petty and vindictive faultfinding" of the opposing party. Frank was not going to head a "smearing squad."[60] The committee's work was to be substantive—it "must, as its contributions to the council of Republicans, create a comprehensive report of policy respecting the long array of stubborn problems confronting us—labor, agriculture, business, social security, taxation, political and economic foreign policy, unemployment, and so on," Frank argued.[61] This was a step toward programmaticism, involving a significant investment in issue research for which "the obvious and immediate result aimed at is the restoration of the Republican Party to power."[62] It could also have broader effects, raising the status of the platform, which had "fallen into contempt," as it was "hastily drawn" and "comes out of the resolutions committee reeking with platitudes and stale cigar smoke."[63]

Their strategy, quite revolutionary for the time, had three main parts. They conducted a large survey of voters, distributing questionnaires to the RNC to forward to county and precinct chairmen. They also held regional conferences with "leaders of various groups—farm, labor, industry, and so on."[64] Finally, they would use "small forums to sound opinion from various groups." Frank himself traveled "to many corners" of the country to collect information, "looking, listening, talking and trying to gauge public sentiment."[65] Additionally, the committee commissioned a survey of Black voters to be conducted by Ralph Bunche, political science professor at Howard University, to better understand why the party had lost so many Black voters to the Democratic camp. In addition to the obvious benefits of information gathering, Frank noted that an "unsuspected asset" of these widespread interactions with groups and rank-and-file party members is that they could "result in the stimulation and consolidation, in advance of the 1940 campaign, of a widespread body of opinion in support of the accepted parts of the committee's recommendations." This attempt to figure out what the public wanted, not just before the next election but more broadly in a programmatic spirit, was "without precedent in American political history."[66] It had been done in Europe, especially Great Britain, but not in the United States.

The committee members worked in a few collective sessions. A few months after their initial meeting in March 1938—which someone "widely known in academic circles for cautious and sound judgement" called "the most remarkable political meeting since the Constitutional Convention of 1787"—they had a summer session, which involved "a week of intensive work by subcommittees and the committee as a whole" on various major issues of the day (including "labor, agriculture, social security, financial policy, relief, civil service and political liberties").[67] The committee invited experts in these areas, "in many cases representing divergent points of view," to participate in this session.[68] Group leaders representing different interests (e.g., the American Federation of Labor [AFL], Congress of Industrial Organizations [CIO], and "management" representatives) were also invited. Regional subcommittees drafted documents, representing "an intellectually honest, economically sound, and politically effective basis of party action," which were then sent up the ladder to the regional committees and central headquarters, who then assessed areas of agreement and disagreement within the party, as well as areas where further research was necessary. The central body served as "a clearing house and also a catalyst" for moving forward when diverging opinions created "stalemate."[69]

It seems that the more they worked on this project, the more they realized how much work was needed. As the regional subcommittees on issues dove into their tasks, Bridges (1939, 302) notes,

> The size of the job was becoming apparent. Sharp differences of opinion inevitably came to light. Considerations of party strategy kept intruding upon the broader problems of what was good or bad, right or wrong for the country as a whole. And the key subcommittees on fundamentals got knotted up on the nature of fundamentals and whether in writing they could be distinguished from platitudes. A great deal of work had been done and not much of consequence had been accomplished.

Initially, many people thought the group would be releasing a report in advance of the 1938 midterms. Indeed, Bridges (1939) notes, "In view of the very short time spent by party conventions in drawing up a platform, six or seven months looked like a generous allotment for doing the job."[70] It became clear, however, that their programmatic goals could not be achieved in that time, not from such a meager foundation.

They released a progress report to the RNC in November 1938. A draft of their final report was sent by the central Frank Committee headquarters to regional subcommittees so committee members could offer feedback by June 1939. The final draft needed to be approved by the whole committee in a meeting in Chicago.[71] The committee presented the final report to the RNC, which then released it in February 1940. Frank also discussed the report in a national broadcast. He again emphasized that this was not itself a platform—writing a platform was the convention resolution committee's job, as it had been in the past—but this report would "aid the resolutions committee with a background of careful, detailed study in recognition of the fact that 'the time is past when a party can hope to produce an adequate platform in one or two evenings in the head and hurry of a national convention."[72] Their work was extensive, and their 35,000 word final report covered major issues of the day, like tariffs and farm policy. This final report, and the effort to produce it, reflected a substantial organizational evolution for Republicans.

After World War II, there was a shift on the Democratic side as well. Harry Truman's "whistle stop" campaign was an interesting development from

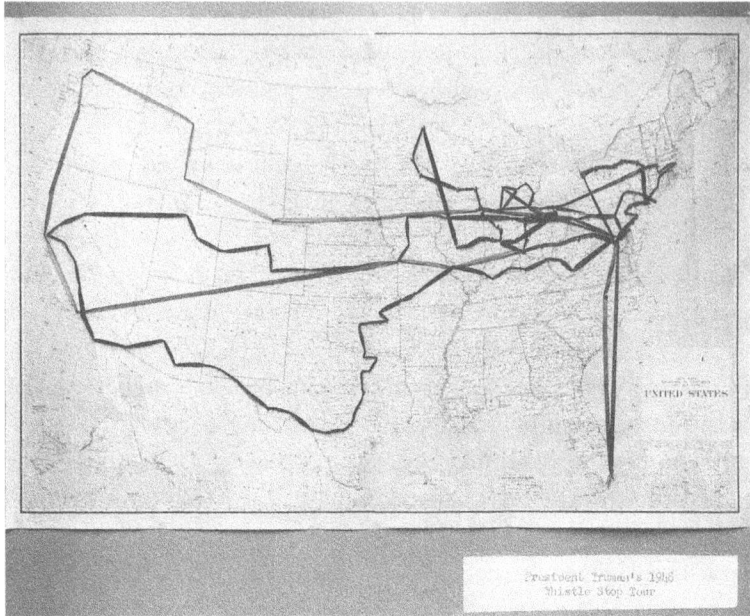

FIGURE 4.4. President Truman's 1948 Whistle Stop Tour.
Photo of U.S. map with ribbons and pins marking the route of President Truman's whistle stop tour and stops on the tour. Caption and photo from the Harry S. Truman Presidential Library and Museum, accession number 2006-175. Credit: Harris & Ewing.

a programmatic standpoint. Without the dynamism of Franklin Roosevelt, from whom he assumed the reins of office when Roosevelt died a few months into his fourth term, Truman faced speculation—seemingly confirmed by polls—that he could not carry the Democratic ticket from the top and would lose the 1948 campaign to his formidable Republican opponent, New York governor Thomas Dewey. Undeterred, or perhaps in response, he embarked on an ambitious railroad journey around the country, making 247 appearances across 206 counties along the way. This so-called whistle stop tour, covering over 31,000 miles and reaching an audience of more than 12 million, involved major speeches in highly populated cities, along with less formal, locally tailored speeches from the back platform of the presidential train car, the Ferdinand Magellan, in many smaller localities. Figure 4.4 shows his route mapped with ribbons and pins.

While this method of campaigning was familiar at the time, Truman's approach was notable for its volume—he made nearly twice as many appearances as Dewey—and style, which included speeches that were more extemporaneous and based on issues.[73] "I have been making a crusade all over this country to tell the American people what the issues in this campaign are," he remarked in a whistle stop speech in Decatur, Illinois, on October 12, 1948. "I am explaining just exactly what this election means to them."[74] Figure 4.5, which pictures Truman delivering a speech in Devils Lake, North Dakota, shows how this setup allowed his words to be projected through speakers on top of the train while also capturing the intimacy of this mode of communication, which allowed people to be quite close to the platform.

Through this tour, the campaign aimed to raise support among several groups, especially laborers, farmers, African Americans, and small-business owners. As the map makes clear, this increase in programmatic action was not directed at the Jim Crow South, which received little to no attention from Truman on his tour. This was the year after southern Democrats sided with Republicans to support the Taft-Hartley Act, severely undercutting the power of organized labor and rattling the already tenuous relationship between southern and non-southern Democrats. Indeed, southern Democrats would end up walking out of the 1948 Democratic Convention in protest over the inclusion of a civil rights plank in the platform. Less than two weeks after that exodus, Truman issued executive orders to desegregate the military and outlaw racial discrimination in the federal civil service. Reflecting rage among southern Democrats, Strom Thurmond proceeded to challenge Truman under the pro-segregation "States' Rights" ticket, winning four states (Louisiana, Mississippi, Alabama, and South Carolina). Truman and like-minded Democrats no longer felt bound to the white supremacist policy inclinations of the Dixiecrat wing of the party, instead embracing a civil rights agenda and courting Black votes. A DNC staff member recalls:

> I think the general consensus . . . was that, quite apart from the right or wrong of the morals involved . . . that you had no choice but to pursue a strong civil rights position and hope that this would enable you to bring out a big minority vote in the key urban industrial states and enable you to carry them; and that there was no point at that junction of trying to placate the South.[75]

Supporting this whistle stop tour was the Research Division at the DNC, created in 1948, and the first entity of its kind for the party.[76] Previously, "during the days of Roosevelt, leading up to this, Charlie Michelson had been sort

FIGURE 4.5. Truman speaking to constituents from his train car platform. "A small boy listens intently from his railroad track perch as President Harry S. Truman makes a whistle stop speech from the platform of his special train. They are in Devils Lake, North Dakota." Source: Harry S. Truman Presidential Library and Museum. Credit: AP Photo/William J. Smith.

of a one-man research operation at the national committee," but no group had been devoted to research.[77] Director Bill Batt recalls that the idea for "a little 'think' group and writing group" of this nature came from Clark Clifford, who wrote a key memo on 1948 campaign strategy while serving as special counsel to the president.[78] There had also been some pressure from "contributors to the party who felt there ought to be some of this kind of activity, that there had not been enough in the past."[79] Around the turn of the year, Clifford discussed the idea with DNC chairman J. Howard McGrath and Bill Batt, who was working in the private sector but interested in returning to public service. They considered whether it made more sense for it to be located in the White House or the DNC. Clifford preferred the latter because he thought it would offer "much more freedom of action."[80] And so it was. The DNC brought the idea to life in establishing the Research Division, giving it a director, a staff, and a budget of approximately $80,000, a substantial sum for the time.[81]

From the beginning, Director Bill Batt recalls, they were "all issues-oriented; the President wanted the campaign to be issue-oriented."[82] They created documents called "Files of the Facts" for twelve topics: human resources, Social Security, education, health, and veterans; agricultural abundance; housing; veterans benefits; loyalty and subversive activities; the 80th Congress and lobbies; labor; civil liberties; foreign policy; prices; natural resources; and opposition research on Thomas E. Dewey. The structure of these documents reflected attention to issue-based party competition. It was decided early on in the division's work that the Files of the Facts would have a particular structure, covering "the Democratic record; quotes from Roosevelt and Truman; what we did; what the opposition said; the Republican record, and Democratic plans for the future."[83] Different staff members specialized in different areas (indeed, Batt recruited them with their particular areas of expertise in mind).[84] For example, Batt "remember[s] distinctly that we got Kenny Birkhead, particularly, because of his background in the field of race relations. He and his father before him had been very active in NAACP matters, and he was very knowledgeable in this whole area."[85] They did not do "original research," relying instead on existing materials (e.g., agency reports, newspapers, congressional hearings) to create their "handy briefs for the campaign." These materials were used for speechwriting, interview preparation, and other campaign activities, and would travel on the train with Truman along his whistle stop tour. The Research Division also ended up getting involved in preparing the president for local stops with information about the locality, important politicians, the issues important to people there that the president should emphasize, and so on. They were also "very valuable in supplying material to the [DNC's] platform committee," according to the DNC's assistant publicity director Samuel Brightman.[86]

And yet, the Research Division reflected tensions in thinking about programmaticism. Although the division's establishment indicates some interest in issue politics, it was kept at a distance from the core of the DNC, figuratively and physically. In fact, the division was initially a secret until the *New York Times* learned of the group and "spill[ed] the beans" about their existence in an August 1, 1948, article that "quite shocked" people in the group, according to one of its members.[87] Asked why he thought the party tried to keep the group a secret, the Research Division's assistant director, Johannes Hoeber, said that he thought it was because the people recruited to the committee had backgrounds in liberal organizations like Americans for Democratic Action (ADA) and the American Veterans Committee (AVC), to which Director Bill Batt had strong ties.[88] Indeed, the *New York Times* article notes this in a somewhat disparaging tone, calling them "zealous liberals, part of a new crop of New Dealers" associated with AVC and ADA. Notably, both of these organizations were pro–civil rights.

The Research Division was placed in a separate building a few blocks away from the rest of the DNC, purportedly because there was not sufficient space in the Ring Building, where the DNC was housed. But Research Division staff understood they were being kept in a separate and inferior space, which was "the hottest office I think I've ever worked in in my life" (Kenneth Birkhead, associate director of public relations for the Research Division) and "miserably noisy" (Director Bill Batt) due to construction on a nearby overpass. Recalls Birkhead, "you had to have a window open to get any air at all, and outside were pile drivers driving piles, and it was not conducive to very concentrated thinking."[89] Inside, they had a "very Spartan setup" with "nothing but a desk and chair." Birkhead mused, "I don't know where they found the desks, but they were Army surplus from about the Civil War."[90]

They did not officially report to anyone at the DNC. Rather, their official chain of command went up to Clark Clifford and the White House staff.[91] Their "basic contacts were with the Truman campaign train," not the DNC, Birkhead recalls. The DNC "sort of wondered about exactly who we were, sitting off in this building up there, and exactly what we were doing."[92] Officials at the DNC did not particularly care for the Research Division. Remarked Assistant Director Hoeber, "I wouldn't say the relations were at dagger's point, but they were kind of exceedingly cool. I think the Ring Building [i.e.,

DNC] fellows considered this long hair crowd as kind of interlopers into their 'professional business.'"[93] Birkhead recalls, "We were considered sort of outsiders if you can put it that way. We were not in the traditional political sense of raising money and putting out press releases. I guess to some of them they thought we were some kind of thinkers or something. We were not politicians in their mind although all of us at one time or another had been closely associated with politics."[94] This wariness may have been related to the fact that the division was a new idea. "I think part of it was that they never really had anything like a Research Division," Birkhead speculates. "We were maybe too erudite for them or something. They weren't sure what a Research Division really did."[95]

This impression is consistent with a stony and somewhat dismissive assessment of the Research Division by Samuel Brightman. Chairman J. Howard McGrath reportedly never commented on or even visited the Research Division, and Hoeber notes that "except for Bill Batt, all of us were really kept away completely from the Democratic National Committee." The Research Division was "not [McGrath's] cup of tea," and the chairman apparently thought money would be better used for campaign finance.[96]

Even cost considerations reflect tensions in thinking about issues at this time. Research was a considerable investment, which was particularly notable given the DNC's financial woes. Hoeber recalls that the committee experienced a few "crises" in which they had "run out of money" and staff "had to wait for our paychecks and so on."[97] In this light, McGrath's concern about cost is understandable; and yet, the fact that he did not consider issue research part of campaign finance is telling on its own.

The nation had by no means reached robust programmaticism. The Research Division was not a permanent institution, ending in early October 1948, though there was "considerable discussion" and "concern" among some people about it ending.[98] There was a long way to go on the Republican side as well. Like the DNC's Research Division, the Glenn Frank Committee was temporary. There were a few young people, similar in many ways to those working in the Democratic Research Division, doing research at the RNC. Hoeber notes that they ran into each other in a restaurant one night and shared a jovial evening of "banter" about potential campaign slogans. But the Republican Party was less invested in this kind of effort at the time. Indeed, Dewey spoke much less about issues than did Truman.[99]

In 1950, APSA argued in *Toward a More Responsible Two-Party System* that the parties needed "stronger, full-time research organization[s], adequately financed and working on a year-in, year-out basis."[100] They would need more organizational strength to accomplish that goal. By midcentury, though they had grown in many ways, the RNC and DNC still did not meet regularly. The national committee "is seldom a generally influential and much less a working body," APSA noted.[101] Since the committees still focused mainly on presidential elections, it is not especially surprising that their activities consistently dwindled thereafter.[102] In a comparative analysis of American and British parties, Ralph D. Casey (1944) observed, "The usual American practice is a feverish construction of a party headquarters staff capable of real organization and propaganda service a few months before a presidential campaign. The skeleton gets flesh and bones on the eve of a national convention or soon after a nominee is chosen. After an election, the major part of a headquarters staff melts away."[103] This changed in the second half of the twentieth century, as discussed in the next chapter. Before getting to that, though, we'll return to the platform-writing process to examine how its evolution after the turn of the century helped create a foundation for modern processes.

Platforms in the First Half of the Twentieth Century

Examining national party platforms in figure 4.1, we can see parties paying more attention to issues over time. The party platforms gradually lengthen toward the end of the nineteenth century, before the imperatives of the Great Depression temporarily focus politics on the most critical issues of the day. By the end of the New Deal period, however, we begin to see a dramatic increase in platform length. National parties clearly change their orientation toward issues, viewing them as more worthy of attention than they were in the past. Notably, this is also around the time when they started building more robust research capabilities.

REPUBLICAN PARTY

During the 1908 Republican National Convention, there were two notable changes from prior years. First, the platform, which was read into the record as usual, included a whole section on how Democrats and Republicans differ. And second, the party took a step toward more formalized procedure for handling intraparty differences, allotting (as announced by the chair) "forty minutes for debate, twenty minutes in behalf of the majority report and twenty minutes in behalf of the minority report."[104] Following this sequence of events, there were votes on amendments, all of which were rejected (see figure 4.3), and the platform was adopted.

Dissent from Progressives generally came in the form of minority reports, which at times faced jeering, laughter, and even hisses and "hooting" when read into the record. The dissent came from two state delegates (one from Wisconsin, one from North Dakota) in 1912, and from only Wisconsin in 1916 and 1920.[105] The floor overwhelming voted against these reports. Despite the lopsidedness, these delegates were given floor time (e.g., twenty minutes in 1912) to express their views. This did not always please the floor, to say the least. When the delegate from Wisconsin read his minority report, which only he signed, in 1920, there was so much disruption that the chairman needed to intervene. In 1924, the minority gave the report an official name: "Platform of the La Follette Progressive Republican Delegates," which was read to the floor by Hon. Henry Allen Cooper of Wisconsin.[106] In the following convention, La Follette himself read the minority report into the record. For a while, it seemed that the whole platform committee could agree except for the Progressive delegates.

Things started to heat up in 1928. Amid the presentation to the floor of a potential platform amendment on agriculture there was a demonstration by delegates from Iowa, Nebraska, Minnesota, South Dakota, and some other western states, as well as a counter-demonstration. The chairman restored order, speeches were then made by delegates from five states (Iowa, Nebraska, New Jersey, Washington, and Idaho), and an additional amendment was offered. This was the most extensive discussion thus far about the business of the Committee of Resolutions at a Republican convention. It ended with approval of the platform by voice vote, though with some dissent evident even in this cryptic form.

In 1932, a demonstration (described in the record as a "parade") broke out when a delegate from Connecticut presented a minority report on the 18th Amendment. Prohibition was clearly an issue that divided the party. As the chairman attempted to restore order, asking the floor whether they wanted to hear the rest of the minority report, "There were cries of 'yes' and 'no' from the floor and galleries and a loud shrill cry from the galleries 'We want beer!' followed by renewed cheering and demands for order."[107] This hubbub was followed by a long and boisterous debate on the platform. The majority report from the platform committee was eventually adopted by voice vote, but with considerable dissent.

Given the time required to write a platform, the floor often found itself waiting on the resolutions committee to make its report, taking extra recesses, allowing speeches on the floor they might not otherwise have permitted, and even offering entertainment. In 1940, for example, when they returned from the recess they took because they were waiting on the platform committee, "the Columbus Glee Club sang several songs and the band played." When the committee still was not ready, they had to take another recess.[108] The process had extended to ten days by 1940, a far cry from the thirty-six hours it had once occupied; and yet, it was not sufficient to complete the platform in a timely manner. They had a lot to consider at this tumultuous historical moment, marked by the enduring sting of the Great Depression, an overhaul of federal government responsibilities, and the growing intensity of World War II. Twenty members of Congress testified before the platform committee regarding U.S. involvement in the war, which they opposed.[109] Together, these facts speak to the increasing arduousness of platform writing, and to its nontriviality.

In 1944, there were significant changes to the platform-writing process. For the first time, the committee included one woman in addition to the usual one delegate per state. This would become standard for the party. The committee worked for six days and for the first time divided their work between subcommittees, each with its own chair, for different issues: (1) foreign affairs; (2) agriculture; (3) taxation and finance; (4) labor; (5) foreign trade; and (6) western and Pacific problems. This kind of division of labor into subcommittees provided a way to manage the volume of work before the platform committee at this complex historical moment. This would lead to an even bigger turning point in the following convention, which for the first time would be broadcast to a radio audience.

The convention of 1948 exhibited some notable similarities and differences from earlier conventions. The platform was written during the convention period, as in previous years. The RNC again appointed subcommittees: (1) agriculture; (2) economics and small business; (3) public works, natural resources, and western affairs; (4) veterans' affairs; (5) general governmental affairs; (6) labor and social welfare; and (7) civil rights. The disappearance of the Foreign Affairs Committee likely reflects the fact that World War II was now over. There was now a Committee for Veterans' Affairs, which makes sense given the number of WWII veterans and the importance of the GI Bill, and a Committee on Civil Rights, reflecting rising pressure in many states for civil rights legislation and foreshadowing the increasing prominence of this subject over the next few decades.

The convention of 1948 was also an important turning point in terms of process. Republicans held hearings in which they heard testimony from "scores of witnesses representing widely differing viewpoints." They regarded their comprehensive process and ability to "[engage] in keen debate, hearing all viewpoints and retaining their good humor" as noble and novel. Indeed, platform committee chair Henry Cabot Lodge Jr. asked (rhetorically): "Is there any other country where this kind of thing happens?" Another important development was that the platform committee received assistance from the Republican National Committee's staff and chair, "whose good judgment and tireless energy were indispensable."[110] This reflected significant change, which would continue after the century's midpoint.

DEMOCRATIC PARTY

Democrats made some marked changes over this period, but they did not get quite as far as Republicans. In 1904, the Committee on Resolutions spent only sixteen hours on the platform, which was unanimously adopted by that body and the floor. While compromise was necessary between delegates from the East and the West, in the end they were able to agree, and the platform was adopted without the drama seen at some other conventions.[111] The process was similarly smooth in 1908, taking "two days and nights of constant labor," but characterized by "unanimity and harmony."[112] The platform was then unanimously adopted by the floor.

Things started to heat back up before long, however. In 1916, procedural debates surrounding the platform reignited, someone proposed an amendment regarding Irish independence outside the context of the Committee on Resolutions (which was then referred to the committee), and both a majority and minority report emerged from the committee. The former supported women's suffrage, while the latter explicitly left this matter to states. After a long discussion, the minority report was rejected, and the majority adopted. The process was even more hectic in 1920, when delegates began offering resolutions from the floor early in the convention, in violation of a previously established resolution that all such suggestions should be submitted directly to the Committee on Resolutions (not occupying any floor time with reading at this stage). Someone raised a point of order, sustained by the chair, to enforce the rule. Yet, disagreement on this matter continued, and delegates offered these kinds of resolutions until the end of the second day. Attempts to get the Committee on Resolutions, which had been meeting in a separate space as usual, to release its report early were not successful. The situation remained conflictual when the committee finished its work, as four amendments/minority reports were offered along with the majority report. The convention chair announced that there would be 3.5 hours of debate, followed by votes (mostly voice votes) on amendments offered in minority reports, all of which lost. The majority platform was then adopted by voice vote. This pattern extended to 1924, with minority reports, amendments, and general hullabaloo surrounding the platform's passage.

Over the next five election cycles, between 1928 and 1944, the process on the convention floor was generally quicker and calmer. In almost all of these years, the platform was presented and adopted with little debate or fanfare and almost no amendment activity.[113] The 1932 convention was an outlier, with four amendments on important subjects like the Federal Reserve, social welfare protections, and the 18th Amendment, as well as more discussion and debate. It's not surprising that there would be more discussion in 1932, as the nation was still reeling from the Great Depression. Ultimately, the amendments were rejected, and a platform was adopted by voice vote.

This is not to say there were never any disagreements, or that disagreement would be problematic. As Governor Albert C. Ritchie (MD) noted in 1928:

A party that never differs on vital issues is not a party of progress. It becomes a party of vested interest, sterile, and the party of selfishness and of defeat. It is conflicts of opinion that indicate party life and vitality. So ability to harmonize those conflicts indicates party strength, and therefore I appeal to a Democratic convention for unity, for accord, for subordination of individual judgements and individual predilections.[114]

In this year, the party attempted to achieve such harmony by involving group representatives. Committee on Platform and Resolutions chairman Sen. Key Pittman (NV) said, of the platform process, "The representatives of the farmers, labor, business, the veterans, and women's associations, in fact, every association that desired to express itself before you with regard to the proposed planks of the platform, were given all of the time that they asked. They aided materially in the framing of those planks."[115] On this basis, Pittman asked that the floor trust that the platform had support from key groups like farmers, implicitly discouraging conflict on the floor over the platform.

In other years, however, the smoothness of the process seems to indicate a lack of significant interest in the platform. Indeed, the 1936 Democratic platform was written by one person: Leon Keyserling, secretary and legislative aide to Senator Robert Wagner of New York, who was serving as the chair of the Democratic Platform Committee at the time and who had strong ties to Clark Clifford.[116] "I made the first draft of the Democratic platform in 1936, the entire draft, in Senator Wagner's office," he recalled. Others read the draft and "changed the style and the format considerably, but the content was the same."[117] Keyserling wrote the 1940 and 1944 Democratic platforms as well, and they were published almost exactly as he drafted them.[118] A few people either read a draft (e.g., Wagner, FDR) or came to hear Keyserling read it (e.g., Lowell Mellett, a colleague of Wagner's), but "there were practically no changes." Needless to say, investment in the platform process was limited, at best. In later years, Keyserling would continue to be involved with the platform (e.g., he drafted the economic sections in 1956, and "became really close to the practical aspects of selling some of these [economic] programs" in 1960), but a more substantial process had grown around him.

The process was more heated in 1948, which makes sense given that the platform included a civil rights plank. It was in this year that Truman established the Research Division and made more issue-oriented speeches. After the Committee on Platform and Resolutions' report was read into the record, there were four amendments—three of which were introduced by southern delegates on the matter of states' rights (i.e., thinly veiled anti–civil rights positions), and one from a Wisconsin delegate about equal opportunity employment, personal security, and equal treatment in the military. In this year, southern delegates revolted from the convention over the platform's civil rights plank, and Strom Thurmond would turn against his own party to challenge Harry Truman.

By the century's midpoint, the Democrats' process was not as extensive as the Republicans'. But in 1948, the Democrats were also facing an internal crisis on civil rights, which fractured their nomination process. When one issue could lead to rebellion by a region's delegates, and serve as the impetus for a challenge to the party's candidate from a third party, it is hard to imagine how they could achieve significant, stable programmaticism. There were certainly signs of progress over time, but the party had a long way to go to reach that state.[119]

Conclusion

There are a few key takeaways from this analysis of party institutions and programmaticism from 1856 to 1950. First, it offers alternative measures of programmaticism. Party platforms grow longer, and there are also changes in process, indicating more attention to programmaticism over time, if not in a simple or linear fashion. We can see the parties outgrowing the rudimentary processes for platform writing that existed in the mid-nineteenth century, and making adjustments to their platform-writing processes to accommodate new imperatives and to manage conflict. We also see party leaders increase their focus on issues as a means of interparty competition in speeches and other communications, and make more of an effort toward the end of this period to work on developing issue positions between presidential election cycles (i.e., outside the context of writing the quadrennial platform). The twists and turns of these alternative measures of programmaticism may not perfectly mirror the measure presented in chapter 1, but they tell the same basic story: there was some increase over this first century of competition, but the changes were gradual, and the level of programmaticism in 1950 was still modest compared to the contemporary era.

This analysis also supplements what's presented in chapter 1 by providing insight into why Democrats and Republicans took steps, even small ones, toward programmaticism, as well as what constrained movement in this direction. On the former front, it became clear that early procedures for developing positions in manifestos became strained. The number and complexity of issues grew, such that having a committee go into a room for a few days during the convention and draft a document about issue positions was too tall a task. They could not finish their work before the floor became restless. It also became more difficult to resolve conflict with the rudimentary processes used in the early years of competition between these parties. Needless to say, the Democrats' 1856 solution to vote on each plank separately became untenable very quickly. Over time, the parties tried different ways of allowing people and groups to request particular platform planks, and different ways of managing conflict about the majority platform presented to the floor of the convention. There were often hours of debate and unruliness that frustrated many and did not seem particularly productive. Bolstering their processes for developing positions was seen as a means of dealing with disagreement over an increasing number of issues in an increasingly complex nation.

Consistent with insights from existing literature on parties, innovations in programmaticism were positively related to defeat, whether experienced or expected.[120] This also squares with comparative work, discussed in chapter 2, showing that programmaticism is associated with increased party competition. The RNC created the Glenn Frank Committee after a major defeat in 1936, with party leaders explicitly arguing that new tools for competition were needed and noting that voters were inquiring about what the party stood for. Bridges (1939) identified this as a reason the United States did not have anything like the Glenn Frank Committee until the late 1930s, much later than the rise of programmatic research in Britain. Likewise, the Democratic Party developed its program committee when Truman was expected to lose badly to Dewey in the 1948 election, and like the Republicans in 1936, they were also facing a crisis of party identity and values, in this case over the inclusion of a civil rights plank and FDR's death.

Of course, these were not the only years in which one party was in a difficult position. In earlier years, however, barebones national organizations would not have been able to carry out this kind of work. Lending credence to the argument put forth in chapter 2, party members often talk about the amount of work involved in developing party positions. They needed to gather and be able to sift through and synthesize information, which came from a variety of sources (group leaders, government agencies, surveys of the public, etc.). They needed ways to manage conflict between various interests and personalities in the party. Institutions dedicated to this kind of work, like the DNC's Research Division and the RNC's Glenn Frank Committee, were positioned to help the parties move toward programmaticism even if the system itself would not have been considered strongly programmatic at the time. The parties would build on their experiences with these institutions in the future.

Several factors constrained programmatic development during this period. Existential crises, both domestic (e.g., the Civil War) and global (e.g., the Great Depression and the fear and pressure stemming from the fall of democracies worldwide), commanded attention from political leaders. At the party level, there was also a lack of belief among some members that developing issue positions was important to the party's business, limited organizational capacity, and intraparty division.[121] Conflict was especially strong on matters of race.

Characterizing the relationship between racial politics and programmaticism in the nineteenth and early twentieth centuries is no simple matter. It would be incorrect to say that policy issues were not central to American politics—a civil war erupted over the issue of slavery. In this light, one might be skeptical of the racial oppression hypothesis, that agents and institutions of racial oppression constrained programmaticism. But this is not evidence against the racial oppression hypothesis; in fact, it's quite the opposite. This was largely a sectional conflict—South versus non-South—rather than fodder for interparty competition. So, in that sense, it constrained programmaticism. Moreover, slavery was such an important issue, both for the future of the nation as a legitimate democracy and for parties, that there was not much room for consideration of programmatic development across a wide range of issues.

Overall, there is a lot to learn about programmaticism from the first century of competition between Democrats and Republicans, even though it had yet to skyrocket. While the work of the research bodies discussed in this chapter did not always have the final say in what the party's position would be, they had some agenda-setting power. As Thomson (1939) notes, "A research agency may play a significant role in determining which issues shall be taken up, which given priority of treatment, and which played down or ignored."[122] There is also power in gathering and distilling information on issues. Perhaps most important, the changes of this century—however modest they may seem to the modern eye—provided an important foundation for the more dramatic changes discussed in the next chapter, as well as the high level of divergent democracy we see today.

5

National Party Institutions and Programmaticism, 1950–2020

BY THE TWENTIETH century's midpoint, attention to issues had risen and procedures and institutions had evolved to facilitate position development, but the level of programmatic partisanship was still modest. This chapter traces the continued increase in programmaticism, and the particularly dramatic shift in the 1960s, employing similar guiding questions and strategies used to analyze the period from 1856 to 1950 in chapter 4. This close analysis offers an alternative view of programmaticism to supplement the measure discussed in chapter 1 and reveals the nature and volume of work involved in position development. By examining the perceived costs and benefits of shifting toward issue-based competition, as well as the people and groups who promoted and resisted this change, we can also better understand why it occurred.

Issue differentiation was not forced on parties, nor did it happen naturally. It necessitated party agency in wrestling with the notion of developing party positions on issues, and in building institutions to make such an idea possible. None of this was easy. Consistent with the axioms presented in chapter 2, developing positions on issues required a great deal of work involving a lot of people, resources, time, and agita. It required taking initiative and managing resistance. Both the advocacy and opposition can help us better understand what facilitated and constrained programmatic development. And in raising attention to party organizations, we can see that the current moment, typically discussed in ideological terms, has important institutional components.

This chapter proceeds in three parts, all of which build on the previous chapter. I begin by examining changes in the general institutional activity and capacity of national party organizations since 1950, which helped buttress the increases in programmatic capacity that are this chapter's main focus. This is a key starting point because the "ghost parties" described by E. E. Schattschneider in the 1940s would not have been capable of the kind of programmatic work discussed in this chapter. I then trace efforts within and supported by national party organizations to develop party positions on issues between conventions and institutions built in this pursuit. Finally, I focus specifically on the process of developing platforms and show how it changed over time to facilitate programmatic competition.

Growth in National Party Organizations

Visiting the DNC headquarters in January 1950, a reporter from the *Kansas City Star* was impressed by its professionalism. With "solid wooden doors [that] swing to the committee's reception room," where "Miss Mary Gates lights up with a bright smile," the office was a welcome surprise to this contemporaneous observer of American politics. "The smooth operation at party headquarters gives it the atmosphere of an efficient business office rather than a political pie counter."[1] Parties had progressed since the nineteenth century, but they still had a ways go before a "pie counter" would no longer seem like a reasonable standard of comparison.

Parties have strengthened in many ways since the mid-twentieth century, particularly in response to electoral loss and minority status in Congress.[2] While their time frames differed, both parties developed better, more stable fundraising capabilities and ways to gather information on the electorate for use in campaigns during this period. This reflected and facilitated their increased activities between presidential election years.

One way to gauge general activity and organizational capacity is to look at staffing levels. I compiled data from archives and secondary sources like Klinkner (1994), the Encyclopedia of Associations (EA), and Cotter and Bibby (1980), who in turn drew on work by Hugh Bone (1958, 1971). EA does not always get new data from organizations every year. In this situation, they typically use data received previously. This means that EA data will exaggerate stability, but it can provide a rough estimate of party staff size in the contemporary era (figure 5.1).

Figure 5.1 shows an increase in staffing levels over time. Bars are colored differently to indicate presidential election years (gray) and off-years (black). In 1935, the RNC had only eleven staff members. This is consistent with

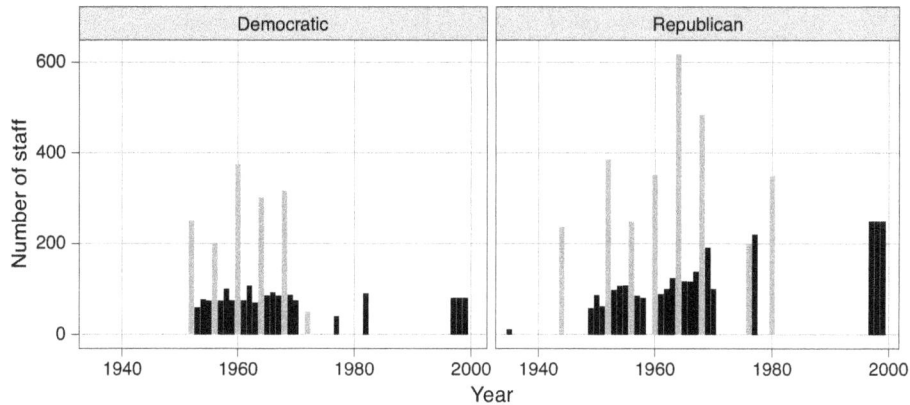

FIGURE 5.1. DNC and RNC staff, 1935–2000.
The data used to make these graphs come from archival documents as well as secondary sources like Klinkner (1994), the Encyclopedia of Associations, and Cotter and Bibby (1980), who in turn relied largely on work by Hugh Bone (1958, 1971). Blank spaces indicate missing data, not necessarily zero staff.

scholars' observations of organizational decline between elections. By the mid-1950s, however, parties were maintaining heartier organizations in non-election years, although staffing levels continued to drop after presidential elections. Between 1952 and 1953, for example, both parties cut their staff by approximately three-quarters (DNC from 251 to 59, RNC from 386 to 98). The between-election staff, however, grew over time, especially on the Republican side.

Parties' meetings also seem to have changed over time in nature and frequency. We can see this by looking at transcripts of committee meetings, which were long included in appendices to transcripts of the parties' national conventions. From the mid-nineteenth century through about the first two decades of the twentieth, the Democratic and Republican National Committees tended not to meet between conventions. They would often have a short gathering right after the convention closed, and sometimes another meeting or two a few weeks later, but they made no true efforts to conduct party business between their quadrennial conventions. By the early 1930s, the DNC started to meet at least once a few months before the convention. In the 1950s, the number of meetings more than doubled, as the party convened roughly every few months. After peaking from the mid-1950s to mid-1960s, the number of meetings, or at least the number of transcribed meetings, lowered. Given that parties maintain robust between-election operations

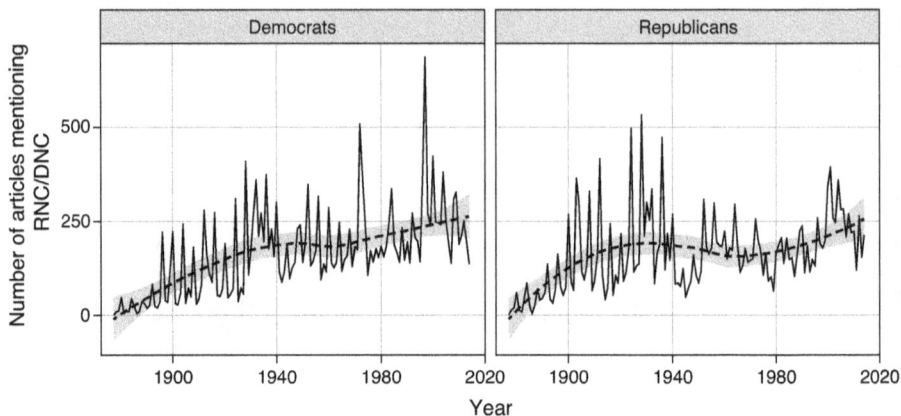

FIGURE 5.2. DNC and RNC in the media.
This graph is based on data from the *Washington Post*, gathered through the ProQuest Historical Newspaper database.

today, it is likely that their modes of convening and communicating changed. Republicans followed a similar pattern, but reached only about a third of the height of Democrats at their peak (three meetings between conventions versus ten).

To get a more continuous measure of national party strength over time, I also consider media attention to the RNC and DNC. This is a coarse proxy, as it is more a measure of prominence than strength, but it's not unreasonable to expect the two to trend together—meager organizations that disband between elections are unlikely to receive much media attention. It would be ideal to have consistent measures of staffing levels, budgets, and bureaucratic complexity (i.e., number of divisions within the organization), but data on those metrics rely on archives, which provide spotty coverage. Media attention offers a more continuous measure. We would not want to rely on this alone, but it is a useful supplement to other ways of examining organizational strength.

Figure 5.2 shows the number of articles per year mentioning the DNC and RNC in the *Washington Post* over time. Raw data are shown in the solid line, and the dashed line is a loess curve with a 95 percent confidence interval shaded in gray. There is an upward trend over time for Democrats and Republicans. This is not simply due to changes in the number of articles over time. The upward trend remains if we look at the percentage of articles mentioning the RNC or DNC.[3]

While none of these measures may be perfect in isolation, together they strongly suggest an increase in party organizational strength and capacity over time. Of course, national parties have limitations even today. The RNC, for example, was unable to stop rogue candidate Donald Trump from winning the party's presidential nomination in 2016, despite widespread distaste among party elites for the style and substance of his political persona and campaign.[4] And national parties in the United States are not as organizationally robust as parties in many other nations, inviting the moniker "hollow parties."[5] This characterization is neither flattering nor incorrect; and yet, it does not preclude parties strengthening in meaningful ways that provide an important foundation for programmatic growth.

Growth in Programmatic Capacity

Political scientist and presidential adviser Charles Merriam, writing in 1921, lamented that "on the side of organization for the consideration of party policies and party techniques [the party] is singularly defective."[6] Party leaders lacked, among other things, "the interchange of ideas regarding national or party politics."[7] APSA, in its 1950 report, argued that the parties also needed greater research capabilities to address what authors considered a troubling degree of programmatic similarity between parties. Over time, the DNC and RNC would make progress on both fronts.

The Democratic Party

Democrats' programmatic efforts during Truman's whistle stop campaign continued after the election. In May 1950, the party held a three-day conference and Jefferson Jubilee, which included panel discussions of major issues like civil rights, welfare legislation, agriculture, labor, business, natural resources, and economic problems. It was a large gathering, including high-profile leadership along with groups (e.g., representing labor, farms, businesses), and was broadcast on radio and television.[8] The panel discussions were modeled after those in regional Democratic conferences in the previous year, evincing organizational learning.

When Frank McKinney assumed the chairmanship in 1951, he expanded the party's programmatic effort. The DNC had put a lot of work into bolstering its organization, but, as McKinney argued in a January 1952 speech,

The machinery of organization is just useless machinery unless the party worker who visits the voter knows how to tell him why he should vote and vote Democratic. . . . We must see that regardless of what the Republicans campaign on, that we Democrats campaign on the important issues, and that those issues are what decide how the American people mark their ballots on November 4.[9]

To this end, McKinney established a new Research Division headed by political scientist Bertram M. Gross, who had previously chaired the APSA Committee on Political Parties and co-authored *Toward a More Responsible Two-Party System*.[10] The Research Division was the party's biggest new investment by far, accounting for over half of the party's new expenses in 1952.[11] McKinney intended for this research staff to operate permanently, in and between election years, "helping to win elections and to carry out party policies through legislative and administrative action."[12]

Their operating plan was to gather information on issues, disseminate it to members of Congress, and publicize it to voters as well.[13] They would end up producing short papers (fact sheets) on twenty subjects, with information on Democratic and Republican orientation toward them. These would become the basis for a campaign handbook disseminated right after the 1952 convention.[14]

Programmatic efforts continued under Stephen A. Mitchell, who served as chairman from 1952 to 1955. In a 1953 report to members of the DNC and state chairmen, Mitchell dedicated a section to the promise "We Shall Tell the Public" and stated that one of the party's main priorities would be "publicizing dramatically and aggressively the activities of the Democratic Party—bringing home to every voter the positions of both parties on every important issue."[15] Under Mitchell's leadership, the Research Division compiled thirty-two fact sheets and collected other material on issues to help lawmakers. "Many Senators and Congressmen have expressed their appreciation for this assistance and the volume of requests for extra copies attests to the usefulness of the material," Mitchell reported to members of the DNC. They would continue this work "in cooperation with the staffs of the Congressional campaign committees."[16] They aimed to be nimble, able to respond to what Republicans were doing. Mitchell noted, "As the Republicans develop particular issues during the campaign, the Research Division will put out prompt and succinct information to assist candidates in dealing with them."[17] Mitchell reported that a member of Congress who had served for four decades said this was the most help he had ever received from the DNC in terms of research.[18]

A central project of the DNC under Mitchell was to establish the National Advisory Council (NAC). The party's "functions and responsibilities have grown with the complexities of modern political campaigns," they noted in an introductory pamphlet. The party needed to engage in more publicity and shoulder "a greater burden" of providing research on issues to members of Congress; no longer would it suffice for the DNC to be "little more than an office with a secretary except during a campaign," as it was before Roosevelt's presidency.[19] The NAC was to help mobilize people into party affairs, raise money, and strengthen the national party.[20]

Notably, the introductory pamphlet on the NAC also said that the party needed to provide more assistance to state and local organizations, which could no longer rely so much on patronage. Underscoring the inverse relationship between clientelism and programmaticism, this document states:

> With the changes that have taken place in the last twenty years local political organizations do not have the same kind of strength they once had. New types of political organizations are called for and different types of people have indicated interest in political activity. In order to attract people to political organization work, the emphasis must be shifted to the motivating factors, such as principle, ideals, and obligation of citizenship. It is the responsibility of the Democratic National Committee to keep abreast of current political methods and to instruct local organizations in their use and application. Consequently the Committee Headquarters must consist of an adequate staff of skilled men and women who are specialists in their respective lines of work.

By this point, the Democratic Party had come a long way since the days of distributing Thanksgiving turkeys to voters and pink slips to staff at its convention. It had a research staff, the NAC, and many fact sheets and other materials to support programmatic appeals. Yet, issue-based competition was by no means easy or well established at this point. As the *Wall Street Journal* observed in 1954, "Democrats Lament Lack of Big Rocks to Toss at GOP Administration." Eisenhower's moderation made this even more difficult, as Democrats were "embarrassed by a shortage of things to oppose" during his tenure. The DNC was aware of this article and kept it in its files.[21]

The heat turned up on programmatic efforts under the tutelage of Paul Butler, DNC chairman from 1955 to 1960. Before he even became chair, Butler implored the DNC's Executive Committee to adapt the party to modern times and issues. The country had changed—becoming far more complex, urbanized, and industrialized—but party organizations had not grown in a commensurate fashion, he argued. The tasks before them were more numerous and challenging, especially as national issues were coming more and more to the forefront of American politics, and party organizations needed to grow to fulfill their responsibilities. There were now "a multiplicity of interests represented by broadly-supported organizations rivaling political parties in competition for public support," and the party that responded best to these new developments would be best positioned to win favor with voters.

Butler believed a 1954 Democratic National Convention could move them toward these goals. "The Democratic Party will not speak in the 1954 elections with a single, clear voice if 435 candidates for Congress and 33 candidates for the Senate have no party platform and thereby are allowed [handwritten note added "as in the past"] to represent their own views as being the official position of our party on vital national issues," he told the DNC's Executive Committee.[22] A midterm convention could show voters that the Democratic Party was rising to new imperatives and offer an opportunity to manage intraparty differences before the 1956 election. "The national convention is the party's chief representative and deliberative machinery for effecting basic political compromises. This party machinery should be used for this purpose more often than every four years," Butler argued.

Not everyone agreed. Pittsburgh machine boss David Lawrence, for example, "pointed out that to 'have a convention and have the linen washed out over television' might exacerbate rather than resolve intraparty tensions."[23] This would not be the last time Butler clashed with others in the party, to say the least. His choices "drew him into ceaseless public conflicts with southern Democrats, urban bosses, and congressional leaders Sam Rayburn and Lyndon Johnson, men who shared a starkly different outlook on the value and function of parties."[24]

While the midterm convention did not come to pass, Butler enacted other innovations once he assumed the reins of the DNC in 1955.[25] He took the 1950 APSA report very seriously and was committed to strengthening the national committee and preparing Democrats to serve as a responsible opposition party that offered true alternatives.[26] The Research Division released a Democratic fact sheet comparing the two parties' platforms, to publicize where each stood at the time. Butler also established an Advisory Committee on Political Organization (ACPO), which brought various experts together to teach people about political organization and create manuals (for instructors, precinct workers, county leaders, etc.).

Heeding the ACPO's recommendation, Butler changed the structure of the DNC by adding four new special divisions—one each for farmers, labor, natural resources, and small businesses—in his "initial effort to locate policy development within the DNC."[27] Previously, there had been only two institutions of this nature: the Women's Division and the Nationalities Division. Although the new divisions operated with limited resources—each with a secretary and small amount of space—they developed relationships with people in government to help them accomplish their aims. They consulted with congressional offices and committees while drafting position papers and statements, which were then offered to campaigns. These resources were used and appreciated by members of Congress. DNC deputy chairman Drexel Sprecher recalled Rep. Thomas Dodd (D-CT) saying, of the Small Business Division's roughly 100 page report, "It's the best damn thing I have for use in Connecticut. . . . This is the best single thing I've ever gotten out of the national committee."[28]

To supplement divisions' limited resources, staff members built relationships with groups outside government who could help them with their work. Each of the four new divisions compiled a list of special interest leaders and recruited a "special director" in each state. Sprecher reported that six regional representatives from the party "often worked closely with state party leaders in building support among various special interest groups, and sometimes they developed good contacts on their own with local leaders among farmers, small businessmen, unions, and other functional groups."[29]

While Butler thought special divisions could help the party progress, he was wary of the existing Nationalities Division, which "had been a big thing for a long time." Indicating distaste for machine-style organizing, Butler "thought the days of the Irishman as such in politics, or of the Poles and the Italians, should be transcended."[30] He wanted to discontinue this division or at least reduce its prominence and dismiss its executive director, who had strong ties to political machines—ideas that faced unsurprising resistance. Ultimately, Butler let go of that effort, but he would help shift the party's style of politics through other means.

The capstone of Butler's endeavor to increase the national committee's responsibility for policy came shortly after the 1956 election, with the creation of the Democratic Advisory Council (DAC) "to coordinate and advance efforts in behalf of Democratic programs and principles."[31] The DAC had the capacity to help create the platform, while managing the party's program between the quadrennial platform-writing process. To accomplish this, they would "continuously study matters of public policy and political activities which are of concern to the Democratic Party, and will seek to formulate suggestions and recommendations for appropriate and constructive policies and actions with respect to such matters, and will engage in other activities in behalf of Democratic programs and principles." In addition to generating and publicizing positions, the DAC could also contribute to efforts to pass legislation in Congress reflecting the Democratic program.[32]

This was in a sense a more formalized version of the Finletter group, which arose after Adlai Stevenson's campaign loss to try to create a policy program that would provide alternatives to Republican positions under the Eisenhower administration. In addition to its namesake and leader, former Secretary of the Air Force Thomas Finletter, the group also included an "informal stable of experts, writers, and politicians to produce detailed memos and speech material for party officials."[33] Many "amateur clubs" had been actively supporting Adlai Stevenson's campaign, highlighting the rise of issue-based political involvement. Though Stevenson was more conservative on many issues than the "amateur Democrats" (to borrow a famous term from James Q. Wilson), his disdain for machine-style politics energized liberal activists who mobilized on issues. And it was thought that issues could further mobilize people. While the Finletter group itself was informal in nature and fluid in membership, it supplied valuable information to Democratic leaders between 1953 and 1956. The DAC would build on this group's work, and Finletter himself would take a leadership role.

Butler asked twenty people to join the DAC as inaugural members. Interestingly, though not surprisingly, very few of the invitees had machine ties. Several had already achieved national-level prominence (e.g., Harry Truman, Adlai Stevenson, W. Averell Harriman). Of the fifteen members of Congress invited, all but one (Democratic Congressional Campaign Committee chairman Michael Kirwan of Ohio) represented states or districts in states with little to no machine activity.[34] The final invitee was Saint Louis mayor Raymond Tucker. While this certainly does not prove that patronage depresses issue politics, it is worth noting that eighteen of the twenty people asked to join the DNC's first major policy initiative were *not* associated with machine politics, and one of the two remaining invitees held a leadership position in the national party.

The DAC was controversial—not everyone who was invited agreed to join. Some were concerned that Republicans, whose votes were necessary to pass bills in a Congress with low party discipline, would be reluctant to support policies originating in a DNC body.[35] Others worried about upsetting members of Congress, whose authority could be undermined by an external policy body like the DAC. This was a major reason why congressional leaders, like Sam Rayburn and Lyndon Johnson, declined participation.

Despite these objections, Butler was determined to define clear and meaningful positions. Unity was a popular concept, a "pretty word," but the party should not abandon "conviction" in its pursuit; for "unity on these terms is only a synonym for sterility and death," Butler argued at the 1960 Democratic National Convention. "There is unity in an ice cube, but not heat," he pointed out. "There is unity in the tomb, but no controversy. A unity which rules out principle is a unity which we Democrats cannot afford if our party is to live and if our Nation is to prosper. The perilous times in which we exist do not allow us the luxury of this kind of unity."[36] The DAC would develop issue stances even if it raised qualms.

The council held its first meeting on January 4, 1957, and proceeded to meet approximately every three months. The DNC stressed the importance of a year-round operation. "The recent election proves the virtual impossibility to have party policy formulated and generally accepted in the brief period from the opening of the Democratic National Convention to the General Election," it stated in a resolution. "We can win in 1960 only if we begin now to hammer out a forceful, coherent policy and to keep communicating it to the public."[37]

By May 1957, they had established ten committees for different issue areas: foreign policy, economic policy, civil rights, urban and suburban policy, labor, farm policy, health policy, Social Security, natural resources, and science and technology.[38] Substantive committees had their own membership and leadership. For example, the Advisory Committee on Foreign Policy had twenty-eight members and a chairman and vice-chairman. They were able to recruit well-respected experts to participate. The Advisory Committee on Science and Technology included two Nobel Prize winners and a number of other researchers from some of the nation's leading universities.

With a great deal of work and conflict resolution, the DAC was able to release fifteen policy statements in its first year of operation, a figure that climbed to sixty-one by 1960. They covered a broad range of subjects, including foreign policy, economic policy, right-to-work laws, Alaska and Hawaii statehood, trade, nuclear testing, immigration, and civil rights.[39] This was no easy feat. Indeed, the *Dayton Daily News* praised the party for "taking up the chore" of this work.[40] Advisory committees would gather materials and draft statements, which would then go to the full council. This process required managing different views. There was disagreement, for example, about economic policy within the liberal Democratic camp, and more specifically between intellectual leaders Leon Keyserling and John Kenneth Galbraith over matters like the potential for economic growth to address poverty. The DAC provided a forum for discussion, and its policy decisions were ultimately made by majority vote.

Stepping back, we can see that in the span of a little more than a decade, there was a remarkable broadening of involvement in program building, demonstrated by the career of Leon Keyserling. Once the solo or near solo author of the 1936, 1940, and 1944 Democratic platforms, he was by the late 1950s still involved in developing the party's program, but in a much more cooperative capacity. He authored an introduction to a series of pamphlets on different issues relating to economic policy, was a member of certain committees for the series (e.g., Human Welfare and the Public Conscience, Housing and Urban Life), and part of the editorial staff for the whole project along with other high-profile minds of the time, like Galbraith and Arthur Schlesinger Jr.[41] But there were committees he was not on, even in the area of economic policy (e.g., farm policy, labor). Wider involvement, in turn, produced more thought and discussion about party policy than existed before. This alone is important.

While opposition from Republican President Dwight Eisenhower and conservative Democrats in Congress squelched many of the DAC's policy proposals, the council still contributed greatly to the party's legislative program. It received a lot of press coverage, including praise by renowned journalist Walter Lippmann, and its messages reached many people.[42] "Despite the lack of short-term success," argues political scientist Philip Klinkner, "the DAC did help to make many of these proposals a part of the Democratic agenda and to help ensure their passage during the New Frontier–Great Society Era."[43] There were some important shorter-term triumphs too. For example, the Democratic Advisory Committee on Agriculture's proposed policy on raising farm price supports was included in the party's 1956 platform.

Perhaps most notably, the DAC played a key role in the party's turn toward a more aggressive and liberal stance on civil rights. The council spoke out during the Little Rock school crisis in 1957, earning significant media attention for criticizing Eisenhower's response.[44] This was momentous, as DNC press secretary Samuel Brightman remarked: "At the time of the Little Rock school crisis, there was nobody in Congress who was getting any headlines or anybody saying that the Democratic Party was in favor of integration, which was going to be pretty important in the '58 election, until the Democratic Advisory Council put out a statement."[45] The DAC would make subsequent statements, continuing to contribute to the party's leftward movement on civil rights, which included a bolder civil rights stance in the 1960 platform.

In this light, it is not surprising that opposition from southern Democrats continued. A July 17, 1959, letter to Hon. Byron Skelton, Democratic National Committee delegate representing Texas, from C. W. McKay Jr., DNC delegate representing Alabama, makes clear that they both wanted to oust Butler. "He is tearing the Democratic Party to pieces," McKay argues. "But, the impetus should not come from the south because if someone from the south instigates it, it will seem like it's all about civil rights and they won't get as much support." In this, we can see how agents of racial oppression worked to constrain programmatic institutions like the DAC.[46] The council had gained some traction, however, which is evident even in McKay's seeming belief that getting rid of the DAC's leader would not be easy. Although there was an initial "boycott," in the words of the *Christian Science Monitor*, "by the Democratic capitol hierarchy and some southern leaders," the DAC later expanded and ended up getting "three of the four Democratic senators seriously considered as presidential possibilities—Kennedy, Humphrey, and Symington," with Johnson "alone outside."[47]

Southern Democrats were not Butler's only source of perpetual challenge. The chairman made no friends among machine leaders when he proclaimed, for example, that "party leaders are fast discovering, some the hard way, that political organizations based solely on patronage, personal favors, and the power and prestige of public office no longer enjoy the tremendous effectiveness they once possessed," and that the party needed to be "first and foremost an 'issue-oriented' organization."[48] Machine leaders joined southerners in attempting to unseat Butler as chair several times. When he finally announced that he would be stepping down as chair the day after the convention ended, he did so with a cheeky nod to his unpopularity in some quarters: "I will retire at that time and not a day later, and in spite of some helpful suggestions which have been made, not one day sooner. (Applause)."[49]

In addition to noting challenges, it is also important to consider what facilitated the DAC's work—specifically, the role of the DNC. Pulling off this operation with a meager national organization that went dormant between elections would have been difficult. Though the DAC operated with its own membership and administrative committee (Butler, Thomas Finletter, and former solicitor general Philip Perlman), it was financed by the DNC.[50] The DNC also had a group of staff assigned to assist the DAC and provided the council with supplies and services (e.g., issuing press releases). A national committee without a permanent headquarters or staff could not have provided this type of support.

Taking a step back in our examination of programmaticism over time, it's worth noting that even this significant increase in attention to issues under Butler was not in a spirit of cut-throat competition. In an early statement of purposes of the DAC, published in January 1957, the council wrote: "First and foremost we are interested in furthering positive, constructive measures. We shall not hesitate to agree with the Republican Administration when it is right. But we shall also be fearless and unsparing in our criticism when it is wrong."[51] In a general pamphlet (officially a "policy statement"), *The Democratic Task during the Next Two Years*, published shortly after the 1958 midterm elections, the DAC stated: "Under our Constitution, we will have a Republican Administration for two more years. The Congress must of necessity cooperate with this Administration. The effort must be to lead the Administration into doing the best of which it is capable."[52] There was a recognized difference between responsible and total opposition.

Paul Butler suffered a fatal heart attack in 1961, at age fifty-six. Butler had been instrumental in the DAC's successful inauguration, as Charles Murphy noted in a letter to Harry Truman in 1957. "I know we could not have gotten that started without Paul's support and cooperation, and I very much fear that we could not keep it operating in the future if he were replaced as Chairman. In fact, you will remember how hard we tried when you were in the White House to get something of this kind going and even then we never could get it done."[53] Butler was an important agent of programmaticism, building institutions and giving attention and traction to the concept of issue-based competition, as well as ideas for its implementation.

The DAC disbanded when the chairmanship transitioned to Connecticut machine–connected politician John Bailey. He jovially disparaged the DAC: "There was no necessity for it whatsoever and I think it was one of my most brilliant thoughts to do away with it! [Slight chuckle]." He argued that traditional party organizations, with which he was deeply rooted, played a role in Kennedy's successful campaign. But he also felt and observed disappointment after the election. "My people, my local leaders would come and say, 'Oh, God. What did we win this election for?' You see, the amount of federal patronage that goes into a state is not very much. It used to be."[54] Even during the tenure of a chair who proclaimed, "I, as chairman, set no policy," it was clear that the party was evolving.

Despite Bailey's disinterest in continuing the DAC and pursuing issue-based politics more broadly, work done in the 1950s would provide an important foundation for programmatic spirit and action. While the DAC may have disbanded, key members like Adlai Stevenson, Thomas Finletter, and W. Averell Harriman joined the Kennedy administration, bringing Butler's legacy into the 1960s. Midcentury work on issues also provided a key foundation for major reform efforts in the late 1960s and early 1970s.

After an uproarious 1968 Democratic National Convention, in which Hubert Humphrey received the nomination without a single primary victory, the embattled party enacted a set of structural and procedural changes known as the McGovern-Fraser reforms. These would end up affecting the whole party system, as the RNC made reforms following the Democrats' adoption of McGovern-Fraser, and many state legislatures controlled by Democrats would change election laws, affecting both parties. Although no specific selection method was mandated, delegates were no longer permitted to be independent agents; they had to be allocated to candidates based on voter support. This led to a proliferation of primary elections, which persist today, and changed the logic of campaigning such that candidates work to gain favor from different groups within the party.[55] This was an assertion of power of the national party over state and local parties, and it contributed to an ongoing centripetal shift in the locus of party power. These reforms also allowed issue-focused groups to participate in and exert power over the nomination process more than ever before.

While the McGovern-Fraser reforms are best known for the changes they made to nomination rules, they also affected party organization and facilitated a shift toward more issue-based competition. A Commission on Party Structure and Delegate Selection held a series of hearings throughout the country to take stock of and evaluate existing procedures. Support for programmaticism came from key figures, including McGovern and Edmund Muskie, who had been at the bottom of the Humphrey ticket and had presidential aspirations for 1972. Many noted that the electorate was more educated and motivated by issues than it had once been, and old clientelistic-style politics was not going to be a winning strategy for the party. In the words of Sam Beer, who played a key role in reform efforts, "There are votes in issues."[56]

There were echoes of the Butler years in the McGovern-Fraser Commission's efforts. Fraser "made suggestions in 1969 and 1970 to his own panel and to James O'Hara's Commission on Rules on reforming the DNC, establishing a Democratic Advisory Council-style research arm, and drafting a party constitution."[57] Some of the same people were also involved, like Neil Staebler, who had chaired Butler's Advisory Committee on Political Organization. Opposition to these efforts was also familiar. As the party worked to draft an official charter, many people wanted to move in a programmatic direction, while others—particularly southerners and machine-connected politicians—did not. The resulting charter reflected a compromise, but this was still a step toward programmaticism.

Developments in civil rights politics were also an important precursor to the McGovern-Fraser reforms. Influenced in part by the DAC, the party took a stronger civil rights stance in 1960 than it had in the past. At the convention in 1964, it became even clearer that civil rights could not be pushed to the side for the appearance of unity within the party. The Mississippi Freedom Democratic Party (MFDP) challenged the credentials of the state's regular delegation in 1964 and put forth its own. Though the MFDP did not get much from the party in the short term, being offered two at-large seats while the segregationist delegation was allowed to proceed as the official Mississippi delegation, they "left a lasting institutional legacy."[58] For the 1968 convention, the party announced that discrimination would not be allowed with respect to state delegations and set up a Special Equal Rights Committee within the DNC to evaluate and come up with ideas for how to manage the problem. This was not merely a symbolic gesture, as "the panel's ultimate report would provide a key mandate for the more sweeping reform commission created in 1968."[59]

The McGovern-Fraser reforms' reputation as pivotal in American party history is well-earned. These reforms and their aftermath, described by scholars like Sam Rosenfeld (2018) and Adam Hilton (2021) among others, altered how parties work in a manner that ultimately, if not simply, shifted the nation toward more issue-based competition. But they were not starting from scratch. If we want to understand when and why the party system shifted in this way—and why it did not happen earlier, when the nation's level of economic development would have predicted—it's critical to look before the riotous 1968 Democratic National Convention. A lot of work buttressed the party's ability to move forward at the pace it did at that time. Democractic reformers in the late 1960s and 1970s were standing on a large body of work on party positions and ways to develop them. Republicans had engaged in this kind of work as well.

The Republican Party

Electoral losses led to debates among party members about whether so-called me too style politics was hurting them and motivated many Republicans to advocate for a more programmatic style of party competition.[60] There was a widespread notion that Republicans had gone along with the Democrats' New Deal brand for too long and needed to build their own distinctive program.

A corps of Republicans stood ready to act on these concerns; Democrats were not the only ones infused with "amateur" spirit during this period. After World War II, there was "a great flourishing of organization-building and political activism by largely middle-class issue-driven conservatives" in the Republican Party, notes Sam Rosenfeld.[61] These new activists would help motivate and execute programmatic work.

Guy Gabrielson, chair of the RNC from 1949 to 1952, noticed these demands at the beginning of his tenure. "Throughout all of 1949," Gabrielson reported in a meeting of the RNC, "in both political and fund-raising activities, our workers were confronted with the question 'What does the Republican Party stand for?'" This was a well-founded inquiry, given Dewey's stinging defeat in 1948 to a much more issue-focused Truman, and one-off answers were not going to suffice. "No matter how sure you individually were as to what the Party stood for," Gabrielson remarked, "there was general insistence upon some statement of a composite and official character."[62]

Policy committees were created in the RNC and in both chambers of Congress to write a statement of "Republican Aims and Policies."[63] Each committee met to come up with an initial set of ideas, and then they joined to reach a "tripartite agreement."[64] In November 1949, before the RNC Policy Committee's first meeting in January 1950, Gabrielson sent a letter to Republican officials and workers asking whether they thought the party should create a list of principles before the 1950 campaign, and if so, what it should contain.

They solicited answers from "as wide a cross-section of Republican thinking as we could quickly reach" and got "thousands of letters" from individuals and groups in response.[65] Almost everyone (96%) said they should release such a statement, and they got many suggestions about what issues it should cover (e.g., foreign policy, labor, agriculture, Social Security, etc.) and how.[66] RNC staff read and aggregated this information—a task that would have been well beyond national party organizations' capabilities a few decades earlier.

Programmatic work continued and was further institutionalized under Chairman Meade Alcorn, who—with strong support from President Eisenhower and the RNC—established the Republican Committee on Program and Progress (RCPP, or Percy Committee) in March 1959.[67] The committee's chairman, industrialist Charles Percy, came to the position with an impressive résumé of private and public sector experience. He was to lead the charge to develop party positions on issues.

Alcorn planned the RCPP's first meeting for March 13–14, 1959, well before the 1960 election. Copies of the 1956 Republican platform were distributed at that time, and copies of the 1956 Democratic platform were distributed about a week later, "with the thought that it will help point up the differences between the two parties."[68] The Percy Committee's task was not just to consider what a Republican policy program should be in 1959, but also to "take a long and penetrating look at the future."[69] They settled on 1976 as the end of their period of focus, which would mark two centuries since the Declaration of Independence was signed. The committee was aiming to meet the imperatives of a rapidly changing world. As Percy wrote in a letter to RNC's new chairman Thruston Morton in October 1959, "We proceeded from the premise that we are entering an era which will open new universes to man—a new world with unique opportunities for human advancement, and tremendous challenges."[70]

The RCPP's membership was broader than that of its contemporaneous Democratic counterpart. Whereas Lyndon Johnson and Sam Rayburn reviled the DAC, Republican minority leaders of the House and Senate, Charles A. Halleck of Indiana and Everett Dirksen of Illinois, were members of the RCPP.[71] It also "included men and women of broad knowledge in such fields as education, labor, agriculture, business, religion, medicine, economics, law, government and politics."[72] The members were generally moderate which makes sense given that Eisenhower—once recruited by both parties—called for the committee, and it was less conflictual than similar efforts on the Democratic side.

They solicited advice from several people officially connected to the party (e.g., RNC members, contemporaneous and former officeholders at the national and subnational level, all Republican candidates from the 1958 election cycle, etc.) as well as from people outside the formal party organization (e.g., group leaders, academics, business leaders). RNC staff distributed a letter to more than eleven thousand people, asking for their views on specific questions relating to programmaticism—what principles they thought the party should and should not embrace, and what they saw as the biggest problems and opportunities for the party and nation over the following decade or so.[73] The committee received many letters in response from prominent figures (e.g., several university presidents, a member of the U.S. Senate Committee on Armed Services, the chairmen of the boards of General Electric and AT&T).[74] Between responses to this particular letter and communication from people who learned of their work and contacted them, the committee "received over 11,500 communications of ideas, suggestions and proposals," which members said they "carefully studied in order that the broadest possible range of American thought can be brought to bear upon the work of the Committee."[75]

To manage the volume and breadth of work before them, the Percy Committee created four task forces: National Security and Peace, Human Rights and Needs, the Impact of Science and Technology, and Economic Opportunity and Progress. The task forces themselves ranged in size from nine to fourteen people, and many more contributed to their research. They interviewed government officials and other policy experts, and RNC staff sent them "numerous books, articles and government documents which would be helpful to them in their work."[76] Each task force held a meeting in April 1959, and then a full committee meeting was held from April 30 through May 3 in Highland Park, Illinois, at which they held sessions on different issue areas (economic policy, labor policy, farm policy) involving formal remarks as well as discussions.[77] Task forces then held a series of two-day meetings in May and June, drafting 6,000–10,000 word reports, which they submitted to the full committee a few weeks before their third and final meeting in mid-July. This process highlights the amount of work, coordination, and resources involved in the development of party positions across multiple issues.

The final report, *Decisions for a Better America* (aka Percy Report), was initially released in October 1959 as a series of four pamphlets. Given their popularity, the whole product was also published by Doubleday as a paperback available in retail stores. This was "the first time that an American political party has produced a statement of principles and Party position on basic issues of public policy which has been deemed worthy of Trade Book publication and circulation to the mass reading public."[78] The report covered many issues, including foreign policy, unemployment compensation, education, atomic power, trade, health insurance, housing, and tax reform.[79]

Congressional Quarterly noted, in its coverage of the report, that it provided "ammunition" for upcoming elections.[80] Candidates used material from the report in speeches and town halls, among other things. It was "talked about as the foundation for the [1960] GOP Convention Platform."[81] President Eisenhower asked that heads of agencies receive and share it; Vice President Richard Nixon and members of Congress used it in speeches; Charles Percy fielded calls from cabinet members about it; and state organizations distributed it to people in mobilization efforts.[82]

The press also took note. Major news outlets like the *New York Times*, *Daily Boston Globe*, and *Washington Post* covered the report and the work leading up to its release. The mixed response was captured well by Roscoe Drummond of the *New York Herald Tribune*: "The Percy committee report is obviously not the final answer to the Republican party's need for a restatement of program and goals," he wrote, "but it is an eminently good beginning."[83] So too can the report's complex significance be seen in coverage by the politically and culturally iconic *Life* magazine. In a September issue, *Life* had implored the parties to "inform the American people where they stand upon major issues of the day, and those which are invalidated for the future." In October, after the Percy Report was published, the magazine noted, "Somewhere in these reports are the issues that a peaceful and prosperous nation like ours should be thinking about now and preparing to vote about next year."[84]

This is certainly faint praise, and consistent with academic judgment that the report "covered a laundry list of policy issues but did little to dispel Modern Republicanisms's reputation for vague philosophical straddling."[85] Nevertheless, the Percy Report was notable not just for the content of its pages but also—perhaps even more—for the process of its creation. It got the party to wrestle with the notion of competing with ideas and to experiment with ways of doing so. They gathered a considerable amount of information about what people thought a Republican program should look like, and how it might be used to benefit the party electorally. The process produced a number of statements and papers by different people about what it meant to be Republican, substantive differences between Republicans and Democrats, and so on.

They were working through these difficult ideas and tasks, individually and collectively.[86] The end product might not have been perfect or even great, but at this point in the parties' difficult transition between forms of competition, it reflected progress.

It's important to pause here for a moment and note that attempts to shift toward programmaticism under Alcorn and his contemporaneous Democratic counterpart, Paul Butler, were not unbridled. The two chairs had a good relationship, with many hearty debates, and they had agreed that issue competition should not extend to all matters. For example, they deemed foreign affairs out of bounds. "Paul and I had agreed that his people weren't going to get into this area, and our people wouldn't, except as this became a part of legitimate debate on the floor of the Senate and the House," recalled Alcorn in an oral history. "In other words, as his people stumped around the country and as he and I did, we weren't going to talk foreign policy. Agree. Everything went fine."[87] Fine, that is, until Senator George A. Smathers (D-FL) criticized Eisenhower-Dulles policies relating to offshore islands in a speech delivered in his home state, a "clear violation of the understanding Butler and I had," stated Alcorn. He was not happy but was inclined to let it go. John Foster Dulles, however, was irate, which led Alcorn to ask Vice President Nixon to issue a statement written by Dulles. Subsequent interviews with the press led to a misunderstanding that Dulles was criticizing the vice president, generating more news stories and infuriating Nixon. He, as history shows, would recover from this particular political setback. Nonetheless the whole sequence of events—the accord and the chaos that ensued when it was broken—shows that boundaries on party competition were valued. This stands in sharp contrast to the present day, when nothing appears to be off limits.

Programmatic work continued after the Eisenhower administration. In 1962, Senator Kenneth Keating (NY) called for an All Republican Congress (ARC). This was to include twelve senators who had recently released a statement of Republican principles, which Keating characterized as an unofficial midterm platform. ARC would build on and publicize this effort. Underscoring the obvious but easily overlooked point that transitioning toward programmaticism requires a great deal of work and institutional capacity, Keating proclaimed:

> It is my eager hope that such a body, adequately staffed, will provide a new forum and a ringing new voice to clarify, dramatize and publicize affirmative Republican positions and to challenge the opposition. A key word in

this projection, however, is 'staff.' Few people outside Washington realize the need for researchers, lawyers, investigators, writers and other technical aids to study, develop and publicize party positions. Official demands, endlessly devouring the days and nights of our lawmakers, place qualified assistance at a premium.[88]

This personnel included, in his vision, members of the ARC, as well as staff in Congress, the RNC, and large cities. This would give the party "the men and machinery to develop issues properly and take its case to the people." The effort would be worthwhile because "[to] attract the allegiance of thoughtful persons, it is important that we crystallize how we differ from Democrats." It appears that the ARC never materialized in accordance with Keating's vision. Nonetheless, this argument from someone who had served six terms in the House before joining the Senate is instructive.

The party would move in this direction. The RNC's Research Division engaged in policy research, with all staff members expected to be generalists as well as having a specific area of specialization. This research could serve "the positive purposes of assisting in the formulation of a Republican position on questions of public policy or of explaining and justifying the position taken by Republicans on such questions, or it may have the negative purpose of criticism of the position taken by the opposition."[89] The Research Division released 116 major reports on various topics between 1965 and 1968—over 100 more than the number produced during the previous three years.[90]

Another medium for programmatic growth was the Republican Coordinating Committee (RCC), established in 1965 to build a stronger, more moderate program after a landslide defeat of the party's prickly presidential aspirant, Barry Goldwater. Over the previous few years, Goldwater's supporters had gained significant control of the RNC, to the distress of more moderate Republicans. Led by RNC chairman Ray Bliss, the RCC was composed of many high-profile Republicans, including Dwight Eisenhower, several former presidential nominees, senators, House members, governors, and RNC vice chairmen, along with the president of the State Republican Legislative Association.[91] A pamphlet explaining the group and its purpose showcased involvement of high-profile party members, but this was not meant to be an insular effort. The RCC's mission was: "(1) to broaden the advisory base on national party policy; (2) to set up task forces to study and make recommendations for dealing with the problems that confront the people of our nation;

and (3) to stimulate communication among members of the party and others in developing a common approach to the nation's problems."[92]

To this end, the RCC held regular meetings—eight by the end of 1966—and created task forces on different issues, ranging from foreign relations to fiscal and monetary policy to senior citizens. This was quite novel for the RNC, which had been focusing primarily on purely organizational developments. They started by establishing five such task forces at their first meeting in March 1965, each of which would include a governor, national committeeman, national committeewoman, and state chairman, "to stimulate intra-party communication."[93] They expanded to six task forces in 1966 that, in addition to the work of their own members, "utilized the talents of some 115 Republicans from all levels of government, politics, business, labor, and the universities" and had thirty-five people in staff or consulting roles.[94] In December 1966, the RCC announced an additional two task forces.[95]

Their output was voluminous and well publicized. The task forces wrote reports on different topics (e.g. "Homeownership," "Clean Air," "Our Older Citizens," "The Restoration of Federalism in America"), which they submitted to the RCC.[96] The RCC released a number of position papers—eighteen plus two supplements by the end of 1966 alone—and many more brief public statements. The paper on cost of living had a circulation of approximately 350,000, though most circulations were lower (averaging around 15,000). The RCC's work also graced publications of the RNC and the Congressional Committee, which together reached approximately 250,000 people per month, captured airtime on the RNC's radio program Comment, which was distributed to 1,700 radio stations across all states, and "received considerable attention within their specialized fields" (e.g., the paper on "Housing and Urban Development" was reprinted in a trade magazine).[97]

The RNC played an important role in this step toward programmaticism in several ways. The RCC was funded and staffed by the RNC and led by the RNC's chair, Ray Bliss. The RNC's Research Division provided key support for the RCC's efforts in production and promotion of issue stances. In Bliss's 1966 chairman's report to RNC members, he explained: "Research personnel served as secretaries or staff directors to the six task forces and were involved in the research, writing, editing, and administrative problems of producing position papers adopted by the task forces and approved by the Coordinating Committee" and "actively promoted the distribution and use within the Party of these documents which played a major role in coordinating Republican campaign efforts."[98] The RCC also benefited from the RNC Publicity

Division's work to expand the party's radio program from 200 to 1,700 radio stations.[99]

Given its wider membership (i.e., including congressional leadership) and aim for unity, the RCC was not as hard hitting or provocative as the DAC.[100] Despite this, and the fact that the RCC only lasted until 1968, it contributed significantly to the formation of party policy. Holding twelve meetings between March 1965 and May 1968, it "provided an internal forum for discussion between party factions and thereby helped to unify a badly divided party."[101] It was, in the words of its chairman, "the first successful effort of either major political party to bring together all elements of the Party into a single, continuing body devoted to the formulation of positions on issues of public policy."[102] Given the source, this needs to be read with caution; but even if it is an exaggeration of success, that an RNC chairman would want to make this statement is notable in terms of the party's orientation toward programmaticism.

These efforts were made with electoral competition in mind, and the RCC's work was in fact used in the 1966 and 1968 cycles. In a chairman's report, Ray Bliss stated:

> Through [the RCC] the Party was able to take a stand on public problems with reasonable speed while at the same time insuring [sic] wide acceptance of these positions through the prestige of the Committee and its members. The 18 papers were widely used by candidates as background, as speech material, and as source matter to help develop their own personal positions on current issues. In addition, the publicity obtained by these papers helped form a public image of a Party concerned with public problems and willing and able to offer positive, alternative solutions to those problems.[103]

The platform committee would draw on the RCC's work in writing the party's 1968 platform.

Chairman Bill Brock resumed and intensified these kinds of activities during the Ford administration through Republican Advisory Councils (RACs). Ford, a "key architect" of the RCC, wanted a new iteration of that organization.[104] He was not alone—others in the party also thought it was time for the RNC to take a more active role in policy development. Klinkner reports, "According to Roger Semerad, an associate of Brock's who later became director of the RNC's policy councils, both he and Brock discussed the need for a 'serious and substantive vehicle' for policy discussion within the party. Such a policy group would bring various points of view into a 'common working environment' with the intention of providing the party with a coherent policy statement for the 1980 campaign."[105] They began by establishing advisory councils for five issue areas in 1977 with a total budget of $100,000, a small staff, and four hundred members.

As planned, these meetings had major consequences for party policy. Many members of the RACs also served on the 1980 platform committee, most notably Roger Semerad, who was director of the former and executive director of the latter. The council's contributions were not simply rhetorical—they also extended into the policymaking process. The concept of "supply-side economics," perhaps Ronald Reagan's most notable legacy, was introduced to a broad range of party members through the Advisory Council on Economic Affairs. The party endorsed a supply-side bill (the Kemp-Roth bill) in 1977, and the RNC worked to apprise current and aspiring Republican officeholders of the proposal and the underlying economic theory. This "helped explain how supply-side economics became, in Rowland Evans and Robert Novak's words, 'the GOP's first universally recognized economic theology since the protective tariff.'"[106]

Like the DAC, the RCC and RACs were products of stronger party infrastructure. It would have been very difficult for a noncontinuous party organization to support these kinds of long-term efforts at issue development. They needed money, staff, and other resources that the paltry national organizations of the early twentieth century could not have provided. The history of these councils also shows that major issue positions do not simply appear—they require work and compromise, which a strong national party organization can facilitate.

Brock's issue councils, like other similar efforts before this, contributed to a shift toward programmaticism even if they did not last long term. Think tanks and other new organizations ended up taking over a lot of the work involved in position development. "These avowedly ideological organizations lacked official partisan ties but, given the ideological sorting underway among the parties, their alliance with the GOP was clear," notes Rosenfeld (2018, 209–10). "This, rather than institutionalized research arms within the formal parties, became the model for partisan policy development." Still, whatever its role today, the RNC was instrumental in pivoting the party toward issue-based competition.

Platforms

In addition to tracing the development of processes and institutions for position development in the party broadly, it is also worth zooming in on platform creation, which has undergone significant changes over time. Empirically, we can observe that many people inside and outside the party (i.e., in associated groups) view the platform as a target. This underscores the point that the platform is not to be dismissed. It may not have the force of law, but it reflects and exudes power—people fight to have planks included or excluded, and presumably they go to such trouble because the platform's contents are of some consequence.

Platform length offers a simple view of programmaticism from a technical and analytical standpoint, but it is instructive nonetheless. It tells us something about the value parties place on explicating positions formally. Figure 4.1 shows that, as in the programmaticism trend shown in chapter 1, platform length does not climb steadily over time. Rather, it rises modestly and temporarily around the turn of the twentieth century, and later exhibits a sharp escalation. The change in platform length predates the change in differentiation, which makes sense; it's reasonable to expect a rise in distinction on issues to lag a rise in attention to platforms by a bit. There are also some outlying years, like 1988, when Democrats released a very short document, and 2020, when Republicans did not write one at all. Nevertheless, the takeaway is clear: there are significant changes in platform length around the mid-twentieth century.

The change in platforms is evident even in the physical documents. The Republican platform from 1860 was brief enough to be printed in poster form. By 1924, it had become a pamphlet that could accommodate more content. By midcentury, it took the form of a thicker, more serious-looking booklet. In 2016, it was a sixty-six-page single-spaced document with a professional, sharp front and back cover, reflecting the fact that the platform committee had a graphic designer on staff at this time. The form of presentation, alongside the length, signifies greater import over time. We would not rely solely on a measure of programmaticism based on what the platform documents look like; nonetheless, that both parties chose to present their platforms in a more complex and impressive package complements other measures of programmaticism.

The increasing distinction between Democratic and Republican platforms indicates that the added content was largely substantive, not just an increase

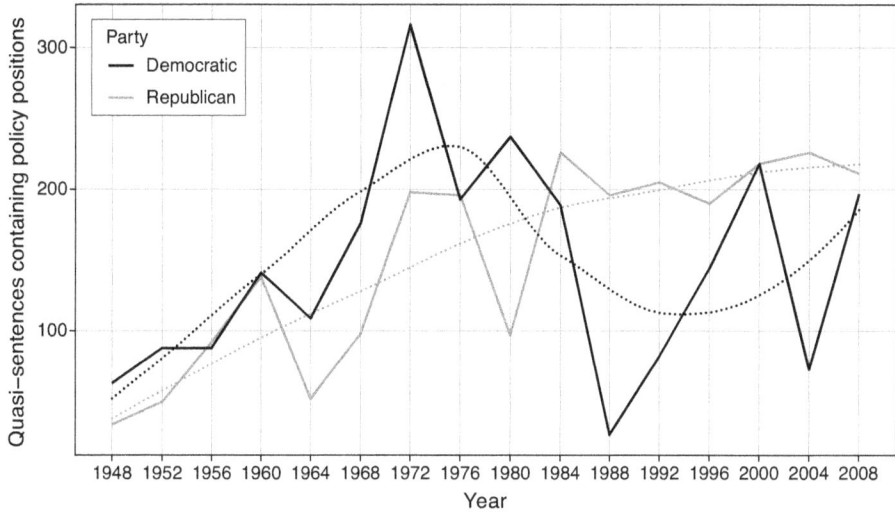

FIGURE 5.3. Policy positions per platform, 1948–2008.
This graph shows the number of policy positions contained in the Republican and Democratic Party platforms over time. The solid lines reflect the raw data and the dotted lines are loess curves. Platform data come from the Comparative Agendas Project, with original coding added for positions.

in vague patriotic language and the like. I buttress this inference by examining the number of policy positions in each platform at the quasi-sentence level.[107] Quasi-sentences were coded 1 if they explicated, or at least strongly alluded to, some kind of public policy action, 0 otherwise. This was a strict standard, excluding support for principles without reference to any type of action; language about priorities (i.e., saying something is important); vague calls for more or less spending on something; discussion of goals or needs without reference to any type of action; explanation for a policy position; criticism of a policy, proposal, or principle; criticism of the other party; and directives for the private sector or citizens. For example, it is not enough to state a vague goal or need (e.g., reducing the achievement gap between students of different racial groups). To count as a public policy position, a quasi-sentence would need to be more specific about what government should do or not do to achieve that goal. Platform data come from the Comparative Agendas Project, with original coding added for positions, and cover the period from 1948 to 2008.

Figure 5.3 displays the results. Solid lines reflect raw data, and dotted lines are loess curves. The smoothed trends (dotted lines) show a rise in policy positions in both parties' platforms over this period—they are much more numerous in 2008 than in 1948. The trend is steadier for Republicans than for Democrats, but this is mostly attributable to the outlying case of 1988, when Democrats released a very short platform. We can see this trend in the raw data as well, and these solid lines show a particularly large increase for both parties between 1964 and 1972. All of these results offer support for the racial oppression hypothesis, especially since concerns about racial issues becoming more prominent contributed to Democrats' decision to have such a short platform in 1988, as discussed in more detail below. There appears to be an "unlocking" of sorts after 1964. It is as if there were compressed gas in a container, which then exploded. When programmaticism rose, it shot up. This can help explain how, after a long period of lower programmaticism than would be expected based on economic development, it has risen to a worldwide high.

As we move from a bird's-eye view of the platforms themselves to an examination of the process by which they were created over time, complementary evidence for a shift toward programmaticism mounts. Scholar Paul T. David (1971, 311), speaking broadly about both parties, noted:

> The amount of preparation, staff work, and committee activity embodied in the national party platforms of the two major political parties has increased greatly since 1944 . . . The input of work at high political and professional levels that is reflected in the total quadrennial platform drafting effort has quite possibly increased by about an order of magnitude, that is, by 10 times. The increase has occurred progressively throughout the period since 1944.

We can gain further insight into programmaticism by examining each party's process in greater detail.

Republican Party Platforms

The Republican platform process evolved during the 1950s with assistance from the RNC. The number of issue subcommittees continued the expansion that had started earlier, reaching ten in 1956.[108] They also continued to hear voices from outside the RNC, "taking testimony from scores and scores of witnesses in the public hearings, and then in executive session undertaking the tremendous task of putting into appropriate language the thoughts which we wish to express."[109] In a novel development, they refrained from reading the platform into the record at the convention because it had already been "widely publicized in the press and on the radio and television and, indeed, the 1956 platform has received more publicity and is now better understood than any platform presented to any previous Convention."[110] The platform was then adopted by voice vote. The chair of the platform committee made a point in his 1956 convention speech to "express for the Resolutions Committee our appreciation to Dr. Floyd E. McCaffree, director of the Research Division of the Republican National Committee, and his able assistant, Miss Elizabeth Fielding. Without their help and the help of their capable staff, it would have been impossible for this committee to have done its job so effectively and efficiently."[111]

The process became even more complex in 1960, a year that, Paul David argued, "undoubtedly represented a new high for its time in the number of manhours of dedicated labor" committed to the platform on both sides of the aisle.[112] The chair noted in his speech that it was challenging to create "the first true political platform of the age of space."[113] The world had modernized, and the platform committee needed to evolve with it. This time, though they didn't start writing until the convention, work on the platform started much earlier with the Committee on Programs and Progress, whose efforts received high praise from the platform committee chair at the convention.[114]

Throughout the 1960s, the platform committees tended to convene "at the beginning of the preconvention week, first to hold public hearings and then to complete committee work on the final text of the platform."[115] They heard testimony from a wide range of groups, including the United States Chamber of Commerce, the Polish American Congress, Student Nonviolent Coordinating Committee (SNCC), and the AFL-CIO. "The goal of our platform Committee," the 1960 chair explained, "was to set down in one document some realistic answers to the needs and problems of the American people."[116] This was achieved, he argued, "after honest debate, great deliberation, exchanges of view, and this is the part of a campaign that's worth all of the effort that we put into it because a free society is only strong so long as its people understand the problems, the challenges and the opportunities that this Nation faces in the years ahead."[117] The platform committee also made a bigger show on the floor of the convention than they had in the past, showing videos of different leaders speaking to issues. They again dispensed with reading the platform into the record, as copies had been distributed to delegates along with the press. It was adopted by voice vote.

This approach extended into 1964. The party held four days' worth of hearings, which included testimony from approximately 150 people and organizations in addition to lawmakers and others in government.[118] In presenting the report from the platform committee to the floor, Congressman Mel Laird of Wisconsin (chairman of the Committee on Resolutions) argued: "Platforms are important. As a matter of fact, they last longer and are more important than any individual within our Party."[119] And, Laird was careful to specify, this was a platform for the party as a whole, not just for Congress or governors or any other individual person or institution. Creating the "program we wish to present to the voters of this Nation this November" was challenging and involved a great deal of conflict, he noted. In a break from past conventions, when delegates would often argue over amendments on the floor, Laird discouraged this kind of debate. "Nothing is likely to be changed by surveying once more the same alternatives which have been so carefully scrutinized in committee during the past week. Rather, the result would be to encourage our common foe—the Democratic Party—to seize upon our differences and divert us from the important task, the retirement of the present Administration in favor of a Republican President. (Cheers and Applause)."[120] A minority report was offered alongside the majority report, and several amendments proposed and considered. In the end, all amendments were rejected, and the platform was adopted by voice vote.

By 1968, the party made the process longer and more complex. The platform they presented was "the result of several months of diligent work culminating in a full week's revision by 102 Delegates from all over the country."[121] There were seven platform subcommittees, the chairmen of which made up the Temporary Platform Committee. The RNC held televised hearings in the week before the convention. Morning sessions were spent on remarks by high-profile Republicans, largely informed by the work of the Republican Coordinating Committee, and afternoon sessions were devoted to the work of the platform subcommittees. Various interest group representatives participated in these sessions. After four days of these hearings, the platform committee held an executive session lasting thirty-three hours, working until a few hours before the final document needed to be released. "Reportedly," says David (1971), "the sessions were devoted to active debate, many votes, and much revision of the previously prepared text."[122]

The convention was then a time for sharing, not debating the platform. Rather than reading the document into the record verbatim, several different people discussed its principles. While Governor George W. Romney of Michigan was allowed to present a proposal to the platform committee and engage in a discussion about it, the committee ended up deciding that the platform "should not be reopened for new language" at that point.[123] It's clear that the party had been trying hard over the past few conventions to avoid floor conflict, having discussions about issues before that point. By the time of the convention, they wanted to present a united front on the platform. And, indeed, the platform was adopted by voice vote without a formal amendment being offered by Romney. To do so would have been "unwise," he conceded, as "[a] floor battle over this amendment or any other could prove divisive and detract from the strength and the appeal of this Platform and of our Party."[124]

Attention to issue-based competition was even more evident in 1976. Before the convention began, delegates spent ten days working "to address thoroughly in unprecedented open sessions every major issue they perceived in this nation."[125] During this time, having broken into seven subcommittees, they drafted the 1976 platform, the full text of which was available for delegates to examine at the convention.[126] At the convention, Iowa governor Robert D. Ray, chairman of the Committee on Resolutions, offered a summary along with encouragement to read the whole platform and compare it to the Democratic Party's 1976 platform. "We want you to compare the two," Ray stated. "You will see basic differences in how the major political parties propose to represent you."[127] The proceedings were not quite as unified as leaders had hoped, but they did not spiral out of control. In response to a rise of some disorder, the chair reminded delegates of new strict rules for offering amendments. To be offered to the floor, an amendment needed prior support from a quarter of the platform committee. Two amendments met this standard. The first, regarding abortion, was given twelve minutes of debate split between each side, after which it was rejected by voice vote. There was twenty minutes of debate allowed on the second amendment, regarding foreign policy, which was then adopted by voice vote.

The process grew significantly more complex by 1980. Republicans held a set of regional hearings over a period of six months "in some ten cities throughout the United States and listened to Americans from all walks of life."[128] Delegates received printed copies of the platform, which various people presented to the floor in abridged form. It was then adopted by voice vote. A delegate from Hawaii asked to suspend the rules to talk about the platform, and a delegate from Massachusetts expressed similar sentiments. Because they did not meet the necessary requirements for offering a resolution, and such requirements were enforced, these small expressions of dissent unceremoniously fizzled.

The trend continued from there. In addressing the floor of the 1984 convention, Mississippi congressman and Committee on Resolutions chair Trent Lott noted—in sharp contrast to earlier years, when the platform was written over the course of the convention—that "this morning we have reached the culmination of a long process involving hundreds of people, thousands of hours and millions of words over the course of a year."[129] As in 1980, the platform-writing process was not insular as it had been earlier in history; in addition to members of the platform committee and other delegates, they "heard from Americans from all over the country on every issue that was covered in this platform."

This process was not easy, to say the least—according to Lott, it involved "discussion, debate, analysis, argument, and research and reflection."[130] There were seven subcommittees, each with a chair and a co-chair, and representatives from each presented parts of the platform. Signaling a move toward programmaticism, Lott stated, "I hope they will convince you, as we are convinced, that this is the most comprehensive and thorough presentation of our Party's position ever, but it is something more here than a collection of views and positions and ideas. Fundamentally it's about the character of our Party, of what it stands for in public policy."[131] This does not mean that the party was unanimous on everything. Indeed, even in the voice vote on the platform, a "chorus of ayes" and a "chorus of noes" could be heard. The chair deemed that the ayes won, and the platform was adopted.

Over time, though certain features stayed the same (e.g., two delegates from each state/territory were on the platform committee, and they continued to have subcommittees), the platform process changed in a few notable ways. The platform committee expanded in terms of leadership and staff, and its operations became professionalized. The party also opened the process more through public sessions. In 1992, it held hearings in four cities before the convention. Some people testified in person, while others contributed in writing. Staff then prepared a draft in advance of the Republican Committee on Resolutions meeting, which was held the week before the convention. At this time, the Committee on Resolutions had a chair and co-chairs, who had their own staff of five, a four-person editorial staff, and twenty-one additional staff members spread across six issue subcommittees. The subcommittees considered the draft first, spending two days discussing and editing their respective sections before passing them on to the full subcommittee, whose section-by-section debate of the platform was televised on C-SPAN.

A little over a decade later, in 2004, the committee had an executive director, communications director, administrative director, parliamentarian, general counsel, special counselor, graphic designer, three platform assistants, an editorial staff, a designated staff member for each of the three chairs, and a clerk for each subcommittee. Many volunteers were also involved in the process. Reflecting continued development over time, the staff in 2016 was even larger and more specialized. A "platform staff" was composed of an executive director, policy director, editor, assistant editor, executive assistant, parliamentarian, counsel, graphic designer, production manager, platform consultant, director of strategic partnerships, three clerks, and an intern. The Committee on Resolutions also had an administrative team of six, two court reporters, and a policy staff of two to three people per subcommittee. This was all in addition to the two to three chairs for every subcommittee (of which there were six); the top leadership of one senator, one governor, and one House representative; and a long list of people who received special thanks for their (presumably unpaid) roles in the process.

Then came 2020, the first time in the history of Democratic-Republican competition that either party did not release a platform. Republicans in 2020 did not even engage in the kind of hurried platform meetings at the convention that were typical in the nineteenth century. It is hard to say for sure why this occurred; candor on political issues often takes time. Indeed, oral histories are typically conducted years after a person has left their position and often cannot be cited during the interviewee's lifetime. Nevertheless, we can consider statements, reporting, and intuition that are available at present. Formally, the RNC released a one-page resolution stating that they "unanimously voted to forego the Convention Committee on Platform, in appreciation of the fact that it did not want a small contingent of delegates formulating a new platform without the breadth of perspectives within the ever-growing Republican movement."[132] They also cited limitations on gatherings and concerns about safety, without explicit reference to the COVID-19 pandemic. If the platform committee had met, the resolution stated, they would have "undoubtedly unanimously agreed to reassert the Party's strong support for President Donald Trump and his Administration," and the party more broadly "will continue to enthusiastically support the President's America-first agenda." This was interpreted by many as a sign of the party's submission to an individual in a manner seen in autocratic states or, in the words of former

National Review editor Bill Kristol, a cult.[133] As a *Slate* headline quipped, "Republicans Announce Their 2020 Platform Consists of Supporting What-ever Trump Wants."[134] Some also argued that the party had arrived at a policy program that, while garnering key support from certain groups, was unpalatable to many and better left off a formal page. This argument was made critically in some outlets, like the *Atlantic*.[135] But even more sympathetic outlets noted that by rereleasing their 2016 platform instead of writing a new one, the party could avoid difficult subjects that had come to the fore of politics. *Fox News* pointed out, for example, that "the 4-year-old document . . . doesn't have any language on new combustible issues like racial justice and police reform or statements in opposition to defunding police departments."[136]

In the end, though it is premature to draw definitive conclusions about the cause of the Republican Party's most unusual decision to skip the platform-writing process in 2020, it is worth noting that this occurred in an election cycle with an incumbent president who made many racially disparaging remarks—sidestepping dog-whistle politics common in the modern era in favor of explicit expressions of racial bias—and during a surge of public attention to racial justice, as the Black Lives Matter movement gained both prominence and support. It stands to reason that many within the party would have found it challenging and risky to comment or not comment on these issues in an encyclopedic statement of party policy.

Democratic Party Platforms

The Democratic platform process also continued to develop after the century's midpoint, with help from the DNC and associated institutions like the Democratic Advisory Committee, as well as outside groups. In 1952, for example, the drafting committee included representatives of the AFL, CIO, and farmers.[137] Several representatives of groups made their case in hearings before the platform drafting committee for particular planks to be added to the platform. Members of the committee could ask them questions, and there was plenty of back and forth and discussion. Interestingly, people testifying were sometimes asked if they also testified before Republicans.[138] Members of Congress also testified on behalf of groups (e.g., Congressman Thomas Gordon of Illinois testified on behalf of all seven Polish members of Congress).[139] This would continue. Platform hearings in 1964, for example, included testimony from representatives of many organizations (e.g., American Textile Manufacturers Institute, International Brotherhood of

Teamsters, National Association of Wheat Growers, the National Right to Work Committee, American Association of Retired Persons [AARP], the National Association for the Advancement of Colored People [NAACP], Planned Parenthood, and the United Presbyterian Church, to name just a few).[140]

In spite of this work, the party continued to struggle with challenges surrounding civil rights. At the 1952 hearings, testimony included the observation: "The depth of regional fear against Civil Rights legislation has become the hallmark of party conventions in recent years. In a measure, this has placed this issue at the top of the platform-drafting problems."[141] It was a problem without an easy solution. On the one hand, southern Democrats were so adamant in opposition to civil rights that the adoption of a pro–civil rights plank led to an exodus at the 1948 convention. On the other, pressure for civil rights legislation was growing. As Rep. Adam C. Powell of New York testified in 1952, "without a strong, unequivocal, forthright stand on this vital matter, we cannot hope to win in November; and therefore we will never have the opportunity to effect our other promises."[142] He proceeded to emphasize that oppression of African Americans' civil rights undermined the nation's strength on the world stage, causing other nations to question the United States and inhibiting effective foreign policy. Paul Butler echoed this sentiment in a speech at the 1960 convention, noting that the world was watching how the United States dealt with civil rights.[143]

The year 1968 was turbulent for the party. More than three hundred witnesses applied to testify in the platform hearings, testimony was covered by the press, and there was significant conflict on issues. Even with a week's worth of hearings before the convention, committee members had difficulty finishing their work by the time of the convention.[144] The platform committee as a whole held a set of hearings on the Vietnam War, and there were also subcommittee hearings on various subjects. They had particular difficulty managing intraparty disagreements on Vietnam, and the committee's proposed position was adopted by a divided vote. Once it reached the floor of the convention, the heat on this issue continued. They had a two-hour debate about Vietnam and eventually rejected an amendment on this subject. The platform was adopted by voice vote, but the process wore on many involved.

The relative chaos and attention to a wide range of issues continued in 1972, with the McGovern-Fraser reforms in place. The Platform Committee had increased in size (to 150), and regional hearings had been held in twelve cities across the country to try to make the process more open after the tumult of 1968.[145] Many groups participated. But further steps would be needed to reduce conflict at the convention. After different parts of the platform were presented by different delegates, many people introduced amendments and minority reports on various issues, including prayer in public school, racial equity in education, gun control, Vietnam, busing, welfare, judicial reforms, and equal rights for people of all sexual orientations. This took a significant amount (approximately 20 percent) of the convention's time and was not an efficient way of managing intraparty differences.

For the next cycle, Democrats had full-time staff working on the platform for six months. Presidential campaign staff, as well as mayors, governors, and members of Congress were also involved. They reached out to many groups and asked them to testify or write statements. There were hundreds of hours of hearings nationwide involving more than five hundred people, with additional testimony collected through written statements. As Platform Committee member Marian Humes of Illinois remarked to the convention floor, they worked very hard to reconcile differences and reach compromises before the convention, which involved many voices. "The Platform Committee must have heard at least six different solutions, or even more, for every problem, and we probably listened to solutions for problems that haven't been discovered yet," Humes said. "But after we identified our differences, we sat down over long days and long nights. We looked for common ground and for the strengths in each other's points of view. In this process, a great many people put their pride of authorship behind them, and we found we could agree."[146] Following all of this, a platform drafting committee worked to write a document. In this light, Humes asked the delegates to reject a proposal that would allow discussion of a platform plank if at least three hundred delegates from at least ten states signed it. Perhaps remembering the previous conventions, delegates voted to reject the proposal. The platform was later presented to the floor through remarks by different people who spoke about different issue areas (e.g., Coretta Scott King talked about civil and political rights, Richard Daley talked about urban issues, etc.). The platform was then adopted without the kind of breathless presentation and discussion of amendments and minority platforms seen in previous conventions.

Similar sentiments were expressed in 1984. The party was trying to identify and diffuse as many conflicts as possible before the convention. After

explaining the work and reconciliation of differing views done before the convention, Platform Committee chair and Birmingham mayor Richard Arrington noted that there would be no floor amendments and encouraged anyone
who wanted to improve on the platform to get involved in the process of policy development with their state party and the DNC. This does not mean that
everything was resolved preconvention. The committee chose five parts of the
platform to open somewhat to floor input through the presentation of minority reports that the floor could consider. "We would be untrue to our name,
not to mention our reputation, if we did not engage in sharp debate where
our differences are strong," said Arrington. "But given the extraordinary range
of our agreements, the fact that we perceived fewer than a half dozen areas of
difference is not a sign of Democratic Party weakness."[147]

The contrast between how platforms were once treated at conventions and
how they were treated by this point is stark and deserving of serious consideration. The platform was no longer simply read into the record by the platform
committee chair. Rather, it became customary for different people to offer
remarks on different parts. At times, these opening remarks summarizing the
section of the platform (e.g., about housing, foreign policy, etc.) were followed
by planned speeches presenting minority reports or amendments, and votes
thereon. These speeches reflect increased interest and stake in the platform by
a wider variety of people, as well as a more organized, planned process.

The Democratic Party made a conscious decision to "devalue its platform"
for the 1988 election cycle.[148] Chairman Paul Kirk stated that the platform
should be "brief and readable . . . reflect[ing] timeless truths and unifying
principles," and other party leaders concurred.[149] This was a significant break
from the longer, more detailed platforms of recent election cycles, and less
than 10 percent of the length of the 1984 platform in particular. In taking
this approach, Kirk "was responding to the argument that one reason for its
electoral defeats was that the Democratic Party had become the party of 'special interests,' while the Republican Party merely represented the interests of
'Americans' without such special interest distinctions."[150]

This choice—like Republicans' unusual decision to not release a 2020
platform—is instructive, with ties to racial politics. To some extent, Democrats' concern about being a "special interest" party may have been attributable to holding more open platform hearings in recent election cycles
than Republicans, and offering greater access to the nomination process and
(limited) empowerment of underrepresented groups through the McGovern-
Fraser reforms.[151] But it also seems like more than a coincidence that this

rather dramatic action occurred in same year that Jesse Jackson mounted a formidable primary campaign, earning 29 percent of the vote (second only to Michael Dukakis, who won with a 42 percent plurality), improving on an already historic 18 percent in the 1984 Democratic primary. During the platform hearings, which included people from both campaigns, there were disagreements about whether the platform should be more general, as preferred by the Dukakis camp, or include more specifics, as preferred by the Jackson camp.[152] Dukakis, and others concerned about putting forth a Black nominee, largely got their way.

After Dukakis lost in a landslide to George H. W. Bush, the party returned to a more extensive platform in 1992, drafted by a diverse group that was slightly less than half women and half racial minorities, and whose members included national party elites (e.g., members of Congress, DNC officers), subnational leaders (e.g., mayors), and some activists (e.g., supporting labor, Israel, gay rights, etc.). After public hearings, staff wrote up a report that the platform drafting committee could use in its work. People associated with the Democratic Leadership Council, members of think tanks, and other policy analysts and activists also contributed to the platform and were acknowledged in platform committee documents.[153] DNC staff managed the logistics of these meetings, a task that would have been well beyond their capacity a few decades earlier. Indeed, this process was a far cry from 1936–1944 when Leon Keyserling essentially solo-authored the Democratic platforms. The full platform committee met for only one day, relying heavily on the work done before this point. And the 1992 convention was not a site of significant conflict resolution, as past conventions had been. "For the most part," observed scholar L. Sandy Maisel, "the presentation of the platform to the national convention was an opportunity to showcase party leaders and to discuss the candidate's views."[154]

This will likely sound familiar to observers of contemporary American party conventions. The party has continued to expand its platform staff, hold platform hearings, and put forth increasingly comprehensive platforms.[155] Having work on the platform, along with other party business, generally done beforehand allows the convention to be more of an event than a meeting for the party. And as the process for writing platforms has become more complex, and more people inside and outside government have participated, it "promotes intraparty communication between the party organization and its elite members" and gives more people a stake in the resulting platform.[156]

Conclusion

This chapter supports the theory of programmaticism presented in chapter 2. Lending credence to the national party strength hypothesis, I show that national parties grew in ways that contributed to parties' ability to develop issue positions, which are critical to programmaticism. They help with the arduous, conflictual work of position development, and play a useful organizational role in this process. While national party committees may not be neutral in conflicts between different parts of the party (e.g., its presidential and congressional wings, for example), they are the institutions best positioned to think ecumenically. They are more likely to work to resolve intraparty conflict than add new positions to the table.

The argument is not that national party organizations were the sole drivers of programmatic growth. Indeed, no one institution or force could single handedly account for such a complex phenomenon. But, they provide an important foundation and coordinating function. Illustrating this point, a group of congressional Democrats in the 85th Congress (1957–58) tried to develop and mobilize around a legislative program against the "conservative coalition" of Republicans and southern Democrats. Led by Eugene McCarthy (MN), Lee Metcalf (MT), and Frank Thompson Jr. (NJ), and backed by approximately eighty other members, they used the 1956 platform as a starting point for their work. "Except on a few key issues," however, "these efforts were crippled by lack of organization, lack of staff and by legislative machinery inadequate to sustain a coordinated operation," according to a pamphlet introducing the Democratic Study Group (DSG), which formed in 1959 to try to manage some of these problems. The DSG would then coordinate with the DNC and DAC—both under Paul Butler's leadership—in the 1960 election season.[157]

We can also see in this history of programmaticism that both machine-connected politicians and agents and institutions of racial oppression militated against programmaticism. On the Democratic side, evidence arises in these groups' opposition to building institutions (e.g., the DAC) that facilitated programmaticism and to people (e.g., Paul Butler) spearheading such efforts. Outlying years for platforms are also instructive. On the Democratic side, the notion that racial oppression inhibits programmaticism is evident in the anxiety surrounding Jesse Jackson's formidable bid for the Democratic nomination in 1988, the highly visible tension between Jackson's preference for a specific platform and Dukakis's preference for a vaguer platform, and especially in the party's dramatic choice to not only heed Dukakis's preference but also cut their platform by over 90 percent from the previous year, bucking a long-time positive trend in platform comprehensiveness. On the Republican side, it seems like more than coincidence that their decision to rerelease their 2016 platform rather than writing a new one in 2020—a first in the history of competition between these two parties—came at a time when their incumbent nominee was making explicitly racist remarks and a movement for equal rights for Black people in the United States was gaining significant strength and traction.

This history offers insight into not only what parties do, but also what they are. As discussed in chapter 1, there have been debates over the extent to which parties should be considered groups of politicians (as in the traditional view) or groups of groups (as in the UCLA school, or group-centered theory of parties). I find that groups helped with position development and became more entwined with parties in this process. As parties became more programmatic, group-party relationships became more exclusive. Whereas midcentury scholars like Schattschneider, Truman, and Greenstone noted that groups tended not to ally with parties and vice versa, Fine (1994a) finds that less than half (45%) of interest groups testified at both the Democratic and the Republican platform hearings (27% testified only at Republican hearings, and 39% testified only at Democratic hearings). Analyzing the 1992 process, Maisel (1993–1994) notes that very few groups got what they wanted from both party conventions. Parties today are more group centered than they once were. We need not spend excess time debating the merits of the traditional view of parties or the new group-centered theory of parties. Ultimately, they are both useful, but they do not always apply equally in all historical moments. By analyzing how Democrats and Republicans have competed with each other over time, we can see that the very nature of parties is dynamic.

6

Party Competition and American Democracy

When there is a crack at the national level between political parties, between religious groups, or between other groups, that's when the virus gets a crack that it can exploit and defeat us. So number one is the national unity; working across party lines. . . . The focus of all political parties should be to save their people.

—DR. TEDROS ADHANOM GHEBREYESUS, DIRECTOR-GENERAL OF
THE WORLD HEALTH ORGANIZATION, APRIL 8, 2020, PRESS
CONFERENCE ON COVID-19

THIS BOOK is about a theoretically pro-democratic development—the rise of party competition over public policy—in the United States, which has the highest level of such competition in the world. And yet, as I was writing the first few chapters, the nation was reeling from the COVID-19 pandemic, having fared worse than many other industrialized nations. Despite pleas by World Health Organization director Tedros Adhanom Ghebreyesus and many others, party divisions emerged in the United States regarding the extent to which the virus posed a serious threat, not to mention strategies for curbing its spread across the nation and the globe. Such disagreement inhibited the government's response to this public health crisis, with deadly consequences, contributing to already brewing concerns about democratic backsliding in the United States.

We face now a new set of questions: What are we to make of this style of divergent democracy philosophically and practically? How should we think about programmaticism as a means of democratic competition? What can this study of programmaticism since 1856 teach us about where we might go from here? We can start by addressing ways in which this analysis helps dispel the myth of moderation that pervades retrospective views of U.S politics.

The Myth of Moderation

In contemporary political discourse, there is often a sense of nostalgia for a time when the nation's parties were less polarized. The implication tends to be that parties had been moderate and lost control of that preferred state. Polarization scholars have challenged this notion. The U-shaped curve in polarization over time—high in the late nineteenth and early twentieth centuries, lower in the mid-twentieth century, then rising to a historic high today—suggests that polarization has been the norm in U.S. history, and the exception has required virulent intraparty conflict over civil rights.[1] That is not exactly a state to which we should want to return in a liberal democracy. In fact, there's a strong case to be made that the so-called world's oldest democracy has only really been a liberal democracy since it meaningfully enfranchised its Black citizens in the 1960s.

Of course, I have argued that polarization and programmaticism, while related, are not the same. The fact that programmaticism does not follow the same U-shaped curve as polarization underscores this point and the importance of measuring programmaticism, not relying on polarization as a proxy, conceptually or empirically. The measure presented in chapter 1 is an important contribution to American politics literature, and the methodology used to generate it can be applied to other nations to help address the lack of historical data on programmaticism worldwide.[2]

Looking specifically at programmaticism further undermines the narrative of a once-moderate nation gone haywire. The history of party competition presented in this book is not about thoughtfully centrist positions among Democrats and Republicans transitioning to polarized extremes. When programmaticism was low, it wasn't because the parties had carefully considered the issues of the day and happened to agree on appropriate party positions; rather, attention to developing policy positions and attention to issues as a means of party competition were low. As we contemplate where we've been, where we are, and where we want to go, we should avoid a "be careful what you wish for" narrative (in response to the 1950 APSA report) or a plea to return to moderate days. The right retrospective comparison is not "moderate" versus "extreme" but the politics of high programmaticism versus the politics of machines and Jim Crow.

Programmaticism as a Macropolitical Indicator

Programmaticism is generally considered a sign of progress for a party system, and there are good reasons for this, particularly given the inverse relationship with clientelism shown in prior comparative work, as well as this book's study of the United States over time. This is not simply a correlation—I find that the machinery of clientelism impeded reformers. Even New Dealers, who transformed the American state, had to contend with machines and cooperate with them in many cases. Clientelism is thought to suppress economic development, which has broad implications for a nation. From a political standpoint, clientelism breeds and nurtures political monopolies, which by their very nature face electoral acccountability that is suboptimal at best and at worst nonexistent.[3] Under more programmatic systems, politicians have greater motivations to provide public goods.[4] For these reasons and others, efforts to understand how to reduce clientelism and increase programmaticism, particularly in developing nations, have been mounting.

Yet, the virtues of programmaticism—in general and in relation to clientelism—are neither simple nor absolute. Clientelism can allow politicians to build diverse coalitions that might not otherwise be possible without material incentives, as well as subdue intergroup conflict.[5] Guaranteed material benefits may also be more appealing, especially for poor voters, than abstract and potentially unreliable policy promises.[6] Moreover, benefits from programmaticm might be non-linear or contingent on other features of the political system. The United States is instructive on this front. There is a sense today among many academics and other political observers that Democrats and Republicans have taken issue-based competition too far. Indeed, the extension of political conflict to facts backed by scientific research, the intrusion of conspiracy theories into mainstream political conflict over issues, and the retraction of rights (e.g., voting without undue burdens, abortion access) indicate that issue-based competition is not always good. Democracy can become too divergent.

I argue that we should treat programmaticism as a macropolitical indicator to monitor the health of democratic systems. Like macroeconomic indicators, it probably has an ideal range, to be defined by vigorous discussion among scholars. Deviation may be more common and concerning in one particular direction, but movement outside the range in either direction is probably cause for concern. Just as it is possible for inflation and unemployment to dip too low, harming an economy, so may programmaticism reach heights that are detrimental to democracy. Better understanding this complexity is one of the most important challenges of our time, not only in the United States but also worldwide.

Toward Defining an Upper Bound for Programmatic Partisanship

To start a conversation about an appropriate upper bound, I propose a standard that is grounded in work by Richard Hofstadter. His classic book *The Idea of a Party System* identifies *legitimate opposition* as a concept that the founders could not grasp while trying to construct and learn to live by their own set of constitutional rules and norms after the American Revolution. They did not want parties to play a role in the new republic, forming them grudgingly and instrumentally as a means to lead the nation toward a partyless state— the loathed institutions were to help them persuade or else stamp out their opposition. It took quite some time for them to understand, let alone accept, the notion that different groups could disagree on pro-democratic grounds. Today, we must think carefully about this notion once again. Legitimate opposition is essential to democracy, and parties are its central vehicles. So, what does *legitimate opposition* mean today?

Hofstadter's notion of *constitutional, responsible, effective opposition* provides a strong foundation. The first two parts are especially relevant. By *constitutional,* he means that "both government and opposition are bound by the rules of some kind of constitutional consensus."[7] Oppositional forces are to challenge policy, not the constitutional order itself, and they must do so through public appeals, not threats, violence, or treasonous actions. The ruling party must allow this to occur—it cannot try to shut down a rival party's expression of dissent. If we think about this in the context of programmaticism—a concept well beyond eighteenth- and early nineteenth-century politicians' minds, even as they came to accept the notion of legitimate opposition— constitutional opposition would mean that Democrats and Republicans offer alternative courses of action on policies and express those views in a lawful manner that does not attack, physically or verbally, the nation's system of governance.

Responsible opposition "contains within itself the potential of an actual alternative government—that is, its critique of existing policies is not simply a wild attempt to outbid the existing regime in promises, but a sober attempt to formulate alternative policies which it believes to be capable of execution within the existing historical and economic framework, and to offer as its executors a competent alternative personnel that can actually govern."[8] Unrealistic policy positions would not be considered responsible. We might also think about pronouncements based on inaccurate or insufficient factual information through this lens. A sober attempt to devise good policy starts with the best available evidence.

To be considered an *effective* oppositional force, a party needs to have enough strength and support to be able to win office and "bring to power an alternative personnel." A small radical group would not qualify as effective opposition (and would likely not meet the standards for constitutional or responsible opposition either). Given that third parties, while usually unsuccessful in winning elections, have achieved notable success in influencing major parties' platforms, this part of Hofstadter's conceptualization of legitimate opposition is less helpful for thinking about programmaticism.

The notion of constitutional, responsible, effective opposition provides a useful starting point, as it helps concretize some tenets of pro-democratic opposition that might otherwise be difficult to articulate. But it is a bit too restrictive in its notion of effectiveness. Moreover, it does not provide much guidance regarding the substance of positions beyond their ability to be executed within the existing constitutional order. Plenty of policies throughout American history have been possible to put into action but should be outside the bounds of a liberal democracy, like Jim Crow laws restricting the rights of Black Americans. In this sense, Hofstadter's standard does not offer enough guidance for present purposes.

To identify boundary conditions on "constitutional, responsible" opposition, we can layer into our thinking Robert Dahl's requirements for democracy in a large nation. Dahl grounds his work in the premise that "a key characteristic of a democracy is the continuing responsiveness of the government to the preference of its citizens, considered as political equals." For this to be possible, he argues, citizens must have "unimpaired opportunities" for the following: (1) "To formulate their preferences"; (2) "To signify their preferences to their fellow citizens and the government by individual and collective action"; and (3) "To have their preferences weighed equally in the conduct of the government, that is, weighted with no discrimination because of the content or source of the preference."[9]

These conditions, in turn, require certain minimal protections and opportunities. He identifies eight, all of which are necessary for the weighing of preferences, and some of which are necessary for preference formulation and expression. To develop meaningful preferences, people need the "freedom to form and join associations," the "freedom of expression," the "right to vote," access to "alternative sources of information," and to operate in a system that protects the "right of political leaders to compete for support." Expressing preferences requires all of these conditions plus "eligibility for public office" and "free and fair elections." To have citizens' preferences weighted equally, the nation must also have "institutions for making government policies depend on votes and other expressions of preference."[10]

To better account for the complexities of politics, I propose adding a fourth condition to Dahl's list: in a democracy, people must have their *interests* protected and weighted equally in the conduct of government, even in the absence of expressed preferences. Party elites have privileged access to technical and sensitive information, as well as more time to digest it given that politics is their profession, and they must act responsibly in this context. At minimum, they should resist the urge to exploit information asymmetry. To the extent possible, they should work to educate their constituents about issues to facilitate the formulation of informed public preferences. When this is not practicable, they should act in ways that reflect equitable protection of people's interests and refrain from vacuous and misleading partisan posturing.

Putting the revised standards of Hofstadter and Dahl together, an issue can contribute to constitutional, responsible opposition only if distinction thereon would not violate key democratic underpinnings. Some problems may not have two significantly different approaches that still allow government to weigh equally the preferences of citizens, freely formulated and expressed. Sometimes, it may not even be possible for members of the electorate to develop meaningful, informed preferences. In these cases, party competition is not appropriate and may in fact damage democracy.

Finally, we can borrow insight from top scholars of democratic backsliding, Steven Levitsky and Daniel Ziblatt, whose timely book *How Democracies Die* has gained attention in academia and beyond. Levitsky and Ziblatt note that the days of democratic collapse under flames of coups d'état or other dramatic usurpations of power have largely passed. Today, democracies tend to erode slowly at the hands of elected leaders through technically legal means. Democracies need not only rules but also norms to survive. In the United States, they argue, two norms have been particularly important for the stability of its checks and balances system: mutual toleration and forbearance. By mutual toleration, they mean "the understanding that competing parties accept one another as legitimate rivals."[11] In this, we may hear echoes of Hofstadter's concept of constitutional opposition. The second norm is particularly important for present purposes. Forbearance, they state, is "the idea that politicians should exercise restraint in deploying their institutional prerogatives."[12]

Together, concepts offered by Hofstadter, Dahl, and Levitsky and Ziblatt can move us closer to specifying a healthy range for programmaticism. In competing over issues, parties need to stay within the realm of legitimate opposition. I have taken this concept from Hofstadter and updated it for challenges we face today. We can think here at three levels: positions, issues, and programs. Certain issues, like the right to vote freely without pressure or undue restriction, are out of bounds because no alternative position befits democracy. In some cases, the issue area itself might be within bounds, but certain positions are not. The parties can disagree about tax laws for nongovernmental organizations, for example, but cannot take positions that would make it impossible for such organizations to exist. It is also important to consider the parties' entire programs, the set of issues on which they compete with each other at any given time. These programs must indicate forbearance, addressing a collection of issues reflecting thoughtfulness about what is included as well as what is not. Parties may compete on any issue on which there is room for legitimate disagreement; but if they compete over every issue that meets this standard, the system will be embroiled in conflict, undermining leaders' ability to manage important problems of the day and eroding confidence among voters.

The analytical history presented in previous chapters can help us wrestle with these ideas. We can learn from situations the United States passed through on the road from low to high programmaticism, and adapt ideas that arose along the way. On the former front, the brouhaha set off by George Smathers's speech criticizing Eisenhower-Dulles policies regarding offshore islands is more than an amusing historical anecdote; the agreement between parties that foreign policy would be off-limits in competition is an example of forbearance. They were not going to compete on every issue and in fact could agree on an area in which they would abstain. "No-fire zones" like this are essential for progress in some areas. There is a rigidity to voter-facing policy positions that can make problem solving, which generally requires politicians to be nimble and willing to compromise, difficult. If we want to rein in programmaticism, helping parties find these no-fire zones will be important.

There are many potential ways to accomplish this. One strategy, which also has the benefit of exposing both parties to the same information, would be to replace the current system of separate Democratic and Republican platform hearings—an innovative and pro-democratic improvement over hurried conversations between platform committee members in conference rooms at the parties' quadrennial conventions—with a combined set where people and groups speak before both parties at once. After hearing the same testimony, parties could consider which issues meet the amended standard of legitimate opposition and, among this set, identify issues on which they agree—and can relay this to voters with confidence that their opposition will not undercut or outbid them—and issues on which divergent views would provide voters with meaningful alternatives. This could allow some breathing room for shared interests that can and should cross party lines, like protecting freedom of the press, counting votes accurately, and fulfilling financial obligations.

Lessons about Polarization

Throughout this book, I discuss the relationship between programmatic partisanship and polarization. My starting point, which remains fundamental, is that we need to talk about this as a relationship—the two concepts are not synonymous. I show that polarized voting in Congress can exist without major widespread differences in program. Indeed, polarization was high in the late nineteenth and early twentieth centuries, but programmaticism was not. The former should not be used as a proxy for the latter. This has been tempting, as we have had a measure of polarization for some time but no long-term measure of programmaticism until now. The measure presented in this book can be used in future work needing a measure of issue differentiation over time.

While they may not be interchangeable, it remains important to consider programmaticism in studying polarization. They are related theoretically and empirically. As parties take alternative positions across an increasingly wide array of issues, distance between them also increases. This can manifest in different ways, including voting in Congress. It is not a foregone conclusion that programmaticism will encourage uncompromising and even hostile attitudes that make Democrats and Republicans appear like repelling magnets who cannot connect even if forces like the need to govern during crises are pushing them together; but it does not require much in the way of mental gymnastics to get from one to the other. From an empirical standpoint, programmatic partisanship and polarization have trended together over the past half century, both to historic heights.

As the nation grapples with hyper polarization—which many view as a critical problem impeding governance—it is important to consider the nature of party competition. Strategies for managing polarization must contend with the fact that we have a different type of party system today than we had before. To be sure, one tool does not account for all party competition today or in the past, but as this book shows, the balance between tools has shifted. Programmatic systems have different dynamics than clientelistic systems. Successful strategies for responding to polarization will need to take this into consideration.

It is also important to account for programmaticism because, while its dynamics might be subject to adjustment—I hope, for example, that it will be possible for the parties to define more thoughtfully issues on which they will compete and issues on which they will not—it is likely to endure. Programmatic partisanship has a strong relationship to modernization, as well as to bureaucratic and party organizational strength. The United States has faced and will continue to experience economic recessions, but a reversal of modernization is hard to imagine.

Finally, the analysis in this book underscores the importance of paying close attention to institutions. Polarization is a classic example of a phenomenon that's typically considered in ideological terms. Inquiries into this topic often take some form of the question: why have parties become more extreme, and what might be done to make Democrats and Republicans think and behave differently? While not wrong, this overlooks the critical organizational foundation of modern polarization. For Democrats and Republicans to vote their party's position across a wide range of issues in Congress, such positions need to exist. As this book has shown, developing positions requires a great deal of work, which in turn requires organizational capacity. This book, in a sense, tells the story of how and why the base for modern polarization was built.

In doing so, it encourages us to see the achievement here. Given great concerns surrounding modern polarization, it would be easy to think about party differentiation in primarily negative terms. Yet, it is also important to recognize how difficult it was for parties to reach a place where they could engage in issue competition. We need to think not only about ways in which they might have been pushed, but also about ways in which they pulled themselves to this place. This was not a case of activists descending on parties, causing polarization. There was a great deal of party agency in the developments described herein; and if we do not take that seriously, we miss a key part of the story of how and why we got to where we are today, which would inhibit our ability to successfully navigate next steps.

Onward

Scholars, students, and others interested in politics and governance can ask themselves several questions to help advance conversations about programmatic partisanship and its implications for democracy in the United States as well as in other nations. I will lay out a few here, offering a starting point for future work on this critical and understudied topic.

One set of questions involves measurement, which has been a challenge in the study of programmaticism. It would be valuable to have measures of programmatic partisanship in other nations across the development spectrum over time. This book got new leverage over the question of what constrains and facilitates programmatic partisanship by looking at a long period in one nation. The method used to estimate the measure of programmaticism presented in chapter 1 can be applied to other countries with published platforms or other expressions of party doctrine over a long period.

With over-time measures for a wider range of nations, we could also see whether there are cases in which there is a significant downward trend in programmaticism. Under what conditions, if any, does this happen? Is it associated with positive or negative democratic outcomes? If and when countries shift away from programmaticism, what do they move toward? This book has been primarily concerned with forward movement in programmaticism, but backward movement is also of interest. I do not mean the word *backward* to carry a negative connotation. Programmaticism can rise too high, and some degree of abatement may be necessary.

In addition to estimating programmatic partisanship over time across more nations, it is also worth thinking about whether there are alternative ways we could measure this concept that would complement the quantitative and qualitative indicators presented here. How might we capture different attributes or dimensions of programmaticism? Addressing this question can enrich our understanding of the concept and contribute to conversations about an appropriate upper bound.

Finally, we need to know more about the relationship between parties and interest groups. Groups were helpful to parties in developing positions and became more involved in this aspect of party affairs over time. Through this process, group-party relationships naturally became closer. Parties have come closer to the "group theory" model of parties as coalitions of groups, though there are still meaningful differences between them. Looking at campaign finance and other aspects of politics today, we can see many groups lining up on opposite sides of the partisan aisle and parties offering support to different groups. What implications does this have for democracy? This is a big question, the potential subject of many articles and books.

Moving forward, we need to think carefully about the nature of competition between groups for goods and services from government. The classic concept here is *pluralism*, the idea that groups compete in a political marketplace for attention from parties and government as firms compete with each other in an economic marketplace for attention from consumers. While pluralism has always been a controversial concept in political science, given unequal power between groups, it remains helpful, even if we use it to consider how to make such competition more fair. In the context of high programmaticism and tight group-party relationships, we also need to think about groups competing in two different submarketplaces. For clarity, we might call this *bifurcated pluralism*. Within their partisan markets, groups compete in two senses: over the content of policy, and over the party's agenda. In this light, groups trying to enact pro-choice policy, for example, need to contend not only with mobilization by pro-life groups, but also with the strength of other groups within the Democratic coalition who want the party's attention and capital. Research on this front is needed from conceptual and empirical perspectives as we move forward in a strongly programmatic context.

The lessons we might learn from addressing these questions, like the lessons from this book, could apply to other nations in addition to the United States. Given programmaticism's relationship to modernization, and efforts to promote further development in many parts of the world, it's more important than ever to understand the dynamics of issue-based competition and their implications for democracy. The politics of who *thinks* what, when, and how can be productive with responsible boundaries. We must continue the conversation about how and why party systems evolve, and how we can define and promote healthy party competition in the United States and around the world.

ONE OF THE GREATEST impediments to studying programmaticism lies in measurement. Estimating policy positions is difficult. This stems largely from the fact that policy positions are by nature hard to pinpoint. Some scholars have gone so far as to say they are "unobservable and must therefore be treated as a latent variable in empirical work" (Slapin and Proksch, 2008, 706). Indeed, as Slapin and Proksch argue, citing Benoit and Laver (2006b), "although one might have a good intuition about where parties stand relative to each other, the positions themselves are abstract concepts that cannot be observed directly" (705).

In particular, we lack reliable measures of programmaticism over time (Luna, Rosenblatt, and Toro, 2014). This appendix describes existing strategies for measuring the degree to which parties differ in their policy positions, noting their strengths and limitations, and then presents a new strategy for estimating programmaticism in the United States from 1856 to 2016.

Existing Measures

The effort to measure programmaticism directly is relatively new. As Kitschelt and Freeze (n.d.) note, "There is a substantial amount of research on the *substantive positions* parties take on policies and the *relative emphasis* they put on specific policies, but not on their overall programmatic effort, when compared to other efforts parties can make to mobilize voters" (2).

Measuring programmaticism is rooted in the task of measuring party positions. Research tracing the parties' positions on issues has been facilitated by the Comparative Manifestos Project (CMP). This invaluable resource, which began in 1979 as the Manifesto Research Group (MRG), has coded manifestos for parties in more than fifty countries into seven major categories and fifty-six subcategories (Budge, Robertson, and Hearl, 1987; Budge et al., 2001; Klingemann, Hofferbert, and Budge, 1994; Laver and Budge, 1992). Topic-coded party platforms are also available for the United States, owing to a major coding effort led by Christina Wolbrecht (n.d.), through the Comparative Agendas Project (CAP), which employs a larger number of categories (21 major, 221 minor).

Scholars can use data from the CMP and CAP to evaluate the degree to which parties have differed in their issue positions. An influential method, developed by Laver and Budge (1992) and employed by many others, has been to sort CMP issues into *left* and *right* categories, and then calculate the amount of attention each party pays to each in total. This is not an ideal measure of programmaticism, since it does not consider the nature of language used to discuss topics, only the volume of attention paid to left versus right issues. This method also has trouble accounting for issues that don't map cleanly onto a left–right continuum and is not sensitive to the fact that the relative importance of issues may change over time (Slapin and Proksch, 2008). While scholars have developed ways to deal with some of these issues (Gabel and Huber, 2000; Klingemann, 1995), this method is not viable for my analysis because the CMP and CAP data cover only a fraction of the period under study, CMP beginning in 1920 in the United States, and CAP beginning in 1948.

Expert surveys address some of these problems and offer additional benefits. The most comprehensive effort to measure programmaticism directly and systematically has come from the Democratic Accountability and Linkages Project (DALP) at Duke University (Kitschelt, n.d.; Kitschelt and Freeze, n.d.). This project builds on a tradition of using expert surveys to estimate party positions (Benoit and Laver, 2006b; Castles and Mair, 1984; Huber and Inglehart, 1995). The value of this dataset, which is based on surveys of experts taken in 2008 and 2009 about 506 parties in eighty-eight democracies, would be difficult to overstate. The central quantitative measure is an index called CoSalPo, which takes into account "the extent to which parties make internally cohesive appeals on at least a subset of salient policy issues, and distinguish themselves from each other by taking different issue positions ('polarization')" (Kitschelt and Wang, 2014, 48). With a set of broad questions, asked about all parties in all countries, as well as questions specific to particular countries developed in consultation with area specialists, the dataset offers a rich and nuanced view of programmaticism at the time the survey was conducted.

Even with these herculean data collection efforts, however, the study of programmaticism faces major data-related challenges, especially for temporal analyses. The DALP data, while valuable for capturing a specific moment in time, cannot be used for historical analysis. More broadly, expert surveys are too costly to serve as a practical tool for measuring programmaticism over long periods.

To overcome these challenges, I use advancements in machine-learning techniques to estimate programmaticism in the United States from 1856, the first year of competition between today's major parties, to the present using platform data from the American Presidency Project (see chapter 1 for more on this data). I estimate differences in orientation toward issues overall, comparing national Republican and Democratic platforms on the whole and within topic areas for each year. While machine-learning methods cannot substitute for other types of work, they can be a powerful complement, especially for places or times for which traditional sources of data are not readily available.

Overview of Methodology for Topic Estimation

Before positions in specific issue areas can be estimated, it is necessary to identify a set of categories and the text associated with each one. That is, we need to define a topic scheme and code platform sentences according to that scheme. This is a common task in political science in general, and particularly when studying party platforms.

Traditionally, hand-coding has been the go-to strategy for this kind of task. Major projects in this realm include the Comparative Agendas Project and Comparative Manifestos Project described above, as well as the American Institutions Project. There are many benefits to hand-coding, the most notable being human attention to nuance and context. A human brain can detect changes to the meaning of words in particular contexts (e.g., in conjunction with certain punctuation or other words) that a computer cannot recognize without specific instruction.

Nonetheless, hand-coding also carries significant costs, both monetary and analytical. The monetary costs are obvious, given that hand-coding is extremely labor intensive. This makes it slow to develop and hard to replicate. A significant analytical cost, beyond the inevitable human error, is the rigidity of hand-coding schemes across time and space (Lapinski, 2013; Slapin and Proksch, 2008). They are generally developed at a particular point in time, or for a particular period in history, which may or may not be ideal for other times. Issues come and go, and sometimes new issues don't fit neatly into existing categories.

Advances in automated content analysis offer new ways to estimate topics, among other things. They are particularly valuable for historical research because more traditional quantitative data are often unavailable or unreliable for long periods. But even before official, high quality records were kept, people were consistently writing about politics. Of course, textual data are far more voluminous than most other kinds of data—it's much easier to analyze trends in quantitative survey data, for example, than large volumes of text like platforms, speeches, or transcripts. Automated text analysis methods can make an otherwise prohibitively costly task manageable. There are several excellent overviews of the evolution of methods for automatic topic assignment, with summaries of strengths and weaknesses as well as appropriate applications for different techniques, which will not be repeated here (see, e.g., Grimmer and Stewart, 2013; Laver, Benoit, and Garry, 2003; Lucas et al., 2015; and Quinn et al., 2010). Rather, I focus on the method used for this analysis, explaining how it works and why it best suits my purposes.

Structural Topic Models

To define topics and to code platform sentences, I use a new estimation strategy called the structural topic model (STM; M. Roberts et al., 2014; M. Roberts, Stewart and Airoldi, 2013). STM belongs to a family of *unsupervised* machine-learning methods, more specifically in a lineage of probabilistic topic models like latent Dirichlet allocation (LDA; Blei, Ng, and Jordan, 2003) and the correlated topic model (CTM; Blei and Lafferty, 2007) that use word co-occurrence to estimate topics. In contrast to *supervised* methods, in which a researcher codes a set of sample documents and then charges the model with replicating that scheme on a larger set of documents, unsupervised methods do not require the researcher to make such ex ante decisions.[1] In the context of topic modeling, this means that the researcher does not define topics in advance, but rather lets themes emerge from the data.

This can be positive or negative, depending on one's goals. If one is looking to analyze a particular topic, unsupervised topic models could be frustrating because the researcher's topic of interest may not emerge naturally. In such a case, which is particularly likely to arise for a topic receiving a small amount of attention relative to the size of the corpus (e.g., a textual database), a researcher may prefer to use a supervised method that would allow them to train a model to look for that particular topic. If one is looking to characterize the set of topics in a corpus, however, unsupervised methods have the advantage of avoiding biases relating to the researcher's life (e.g., they are working in a particular historical moment in which certain topics may be more prominent than others) and academic expertise (e.g., they may be more likely to notice topics relating to their substantive specialty or the period they most often study). An unsupervised model like STM "allows the researcher to *discover* topics from the data, rather than assume them" (M. Roberts et al., 2014, 1066).[2] While one might be naturally skeptical of a topic scheme derived entirely from the data, research indicates that unsupervised methods perform similarly to supervised methods while also enabling the researcher to uncover topics they might not have otherwise thought to define.[3]

There are two types of unsupervised topic models: single membership and mixed membership. As the name implies, a single-membership model essentially sorts the documents into exclusive categories (i.e., so each document can be a "member" of only one category), a common strategy in hand-coding efforts like CAP. In contrast, mixed-membership models assign a probability that each document belongs to each topic. For a document with laser focus on one topic, the model will likely assign a very high probability to that topic and low probabilities to all other topics. For a document relating to two topics, it will likely assign a moderate probability to those two topics, and low probabilities to every other topic. For each document, the probabilities assigned to each topic sum to 1.

This offers valuable flexibility to researchers. Depending on the application, one might be interested in only the top topic, as one would get from a single-membership model and many hand-coding projects, identifiable in mixed-membership models as the topic with the highest assigned probability. Or one might be interested in any topic with a probability above a particular threshold, whether it's the top topic or not. Mixed membership models are well-suited to the study of platforms because they are better able to handle sentences covering two different subjects (e.g., a sentence identifying what the party perceives to be the two most important problems facing the nation at a given moment). They are also better equipped than single-membership models to handle sentences straddling two topics. For example, should a sentence about school lunch programs be classified under education or social welfare?

In truth, it is both, and mixed-membership models can accommodate this reality. By providing a continuous measure of relevance to each topic, they offer great flexibility.

The topics themselves can be conceived of similarly. Whereas a document is essentially a mixture of topics, a topic is essentially a mixture of words, or a distribution over words reflecting a theme. For each topic, each word in the corpus is assigned a probability of belonging to that topic; and for each topic, those probabilities sum to 1. To interpret the meaning of topics identified by the model, one can look at the top words and exemplar documents associated with each topic.

STM differs from other mixed-membership models like LDA (Blei, 2012; Blei, Ng, and Jordan, 2003) primarily by allowing document metadata (e.g., author, date, etc.) to serve as covariates in estimating topic prevalence (i.e., the extent to which each document is devoted to each topic) and content (i.e., the words associated with topics).[4] Accounting for the possibility that parties might pay different amounts of attention to topics or speak about them in different ways can help the model identify topics more accurately, and facilitate hypothesis testing about the relationship between metadata and topics (M. Roberts et al., 2014).[5]

STMs have been used to study various topics in political science, like media bias (Kim, 2018), parliamentary speechmaking (Geese, 2019), and partisan stereotypes (Rothschild et al., 2019), as well as in other fields.[6] They have not, to my knowledge, been used to study party platforms, but they are well suited to this task. Earlier machine-learning tools like dictionary methods (Laver and Garry, 2000), supervised learning methods (Laver, Benoit, and Garry, 2003), and LDA (Catalinac, 2016, 2018) have been applied to manifestos with success.[7] Moreover, Hillard, Purpura, and Wilkerson (2007) have evaluated the use of supervised machine-learning methods on data from the Congressional Bills Project, which uses the same coding scheme as the Comparative Agendas Project, and find they do well.

Evaluating Topic Model Output

Validation is very important when using unsupervised models because human judgment is not used on the front end. An explanation of different strategies for this stage of the process and details on the validation of topic models used in this chapter can be found in the online appendix. (https://press.princeton .edu/isbn/9780691257969).

Topic Estimation on Party Platforms, 1856–2016

Document Preprocessing

In this analysis, the unit ("document") will be platform quasi-sentences, which are strings of text delineated by semicolons or periods (rather than periods only, as in sentences).[8] For narrative ease, I refer to them as sentences or documents.

All topic models in this analysis were estimated using the *stm* package in R (M. Roberts, Stewart, and Tingley, 2019). The documents were preprocessed according to conventional practices using the package's *textProcessor* function. This includes stemming the words (i.e., such that education, educate, and educated are equated by their common root) and deleting punctuation, numbers, and very common words, also known as "stop words" (e.g., the, also, be, etc.). I also removed words that appeared in fewer than twenty sentences (0.05%) across all platforms using the package's *prepDocuments* function.[9] Very common and very rare words make it harder to discern relationships between words and topics.

I then created a document-term matrix, which is the main input for STM, indicating the prevalence of each word from the corpus in each document. Each document is represented as a vector of terms remaining after the preprocessing described above, with an indication of how many times each term is used in each document. This reflects what is known as a "bag of words" assumption, treating documents as collections of unordered words. While one might be concerned about losing information about word sequencing within a document, this practice has been shown to offer significant gains in computational efficiency with minimal substantive cost.[10]

Model Specification and Topic Level Selection

The primary benefit of a structural topic model over other mixed-membership models is that it allows for features of the documents—in my case, year and party—to be used to estimate topics. This enables us to examine the relationship between topics and covariates. One can use covariates for topic prevalence (the extent to which platform sentences, in my case, relate to each topic), topic content (the types of words used to discuss each topic), or both (M. Roberts et al., 2014).

Given that attention to topics may vary over time, especially over a very long period like the one in this analysis, and parties may talk about the same topic in different ways, the most sensible model would include party and year as prevalence covariates, estimated with a spline for year to allow for a nonlinear relationship and an interaction to allow for the possibility that attention to a particular topic may change over time for one party but not the other, and party as a content covariate.[11] The use of a content covariate in this case will allow for the possibility that Democrats and Republicans talk about the same topic in different ways. Without a content covariate, the model might assign Democratic and Republican utterances about a subject to different topics. As a robustness check, I consider other model specifications as well, results for which are substantially similar (for details, see the online appendix). In all specifications, year is expressed as an integer running from 1 to 41, where 1 represents 1856 and 41 represents 2016.

To estimate an STM, one has to set the number of topics (K). There is no one correct answer regarding the number of topics (Grimmer and Stewart, 2013). There are tradeoffs between different metrics used to evaluate topic models, and the ideal level of K may also vary depending on the goals of the researcher. There are questions for which a smaller number of topics at a higher level of abstraction may be useful, and questions for which a narrower range may be useful. The nested structure of existing topic-coding schemes, like the American Institutions Project and Comparative Agendas Project, reflects this value.

My goal was to produce a coherent and comprehensive set of major political issues. Topics needed to be recognizable as significant, nonfleeting political issues over which parties might compete (e.g., education, health); and, on the whole, the topics needed to cover the range of key issues that platforms would be expected to discuss. I was aiming for a level of aggregation roughly corresponding to the CAP's major topics, of which there are twenty-one.

To select a level for K, it is common practice to run models at different levels and examine the results. I ran 41 models, allowing K to vary from 20 to 40.[12] Standard diagnostic statistics like semantic coherence and exclusivity indicate that the former decreases and the latter increases as the number of topics grows, as is typical for topic models.[13] Because these changes were fairly even in moving from 20 to 40, and semantic coherence and exclusivity are both desirable, these metrics were not especially helpful in pinpointing a specific level for K. This was not surprising, as these diagnostic statistics are known to have limitations and cannot substitute for careful qualitative analysis of the results. Thus, I did a close reading of the topics generated by all 41 models.

This helped me choose a level for K and characterize the topics. STM does not label the topics—it simply identifies coherent themes and assigns them numbers (e.g., Topic 1, Topic 2, etc.). It's up to the researcher to label the topics. I examined the top 15 words and top 30 sentences associated with each topic at each level of K from 20 to 40. A research assistant and I each performed this evaluation independently, and then discussed our results for each topic at each level of K to reach a final determination.[14]

This analysis revealed fifteen topics that appeared in similar form across all or almost all levels of K: (1) law enforcement and border security; (2) culture, arts, and multiculturalism; (3) territories and statehood; (4) transportation and infrastructure; (5) American dream; (6) business and jobs; (7) education; (8) energy; (9) healthcare; (10) economy; (11) national defense; (12) development; (13) social welfare; (14) rights; and (15) foreign affairs.[15] We can be fairly confident, then, that these are robust topics.

In evaluating different levels of K, it makes sense to focus on the coherence of these 15 topics and the appearance of others that help round out the range of topics in American politics. After reading closely the top words and documents associated with each topic, we determined that 32 was the best level for K. It produced the most coherent set of associated words and documents and added the following topics to the scheme: (16) trade and markets; (17) regulation and bureaucracy; (18) land and natural resources; (19) labor and anti-trust; and (20) liberal democracy, at home and abroad. The remaining 12 themes identified by STM were not related to policy issues. For more detail on the topics, including a list of more specific issues to which they relate, see the online appendix.[16]

Figure A.1 shows the proportion of documents (i.e., platform sentences) in the entire corpus (i.e., all platforms from 1856 to 2016) that related to each topic, along with the top ten words associated with each topic.[17] Over the course of competition between Democrats and Republicans, the five most prevalent topics have been the economy, American dream, foreign affairs, rights, and territories and statehood. The last one underscores the value of allowing topics to emerge from the data. A topic scheme created by contemporary scholars may not include statehood, which is now largely antiquated. Indeed, it does not appear in the CAP Master Topics coding scheme. To offer

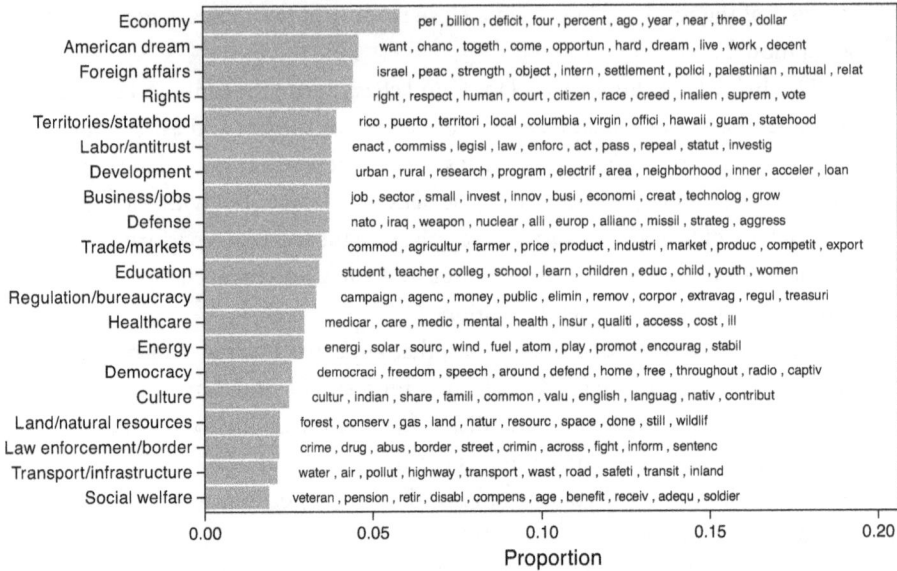

FIGURE A.1. Topic proportions and top word associations. This graph shows the proportion of documents (i.e., platform quasi-sentences) across both parties and all years (1856–2016) relating to each topic, as well as the top ten words associated with each topic. The words have been stemmed for reasons explained in the section on preprocessing.

a sense of exemplary documents, the top five sentences associated with each topic are shown in the online appendix.

VALIDATION

I used several strategies to validate the results of this topic model, including (1) close reading for coherence; (2) examination of attention to topics over time to check for plausibility; (3) comparison of attention to topics in platforms to attention in roll-call votes, using hand-coded data from the American Institutions Project from 1879 to 2010; and (4) comparison of STM's topic assignment for each platform sentence to that of hand-coders from the CAP for the years 1948–2016.[18] Together, they indicate that STM has produced a reasonable topic scheme. For details, see the online appendix.

Overview of Methodology for Estimating Programmaticism

I take a two-pronged approach to measuring programmaticism, looking at platforms on the whole (in which the "document" unit for which an estimate is generated is an entire platform) and within issue areas (in which the "document" unit is the set of sentences on the issue area in a platform). In both cases, I begin by creating estimates for each party in each year using a scaling technique called Wordfish, developed by Slapin and Proksch (2008). Like STM, Wordfish is an unsupervised machine-learning method that does not rely on reference texts. Rather, it generates ideology estimates on a unidimensional scale based on word frequency in the data.[19]

There is an alternative, supervised method for estimating ideology called Wordscores, innovated by Laver, Benoit, and Garry (2003), which uses reference texts at the extremes of a unidimensional continuum to position other texts. While this was a major step forward in computer-assisted text analysis, given its ability to consider the content of issue positions rather than simply attention to issues, it is not well suited to time-series analysis (Benoit and Laver, 2006a; Slapin and Proksch, 2008). Thus, it is not practical for historical studies of programmaticism like the one herein. The benefits and limitations of Wordscores have been covered in depth elsewhere and will not be repeated here (Grimmer and Stewart, 2013; Laver, Benoit, and Garry, 2003; Slapin and Proksch, 2008).

No method is perfect, and Wordfish is no exception. It assumes, for example, that the meaning of words is consistent over time. Nonetheless, Wordfish has several benefits over Wordscores for my purposes. Slapin and Proksch (2008, 708) argue: "The advantage of this new approach is three-fold: its ability to produce time series estimates, the fact that it does not require the use of reference texts because it instead assumes an underlying statistical distribution of word counts, and, lastly, the ability to use all words in every document to estimate the importance of each of these words." Indeed, they argue that the last innovation contributes to Wordfish's advantage in generating positions over time. As they note, "If the political lexicon changes through words entering and exiting the political dialogue, rather than through words changing meaning, our method does take these changes into account when estimating positions" (Slapin and Proksch, 2008, 711).

Wordfish has been shown to perform well in estimating party positions in German party platforms (Grimmer and Stewart, 2013; Slapin and Proksch, 2008) and in Japanese election manifestos (Catalinac, 2016, 2018), as well as in other kinds of documents like parliamentary speeches in England, France, and Germany (Proksch and Slapin, 2010) and party leader statements in Japan (Proksch, Slapin, and Thies, 2011). All Wordfish estimates presented herein were generated using the *Quanteda.textmodels* package in R (Benoit et al., n.d.).

Estimating Programmaticism in Party Platforms, 1856–2016

Document Preprocessing

As with STM, the documents were preprocessed before Wordfish models were run, with words stemmed, and punctuation, numbers, stop words, and very rare words removed. There is no one correct answer to the question of how many documents in the corpus a word must appear in for it to be included in the term-document matrix that's fed to Wordfish. The answer requires careful attention to the nature of the documents and the goals of the analysis. In the present case, a fleeting thought, contained in only one or two platforms, will probably not contribute and may detract from the quality of our programmaticism estimates. Some minimum threshold above 2, meaning that the word would need to span at least two election cycles, seems reasonable. That said, there is a natural ebb and flow to certain issues (e.g., conflicts with particular nations), and so there is also a danger in setting the threshold too high. Moreover, removing words reduces the number of "features" (i.e., unique words) in the corpus. In an article evaluating best practices for Wordfish, Proksch and Slapin (2009) find, through Monte Carlo simulations, that Wordfish performs better as the number of documents and unique words increases. At three hundred unique words and twenty documents, its performance is excellent. One must keep this in mind in setting the minimum threshold for rare words.

From a substantive standpoint, my preferred threshold is 6 because a word that appears in at least three election cycles' worth of platforms seems like it could reasonably contribute to programmaticism, and this also seems like a natural life cycle for certain issues. To be thorough, however, I experimented with varying the threshold from 1 to 8 platforms. The process for selecting this threshold for whole platforms and topics is discussed in more detail below.

Whole Platforms

Looking at platforms in their entirety gives us a sense of the degree to which Democrats and Republicans communicate about issues differently on the whole. This is a reasonably close approximation of the degree of programmaticism in a party system. Of course, not all sentences in platforms are about issues. Especially toward the beginning, they often contain ceremonial language evoking the kind of pomp and circumstance of today's party conventions. They also contain sentences expressing patriotism, optimism "for the future of our great nation," and similar sentiments. We do not want to include

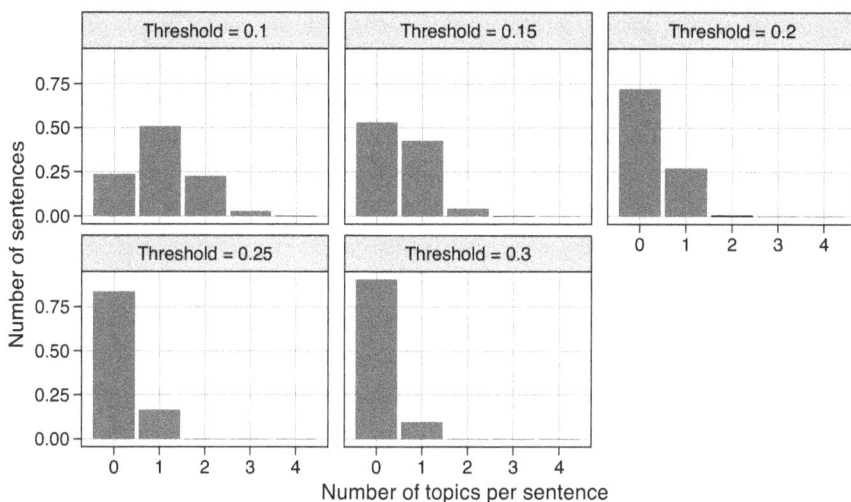

FIGURE A.2. Number of topics per sentence at different
STM probability thresholds.
This graph shows the number of topics per sentence at different probability
thresholds. Platforms for both parties and all years are included.

such language in our measure of programmaticism; rather, we want to focus
on sentences that relate to issues.

STM comes in handy on this front. Unlike single-membership models and
most hand-coding schemes, it does not sort sentences into the closest related
topic (or, in the case of the CAP, a very sparsely populated category for non-
policy); rather, it assigns a probability that each sentence relates to each topic.
This gives us a continuous measure of each sentence's relation to a particular
topic and, by extension, to *any* topic. A sentence that mentions many topics in
a laundry list of issues of the day but doesn't really say anything in particular
about any of them would have a very low topic proportion score for all topics.
By setting a minimum threshold for inclusion in my whole platform analysis,
I can reduce the number of sentences of that nature, along with others unre-
lated to issues, like patriotic puffery, vague disparagement of the other party,
and so forth.

To get a sense of the ideal level for this threshold, and the range to consider
for evaluating robustness, we can begin by examining the number of topics per
sentence at different minimum probability thresholds. Figure A.2 displays this
information. Focusing first on the top left panel, for which the threshold is 0.1,
two things stand out. First, slightly less than one-quarter of sentences in the

platform corpus don't meet this threshold for any topic. This seems reasonable, given the need for transitions between paragraphs and vague patriotic language often contained in platforms. Second, approximately one-quarter of platform sentences meet this threshold for more than one topic. This underscores the value of STM, which allows us to include such sentences in more than one category in the Wordfish analysis by topic. Moving from a threshold of 0.1 to 0.15, there is a dramatic rise in the number of sentences that do not meet the threshold for any topic. We do not want to lose more than half of platform sentences from the analysis. Thus, if we are to set a minimum probability threshold, it should not exceed 0.1.

As expected, the number of unique words declines when a 0.1 minimum topic probability threshold is used, relative to having no minimum, and as we increase the minimum number of platforms in which a word needs to appear in order to be included in the Wordfish model. Even with the topic probability threshold set at 0.1 and the minimum platform threshold set at 8, however, the number of unique words far exceeds the minimum (300) recommended by Proksch and Slapin (2009; see the online appendix). Thus, I proceed with my preferred levels of 0.1 for the topic probability threshold and 6 for the document threshold.

Figure 1.1 in chapter 1 plots the difference between Wordfish's estimates for Democratic and Republican platforms over time, which I take as a measure of programmaticism. The solid line reflects raw numbers, and the dotted line is a loess curve (reflecting locally weighted regression) with a 95 percent confidence interval shaded in gray. The year 1988 has been removed from that graph because it is a significant outlier, a year in which Democrats decided to release a very short platform, as discussed in chapter 5. Its exclusion does not significantly affect the trend (see the online appendix), but it does make the trend easier to see because it changes the graph's scale.

Within Issue Areas

In addition to measuring programmaticim using whole platforms, I also generate measures within issue areas. This is an important supplement because Wordfish assumes that the words in the corpus come from a single dimension (Lowe and Benoit, 2013; Slapin and Proksch, 2008). While Poole and Rosenthal (2007) show that a single dimension accounts for the vast majority of roll-call voting choices (e.g., 92% in the 109th House and Senate), a second dimension has sometimes played an important role in congressional decisionmaking.

Thus, I subset the platforms by topic and ran Wordfish on each subset separately. This is the method recommended by Slapin and Proksch (2008) for estimating party positions in specific issue areas. Before doing so, however, a standard must be set for a sentence to be included in the corpus for a particular topic. While we could just use sentences for which the topic was STM's top topic (i.e., assigned the highest probability of topic assignment), this could lead to a loss of relevant information. Some sentences are truly about more than one topic. Examining the percentage of total platform sentences exceeding thresholds from 0.1 to 0.3 in increments of 0.05, I found that it is quite common for sentences to exceed the 0.1 threshold for a topic even if it was not the "top topic" according to STM (see the online appendix).[20]

In addition to choosing a minimum topic probability threshold, we also must choose a minimum for the number of documents in which a word must appear in order to be included in the Wordfish model. In making these choices, it is important to keep in mind best practices recommended by Proksch and Slapin (2009). While all subtopics appear in at least twenty platforms, so the document threshold is not a concern, careful attention must be paid to the number of unique words left in each corpus (here, the pool of text on each topic) when raising the minimum document appearances for a word to be included in the model. All topics are at minimum close to, and often far above, this threshold with the topic probability set at 0.1 and the minimum document threshold set at 6, as in the full platform analysis (see the online appendix). Thus, these are the levels used for the within-issue analysis.[21]

Figure 1.4 in chapter 1 plots programmaticism in each issue area.[22] These estimates should be taken with a grain of salt for particular areas. If writing a book about a specific issue, one may find it more fruitful to use a supervised model trained to look for specific language known to be associated with that issue. For my purposes, however, the goal was to characterize the corpus and gauge the extent to which distinction between parties is evident within different issue areas. The fact that there is variation across issue areas, both in the baseline level of programmaticism and in the trajectory over time, suggests that the overall estimate of programmaticism shown in figure 1.1 is not simply capturing differences in vague ideology or language style.

Validating Wordfish Estimates

I used several strategies to validate the results of the Wordfish models. Following Slapin and Proksch (2008), I compared the estimates derived from Wordfish to those derived from hand-coded platform data from the Comparative Manifestos Project using the Laver and Budge (1992) method. I also examined the Democratic and Republican parties' positions relative to each other over time. These analyses suggest that the measures of programmaticism for full platforms and topic areas are reasonable and valid. For details on validation, see the online appendix.

NOTES

Chapter 1. The Puzzle of Programmatic Partisanship

1. See, e.g., *The Debt Limit: History and Recent Increases*, Congressional Research Service, 2015; *Reaching the Debt Limit: Background and Potential Effects on Government Operations*, Congressional Research Service, 2015; *Life after Default*, Council of Economic Advisors, 2021; *Q&A: Everything You Should Know about the Debt Ceiling*, Committee for a Responsible Federal Budget, 2023, inter alia.

2. O'Neill (1987, 349).

3. Mathews (2013, 51-52).

4. *Memorial Addresses and Tributes in Honor of Thomas P. "Tip" O'Neill, Jr.*, House Document 103-340 (Washington, DC: U.S. Government Printing Office, 1995), p. 101. See also Farrell (2001).

5. O'Neill (1987, 376).

6. Przeworski (1991, 10).

7. O'Neill (1987, 29).

8. O'Neill (1987, 9).

9. Party differences on issues are not necessarily required for there to be electoral accountability. An "electoral connection" involves members of Congress who are responsive to the preferences of their constituents (Mayhew, 1974). Convergence can provide a path for public opinion to influence lawmakers' behavior. Indeed, lawmakers may be punished by voters for extreme positions relative to their constituents' wishes, and parties can try to become more competitive by moving toward the other party's position on an issue if the other party is more in line with public wishes. For issues to affect voters' evaluation of the two parties, however, some significant distinction remains necessary.

10. See Mayhew (1974) and note 9 herein.

11. In the United States, Grossmann and Hopkins (2016) have shown that the two major parties are fundamentally distinct organizations held together by different types of glue, so to speak. While ideology is a critical force bringing Republicans together, the Democratic Party is better conceived as a coalition of groups, they argue.

12. Cheeseman and Paget (2014).

13. There is variation across definitions in how scholars treat institutions. Some are silent on the subject, focusing more on outputs like policy positions (e.g., Cheeseman et al., 2014a), while others (e.g., Cheeseman and Paget, 2014) include an organizational component. Cheeseman and Paget's (2014) conceptualization of programmaticism requires that "well-structured

and stable ideological commitment constitute the basis for ... the internal organization of the party" along with outputs like the platform. Luna, Rosenblatt, and Toro (2014) take a similar position, including among their criteria "organizing the party in ways that facilitate the construction, diffusion and reproduction of its programmatic platform" (1). Definitions of programmaticism often state that party programs should be a basis for the policymaking process (see, e.g., Cheeseman and Paget, 2014; Luna, Rosenblatt, and Toro, 2014). Of course, parties will not always be able to pass the policies in their program, as exogenous factors (e.g., economic strain) may interfere, they may face prohibitive levels of opposition, and so forth; but, some argue, programmatic parties exhibit a "serious commitment to delivering on promises made in the party campaign platform" (Kitschelt and Wang, 2014, 45). For more on definitions of programmatic partisanship, see Kitschelt and Freeze (n.d.); and Kitschelt and Wang (2014).

14. I do not focus here on legislative behavior on issues, which has received more attention from American politics scholars (e.g., Lapinski, 2013). Future work could examine the relationship between programmaticism, as I have defined it, and lawmaking. Presumably, for elected officials to remain loyal to their party's policy positions, such positions need to be defined.

15. Brady, Ferejohn, and Harbridge (2006).

16. On ideological polarization, see McCarty, Poole, and Rosenthal (2006); and Noel (2013), inter alia; on affective polarization, see Iyengar, Sood and Lelkes (2012); and on social polarization, see Mason (2018).

17. For differences on issues between Democrats and Republicans in the electorate, see, e.g., Abramowitz (2006); Abramowitz and Saunders (2008); Fiorina (2006); and Fiorina and Levendusky (2006). There have been studies of elite programmaticism on abortion (Adams, 1997), LGBTQ+ rights (Krimmel, Lax and Phillips, 2016), and a few other topics (Karol, 2009).

18. Kitschelt and Wang (2014, 45).

19. A similar logic applies to what Herd and Moynihan (2019) call "administrative burdens"—the learning, psychological, and compliance costs required for citizens to engage with public policies. Such burdens are distributed unevenly across the population, making it particularly difficult and degrading for people with fewer resources to secure and maintain access to public policies. This important point relates more to systematic burden on less well-resourced people than clientelistic exchange.

20. Diaz-Cayeros, Estévez, and Magaloni (2016); Kitschelt and Wilkinson (2007a); Mares and Young (2019); Stokes et al. (2013); Weitz-Shapiro (2014).

21. Herbert Kitschelt and Steven Wilkinson (2007b, 324).

22. Stokes et al. (2013, 7). This is consistent with the spirit of a recent definition of policy offered by Karen Orren and Stephen Skowronek, as "a commitment to a designated goal or course of action, made authoritatively on behalf of a given entity or collectivity, and accompanied by guidelines for its accomplishment" (Orren and Skowronek, 2017, 27).

23. Stokes et al. (2013, 8).

24. Cheeseman et al. (2014a, xii).

25. Schattschneider (1942, 1).

26. See, e.g., Adams (1997); Baylor (2017); Carmines and Stimson (1989); Farhang and Katznelson (2005); Karol (2009); and Wolbrecht (2000).

27. The underlying concept was originally developed by Poole and Rosenthal (1997) and has been refined over time by McCarty, Poole, and Rosenthal (2006); Poole and Rosenthal

(2007). For an excellent, clear summary of the mechanics of these scores, see McCarty, Poole, and Rosenthal (2006, chapter 2).

28. Kitschelt and Freeze (n.d.).

29. Lee (2016b, 116). A revisionist perspective has emerged, pointing to some difference. But, Lee argues, these claims still come nowhere close to the degree of polarization suggested by DW-NOMINATE.

30. Layman, Carsey, and Horowitz (2006); McCarty, Poole, and Rosenthal (2006).

31. The Democratic Accountability and Linkages Project (DALP) has created an invaluable cross-national measure, but it covers a limited time (2008–9). Standard measures of polarization (e.g., the difference between the ideologies of the median Democrat and Republican in Congress) often serve as proxies for programmaticism, but party voting in Congress is not a reliable measure of programmatic distinction (Lee, 2016b). The Comparative Manifestos Project tracks party positions over time, but these data only go back to 1945.

32. Platform data were drawn from the American Presidency Project's repository, https://www.presidency.ucsb.edu/documents/app-categories/elections-and-transitions/party-platforms, accessed July 16, 2020.

33. A body of research, spearheaded by Gerald Pomper (1968), has shown that lawmakers' actions reflect platform pledges. Examining the period from 1945 to 1985, Budge and Hofferbert (1990) find a significant relationship between subjects emphasized in party platforms and actual federal expenditures. In an exchange published in the *American Political Science Review*, Gary King and Michael Laver challenge these findings, revealing much smaller effects from their preferred method of analyzing the data. Still, they conclude by noting, "We do not wish to imply that there is no connection between party positions and federal priorities. Instead, we argue that the connection probably does exist: it is just far weaker and more subtle than could be perceived with these data and methods" (King et al., 1993, 747). In Budge and Hofferbert's response, they underscore that the relationship between platform emphases and government expenditures remains notable, with a positive association in 13 of 24 cases in their analysis, and 10 of 24 in King and Laver's. Concentrating on the Reagan era, Royed (1996) finds a reasonably high level of platform pledge fulfillment among both parties—for Republicans, 61 percent in 1980 and 58 percent in 1984, and for Democrats, 48 percent in 1980 and 50 percent in 1984.

34. David (1971, 303–4).

35. Thurmond would go on to win four states (LA, AL, MS, SC), amounting to 7.3 percent of the electoral college vote (2.4% of the popular vote). American Presidency Project, Statistics, 1948, https://www.presidency.ucsb.edu/statistics/elections/1948, accessed September 8, 2020.

36. The year 1988 has been removed from this graph because it is a significant outlier, a year in which Democrats decided to release a very short platform, as discussed in chapter 5. Its exclusion does not significantly influence the trend (see the online appendix), but it does make the trend easier to see because it changes the graph's scale.

37. While Gerring does study a long period (1828–1996), his 1998 book does not provide a systematic measure of programmaticism overall or within a wide range of issue areas over time.

38. Lewis et al. (2023).

39. As a robustness check, I also reran the model with data that included stop words and not stem words. The results were very similar, indicating that the trend is not sensitive to decisions made in the preprocessing phase (see the online appendix).

40. Given my focus on trends over time, I allow the scales on the y-axis to vary across topics. For a version of this graph with consistent scales across topics, see the online appendix. As in the full platform graph, the year 1988 has been excluded because it is a significant outlier. The trend is similar but more difficult to see because of the altered scale when 1988 is included (see online appendix for comparison).

41. Kitschelt and Wang (2014).

42. The relationship is not perfect. Indeed, while there is a general consensus that economic development and programmaticism are related, it is also widely acknowledged that the latter is not a simple function of the former (Kitschelt, 2007; Kitschelt and Wilkinson, 2007b; Kuo, 2018; Lyne, 2007;Magaloni, Diaz-Cayeros, and Estévez, 2007; Stokes et al., 2013).

43. For an excellent new analysis of party organizations and their important role in American politics, see Heersink (2023). See also, e.g., Abramowitz (2006); Abramowitz and Saunders (2008); Fiorina (2006); Fiorina and Levendusky (2006) on the electorate; Lee (2016a) and Lapinski (2013) on Congress.

44. See, e.g., Cheeseman and Paget (2014); Hicken (2011); Kitschelt and Freeze (n.d.).

45. Kitschelt and Freeze (n.d.); Kitschelt and Wilkinson (2007b).

46. Bustikova and Corduneanu-Huci (2017); Hicken (2011); Keefer (2007); Lizzeri and Persico (2004); Shefter (1994).

47. Clark and Wilson (1961).

48. Quoted in O'Neill (1987, 4).

49. See Schlozman and Rosenfeld (2019) and their forthcoming work on this subject (2004).

50. See, e.g., Katznelson (2005, 2013); Lieberman (2001); Quadagno (1996).

51. Rosenfeld (2018).

52. Hood, Kidd, and Morris (1999); Jacobson (2000); Polsby (2005); J. Roberts and Smith 2012; Rohde (1991), inter alia.

53. Bawn et al. (2012, 571).

54. Books associated with this view have made significant contributions to our understanding of party nominations (Cohen et al., 2008), issue position change (Karol, 2009), polarization (Masket, 2011), and reform (Masket, 2016).

55. Krimmel (2017).

56. Schattschneider (1960, 23).

57. This quotation, found on p. 64 of Schattschneider's *Party Government*, is cited by Cohen et al. (2008, 38).

58. Schattschneider (1960, 34–35).

59. Schattschneider (1948, 18).

60. The two parties and even different actors within each party can be shaped differently by changing political and institutional forces, like media and group networks (McCarty and Schickler, 2018). For more on party asymmetry, see Grossmann and Hopkins (2016).

61. Cheeseman et al. (2014b); Cheeseman and Paget (2014); and Luna, Rosenblatt, and Toro (2014); but see Calvo and Murillo (2019); Kitschelt and Wilkinson (2007b); Kuo (2018).

62. Luna, Rosenblatt, and Toro (2014, 7); Stokes et al. (2013).

63. For excellent discussions of this subject, see Kitschelt and Wilkinson (2007b) and Kuo (2018, 14).

Chapter 2. What Constrains and Facilitates Programmaticism?

1. This observation is made by Hicken (2011) in an *Annual Review of Political Science* piece on clientelism. Examples include Keefer (2006); Cruz and Keefer (2010); and Kitschelt et al. (2010). The quotation earlier in this paragraph is attributable to Cheeseman and Paget (2014, 75).

2. Cheeseman and Paget (2014); Hicken (2011); Kitschelt and Freeze (n.d.); Kitschelt and Kselman (2013).

3. This graph uses variables *b15nwe* and *cosalpo_4nwe* from the DALP data for clientelism and programmatic partisanship, respectively.

4. For the high income group, the adjusted r-squared $= 0.17$, $N = 36$, $t = -2.88$. For the upper middle income group, the relationship is statistically significant at the 0.1 level ($t = -1.76$, $N = 26$). For the lower middle income group, the relationship is negative but imprecisely estimated ($t = -0.84$, $N = 21$). The low income category is sparsely populated ($N = 3$), so we should be cautious in drawing conclusions.

5. Cheeseman and Paget (2014); Kitschelt and Wang (2014).

6. Hicken (2011); Hicken and Nathan (2020); Kitschelt (2007); Mares and Young (2019), inter alia. For a useful explanation of different types of clientelism, see Kitschelt (2007). This piece, along with Hicken (2011), also provides a helpful overview of the range of definitions. Mares and Young (2018, 2019) offer a useful distinction between clientelistic strategies based on inducements and threats and between those based on public versus private resources.

7. See, e.g., Bensel (2004); Erie (1988); James (2006); Shefter (1994); Stokes et al. (2013); and Trounstine (2008).

8. Pierson (2000a, 254). Pierson adapted this framework from classic work by economist W. Brian Arthur (1994), who argued that these four characteristics made a particular technology subject to increasing returns.

9. Hicken and Nathan (2020).

10. Thelen (1999, 392). See also North (1990).

11. Thelen (1999, 400–401).

12. Of course, not all voters were receiving patronage. Not all voters need to; parties need to appeal to just enough voters through patronage to build a winning electoral coalition.

13. Direct exchange may bring classic cash bribes to mind, but it can also include other goods and services. Mares and Young (2016) note that voters relying on machines for jobs or social welfare benefits will still feel tied to them. In fact, Mares and Young argue that the latter are even more powerful than cash bribes, which tend to be relatively small.

14. Lyne (2007, 166).

15. This is consistent with Hicken's assessment, surveying the literature on clientelism in the *Annual Review of Political Science*: "Although there is clearly a strong negative relationship between clientelistic and programmatic exchange, it is not a one-to-one relationship. Clientelism is a common alternative strategy to programmatic exchange, but it is not the only alternative" (2011, 305).

16. See Calvo and Murillo (2004); Kitschelt (2000); Kitschelt and Kselman (2013); Kitschelt and Wilkinson (2007a); Magaloni, Diaz-Cayeros, and Estévez (2007); and Stokes et al. (2013).

17. Kitschelt and Kselman (2013).

18. Banfield and Wilson (1965); Chubb (1982); Hale (2007); Kitschelt and Freeze (n.d.); Medina and Stokes (2007); Stokes et al. (2013), inter alia.

19. Dixit and Londregan (1996).

20. Calvo and Murillo (2004); Chubb (1981); Kitschelt (2000); Lyne (2007); Magaloni, Diaz-Cayeros, and Estévez (2007); Scheiner (2007); Scott (1969); Stokes (2005); Weitz-Shapiro (2012).

21. Magaloni, Diaz-Cayeros, and Estévez (2007); Stokes et al. (2013); Weitz-Shapiro (2012).

22. Lyne (2007); Magaloni, Diaz-Cayeros, and Estévez (2007); Scheiner (2007); Shefter (1994); Wilkinson (2007).

23. H. Aldrich (1979); Lizzeri and Persico (2004); Reid and Kurth (1988).

24. Kitschelt and Wang (2014, 50).

25. Changes in particular sectors of the economy can also influence parties' strategies. While clientelism is classically associated with exchanges between parties and individual citizens, certain industries have also engaged in clientelistic relations. As Kitschelt (2007) notes in a study of four wealthy democracies (Austria, Belgium, Italy, and Japan) that held onto clientelism much longer than one might expect, "The 'clientelistic moment' in the 1940s and 1950s when centrist parties with cross-class alliances in Austria, Belgium, and Italy built or at least expanded business-mediated clientelistic empires occurred at a time when heavy industries, engineering, construction, finance, and infrastructure (telecommunications, transportation) were considered the lead industries pushing economic growth" (311). As other industries (e.g., consumer products, technology, service) developed, the balance of business support for clientelism declined. When industries associated with clientelism began to struggle, needing more and more support from government, this strained the economy and tolerance among the business community and the populace for clientelism.

26. Kitschelt and Kselman (2013).

27. This dynamic was noted by Cox (1987) in a historical study of Britain and by various studies of the contemporary era. For example, Magaloni, Diaz-Cayeros, and Estévez (2007) find support for this relationship in examining variation across different areas of Mexico. And Scheiner (2007) notes that urbanization decreased support for clientelism in Italy and Austria as well as in Japan, this study's focus, and expects support for clientelism to further erode as Japan's urbanization trend continues.

28. Ingle (2008); Stokes et al. (2013); Wang and Kolev (2019).

29. Magaloni, Diaz-Cayeros, and Estévez (2007); Scheiner (2007); Stokes et al. (2013).

30. Mares and Young (2019) also emphasize the importance of brokers in their study of clientelism in Hungary and Romania. They note that many types of actors can serve as brokers, including "employees of local municipalities, and economic brokers, such as employers, or moneylenders, or tenant farmers" (6).

31. Stokes et al. (2013, 24).

32. Stokes et al. (2013, 184).

33. See also Bensel (2004).

34. Stokes et al. (2013, 184).

35. Kitschelt (2007); Müller (2007); Scheiner (2007); Stokes et al. (2013).

36. Kuo (2018).

37. Kitschelt and Wilkinson (2007b); Lyne (2007); Stokes et al. (2013), inter alia. Scholars have also have noted a nonlinear relationship between modernization and clientelism (Hale, 2007; Kitschelt and Kselman, 2013; Magaloni, Diaz-Cayeros, and Estévez, 2007; Wilkinson, 2007; but see Stokes et al. [2013] and Weitz-Shapiro[2014]), though this is less relevant to my study because the same is not true of programmaticism—its relationship to development is linear (Kitschelt and Kselman, 2013).

38. Bustikova and Corduneanu-Huci (2017); Hicken (2011); Keefer (2007); Kuo (2018); Lizzeri and Persico (2004); Lyne (2007); Nathan (2019).

39. Chubb (1982); Keefer and Vlaicu (2007); Shefter (1977); Tarrow (1967).

40. Cruz and Keefer (2015).

41. Kitschelt and Kselman (2013); Kitschelt and Wang (2014). This is similar to the curvilinear relationship between economic development and clientelism, and the two are almost certainly related.

42. Bustikova and Corduneanu-Huci (2017); Hicken (2011); Kuo (2018).

43. Challenging Shefter's account, Stokes et al. (2013, 208) argue, "The coalition that developed against patronage and electoral bribery in Britain and the United States was comprised not of bureaucrats and the educated middle classes who favored meritocracy so much as between reformists and party leaders, the latter chafing under their own machines. Their motivation was not to preserve the civil service for their elite-educated sons but to circumvent unreliable brokers."

44. Persson, Tabellini, and Trebbi (2003); Scheiner (2007); Stigler (1972).

45. More specifically, he notes: "Three of the four affluent clientelistic democracies went through an era of fascist rule in the twentieth century after a belated start of industrialization, typically with assistance from an illiberal authoritarian regime," and the fourth (Belgium) had a "powerful fascist movement, but no fascist regime" (305–6).

46. Kitschelt (2007, 312).

47. Kitschelt (2007, 306).

48. Scheiner (2007, 277).

49. These are not the only factors that matter. Hale (2007) also finds that higher levels of clientelism are found in regions of the Russian Federation "when state control over the economy is high, and when ethnocultural networks have been politicized by the state" (250).

50. Baland and Robinson (2008); Frye, Reuter and Szakonyi (2019); Mares (2015).

51. Hicken and Nathan (2020, 286).

52. Voters receiving public service jobs in exchange for political support may continue to support the incumbent because their job security and working conditions depend on reelection (Oliveros, 2021).

53. Hicken and Nathan (2020, 287) nod to the literature on this point: "Where results are publicly reported at fine-grained resolutions, such as for individual polling stations, politicians may still be able to reasonably infer the approximate share of clientelism exchanges that were reciprocated even without investing any resources in tracking individual voters (Gingerich and Medina, 2013; Kitschelt and Wilkinson, 2007a; Medina and Stokes, 2007)."

54. Chauchard (2018); Guardado and Wantchekon (2018); Hicken and Nathan (2020); Muhtadi (2019).

55. See Kingdon (1984).

56. Orren and Skowronek (2004, 116). See also Mahoney and Thelen (2010); and Sheingate (2014).

57. Orren and Skowronek (2004, 113, 108).

58. This is not to say that programmaticism is based only in opposing stances. Parties can attempt to become more competitive by moving closer to their opposition on a particular issue, when doing so would gain favor with voters. Nonetheless, for voters to choose between parties based on issues, there must be some meaningful differences.

59. See also Kennedy (2009); Leuchtenburg (1963).

60. Lee (2016b).

61. Baylor (2017); Oldfield (1996).

62. Of course, institutions do not always play a facilitating role; it's well known that they can inhibit changes in politics, as well as in other areas of life (Pierson, 2000a, inter alia).

63. King and Smith (2005). Other political institutions can help party leaders pay the informational costs associated with position development. Kitschelt and Wang (2014) point to legislative organization as a factor that may facilitate programmaticism. While this remains to be evaluated sufficiently, they argue, it stands to reason that a committee system or other similar institution can help party leaders develop policy expertise, which in turn could support the rise of programmaticism. But, of course, they could simply use this expertise to make short-term policy decisions without committing to particular positions for the party. Thus, I argue, committees may be helpful, but they are unlikely to be sufficient for the growth of programmaticism.

64. Cheeseman and Paget (2014, 80). See also Kitschelt et al. (2010).

65. Cheeseman et al. (2014b, III).

66. Eder, Jenny, and Müller (2017).

67. King and Smith (2005, 75).

68. More specifically, King and Smith (2005, 78) argue that racial orders "exercise governing power in ways that predictably shape people's statuses, resources, and opportunities by their placement in 'racial' categories."

69. King and Smith (2005, 75).

70. See, e.g., Bates (1974); Burgess et al. (2015); Chabal and Daloz (1999); Chandra (2004, 2007); Erie (1988); Hale (2007); Ichino and Nathan (2013); Posner (2005); Post (1963); Van De Walle (2007); and Wantchekon (2003).

71. Baldwin (2013); Habyarimana et al. (2007); Koter (2013); Larson and Lewis (2017); Miguel and Gugerty (2005); Nathan (2016); and Wang and Kolev (2019).

72. Wang and Kolev (2019).

73. Alesina and Glaeser (2004); Alesina, Baqir, and Easterly (1999); Baldwin and Huber (2010); Habyarimana et al. (2007); Luttmer (2001); Miguel and Gugerty (2005); Wang and Kolev (2019); Yakter (2019).

74. Wang and Kolev (2019). See also Morgan and Kelly (2017).

75. King and Smith (2005).

76. Frymer (2017); Katznelson (2005); Lieberman (2001); Mettler (1998); Poole (2006); Quadagno (1996); Ward (2005).

77. Key (1949), inter alia. Wang and Kolev (2019) find that political inequality is not associated with clientelism, but their study included eighty nations, which do not all necessarily have

the same degree of racial conflict as the United States. Moreover, the degree of political oppression caused by Jim Crow laws also led to and reinforced economic inequality between Blacks and whites.

78. Rosenfeld (2018).

79. Hood, Kidd, and Morris (1999); Jacobson (2000); Polsby (2005); J. Roberts and Smith (2012); Rohde (1991), inter alia.

80. As noted earlier in the book, though polarization and programmaticicsm are distinct, the latter does contribute to the former. Thus, explanations for programmaticism are relevant to understanding polarization.

81. Medina and Stokes (2007, 82).

82. Calvo and Murillo (2019); Medina and Stokes (2007); Wilkinson (2007), inter alia.

83. Gerring (1998).

84. For example, writing in the 1990s, Shefter argues, "Patronage continues to this day to play an important role in the party politics of most states of the Northeast and lower Midwest, including those parties (e.g., the Republican parties in Pennsylvania, Ohio, and New York) that draw much of their support from the middle classes" (1994, 24).

85. For details on the impact of the white supremacist order on New Deal program design, see, e.g., Katznelson (2005, 2013) and Lieberman (2001).

Chapter 3. The Dance of Clientelism and Programmaticism

1. See, e.g., Bensel (2004); Erie (1988); James (2006); Kuo (2018); Milkis (1993); Shefter (1994); Stokes et al. (2013); and Trounstine (2008).

2. The positive association between modernization and prorammaticism is discussed at length in chapter 2.

3. Thelen (1999, 388).

4. Carpenter (2001); Schickler (2001); Sheingate (2003, 2014).

5. Orren and Skowronek (2004, 108).

6. Thelen (1999, 370), citing Levi (1999).

7. See, e.g., classic work by Luebbert (1991) and Collier and Collier (1991), as well as more recent models like Bloch Rubin (2017) and Bateman, Katznelson, and Lapinski (2018), among many others.

8. Bensel (2004); Kuo (2018).

9. Kuo (2018), citing Butler (2000). The term "patriot king" appears in Hofstadter's classic (1969) analysis of the party system.

10. Hofstadter (1969); Shefter (1994).

11. R. M. Smith (1993).

12. Milkis (1993, 75).

13. Shefter (1994). This elite grasp on political power was based on "elite networks of the notables and the autonomous craft organizations of the mechanics" (Shefter, 1994, 70). With mass mobilization, Jacksonians were able to overpower these groups.

14. Shefter (1994, 71) notes: "The Jacksonians were free to use bureaucratic appointments as a reward for party service to the extent that they wanted the state to perform only a limited range of functions—chiefly, delivering the mails, distributing public lands, collecting tariff revenues

and driving the Indians further west—and these did not require most civil servants to have skills and training beyond those that ordinary citizens possessed, as President Jackson himself observed in his first inaugural address."

15. Folke, Hirano, and Snyder (2011); Key (1964); Kuo (2018); Van Riper (1958); Shefter (1994). Key (1964) explains this principle succinctly: "The patronage system may be considered, too, as a method of financing party activity. The operation of a party organization requires the services of many men and women. . . . Though much of this work is performed by unpaid volunteers, their efforts are not adequate. Indirectly, a considerable part of party expense is met by the public treasury, and the chief means of channeling public funds to party support is through the appointment of party workers to public office." Quoted in Folke, Hirano, and Snyder (2011, 567).

16. Kuo (2018); Shefter (1994).

17. James (2006, 41).

18. Kuo (2018); Van Riper (1958).

19. Kuo (2018).

20. Kuo (2018, 53) expands on this idea of clientelism as a means of economic development in a later passage:

> Politicians in the nineteenth-century United States combined clientelistic campaign strategies with distributive legislative policies—those that targeted resources to discrete populations—not only as a way to recruit and to reward voters, but also as a broader policy of economic development. Expansion of the postal service, for example, not only provided a way to increase the delivery of goods, but also provided a politically expedient way to reward voters (with positions in the postal service) and districts (with new post offices). Similarly, providing federal grants to canal corporations fostered both trade and development while also promoting local partisan interests. By using distributive policies and patronage, clientelism became "a strategy for the acquisition, maintenance, and aggrandizement of political power" (Piattoni 2001, 2).

Underscoring the low level of programmaticism at this time, scholars have noted that these distributive policies tended not to be principle driven. On this point, Kuo (2018) points to Gutchen (1961), Lowi (1972), and McCormick (1966).

21. Skowronek (1982, 48).

22. Milkis (1993, 6).

23. Engs (2002); James (2006); Keller (1977); Shefter (1994). This is largely attributable to the Civil War and Lincoln's presidency. Lincoln replaced mass numbers of Democratic civil service workers with Republican appointees, guaranteeing loyalty and a clear Republican presence in national government, which in turn fortified the party. As Engs (2002, 64) notes, "It was the biggest political purge in the nation's history to that time, but well suited to providing roots for a party that was less than seven years old in 1861." This went on to become a norm of entrenching Republican influence, thus consolidating the party. Thanks to Annie Iezzi for her assistance in researching and summarizing this phenomenon.

24. James (2006, 39).

25. Kuo (2018).

26. James (2006). The antebellum system was simple in the sense that it served primarily as a way to recruit workers. Scott C. James (2006, 59) notes, "Very little evidence has been found

that the president's appointment power was used to enhance organizational efficiency or punish cadre disloyalty." This changed in the postbellum period.

27. James (2006, 41).

28. For more on factional machines, see Brown and Halaby (1987).

29. Kuo (2018, 4). For this observation, Kuo cites James (2006) and Summers (1987).

30. Wolfinger (1972, 379, 380).

31. Their sample included cities with regional diversity. For details, see their footnote 3.

32. Skowronek (1982, 46).

33. Other prominent scholars have concurred with this assessment, noting for example that the United States "had a swift and rather rapid apparatus (partisan rotation in office) for staffing the agencies of government" (Carpenter, 2003, 468).

34. Skocpol (1992).

35. Cited in Skowronek (1982, 49).

36. Kuo (2018); Skowronek (1982).

37. As Skowronek (1982, 49) notes, "In 1871, federal expenditures amounted to a mere $292 million; 1891 was the year of the 'billion-dollar Congress.'"

38. Skowronek (1982, 4; see also 13).

39. Schickler (2001).

40. Makemson (2004); Thomas (2001). The Mugwumps and associated groups were also sometimes called Liberals, Independents, or other names (e.g., Young Scratchers) throughout their history. The "dominant factions" of the party at the time were known as the Stalwarts and Half Breeds (Shefter, 1994, 73).

41. Shefter (1994, 73).

42. *Puck* originated in the Jacksonian era but later became known as a Mugwump publication.

43. Morone (2004).

44. Blodgett (1962).

45. Skowronek (1982, inter alia).

46. Shefter (1994, 73).

47. Makemson (2004, 180).

48. Blodgett (1980); McFarland (1963).

49. Blodgett (1980, 882). See also Blodgett (1962).

50. Blodgett (1962, 629). See also Blodgett (1980). The notion of Mugwumps as "partyless" men also comes up in a contemporaneous article, "The Opportunity of the Mugwump," published in the *Sewanee Review*, November 1894, 3(1): 1–9.

51. Shefter (1994, 74). See also Blodgett (1962, 1980); X.Y.Z. (1894).

52. Shefter (1994, 74).

53. Feinstein (1975).

54. Blodgett (1962).

55. Blodgett (1980, 881).

56. These quotations appear in Blodgett (1980, 883).

57. Blodgett (1980, 883). See also Makemson (2004).

58. Blodgett (1980, 614).

59. For a rich history of the struggle to pass the Pendleton Act, see Skowronek (1982, chapter 3). At the end of the nineteenth century, there was also an attempt to limit clientelism through campaign finance legislation. This began with an 1890 law in New York and spread to seventeen other states over the next decade. These laws were not very effective, however, as they "applied only to candidates and not to political committees" (Stokes et al., 2013, 240).

60. As Skowronek (1982, 49) notes, "In 1981, the civilian payroll of the federal government supported a mere 53,000 employees; by 1901, it had increased fivefold to 256,000."

61. Skowronek (1982, 48–49); Shefter (1994, 74). For more detail on the ratio of patronage to merit appointments during this time, see Skowronek (1982, 69).

62. Skowronek (1982, 68).

63. Skowronek (1982, 165).

64. Sundquist (1983, 170).

65. Shefter (1994, 78).

66. Sundquist (1983).

67. Skowronek (1982, 44).

68. Skowronek (1982, 286).

69. Skowronek (1982, 45). As Skowronek (1982, 44–45) argues, "These reformers perceived the structural problems of the American state in the industrial age. They cultivated an understanding of the alternative institutional designs found in the great states of Europe. They developed specific plans for a bureaucratic reconstruction of governmental operations, and they were ready to assume control of the new institutions they advocated. In a period in which the established mode of governmental operations was being stretched to the limits of its capacities to govern effectively, the new professionals were the dynamic and creative force on the side of building new systems of control."

70. Kuo (2018, 3).

71. Stokes et al. (2013).

72. Citing Key, Stokes et al. (2013, 229) note: "In southern states, where populations remained more rural and poverty rates high, vote buying remained endemic well into the twentieth century. This was the case even though the hegemony of the Democratic Party and the disenfranchisement of blacks reduced the need and hence willingness of candidates to pay for votes. However, in places where elections were competitive, vote buying persisted well into the twentieth century. Poll taxes afforded opportunities for buying votes." The persistence of vote buying—the most rudimentary and arguably egregious form of clientelism—in a region with high levels of poverty and low levels of urbanization lends credence to the negative association between clientelism and modernization discussed in chapter 2.

73. Cox and Kousser (1981).

74. These oft-cited examples come from a seminal work on vote buying by Richard Bensel (2004, ix).

75. Stokes et al. (2013, 228).

76. As Shefter (1994, 33) notes, "the party that first brings a social group into the political system retains a privileged hold upon the members of that group for decades, and even generations, thereafter." See also Lipset and Rokkan (1967).

77. Folke, Hirano, and Snyder (2011); Kuo (2018).

78. Skowronek (1982).

79. Shefter (1994).

80. Shefter (1994, 80).

81. Sundquist (1983, 170).

82. Kuo (2018).

83. Skowronek (1982, 286).

84. Skowronek (1982, 211).

85. Mayhew (1986); Stokes et al. (2013).

86. Kuo (2018); Stokes et al. (2013).

87. This observation comes from Kuo (2018, 46, citing Martis 1989).

88. See Kuo (2018, 46) for a summary of the use of contested elections as a measure of electoral irregularities in other countries.

89. See Kuo (2018, figure 2.1, 48). Looking at contested elections as a proportion of all House seats from 1860 to 1940, she finds they fell from a high of a little over 12 percent during Reconstruction to less than 1 percent by 1940. There are a few spikes, but the overall trend clearly goes in a downward direction over this period. See Kuo (2018, figure 2.2, 50).

90. Jenkins (2004).

91. Kuo (2018, 54).

92. Adler and Wilkerson (2020).

93. Kuo (2018, 2).

94. Kuo (2018, 90).

95. Kuo (2018).

96. Lee (2016b); Shefter (1994).

97. Milkis (1993).

98. Stokes et al. (2013, 238).

99. Skowronek (1982, 196). For more detail on Wilson and examples of ways in which other presidents, like Theodore Roosevelt and William Howard Taft, were constrained by the existing system, see Skowronek (1982, especially part 3). In summary, he argues, "None of the various combinations of party power and state-building strategy encountered in these years resolved the developmental contradiction between American party structure and the forging of a bureaucratic mode of operations for the national government. Roosevelt had tried to circumvent his party, Taft had tried to use his party, Wilson had tried to lead his party; but none of them could change the provincial coalition form of party in America, and each of them ultimately found the demand for control over national administration incompatible with party government" (211).

100. On the demand for dictatorial executive power during FDR's administration, see Katznelson (2013).

101. An earlier public jobs program also became a tool for machines. Citing Caro (1974), who is quoted in Erie (1988), Stokes et al. (2013, 229) point to the following egregious example: "New York's Tammany Hall machine required party affiliation for applicants for the Civil Works Administration (CWA), a 1933–1934 employment relief program. One Tammany employee boasted, 'This is how we make Democrats.'"

102. Stokes et al. (2013, 229).

103. Erie (1988); Stokes et al. (2013); Wallis (1974); Wright (1974).

104. Kuo (2018, 59).

105. Erie (1988).

106. Erie (1988, 134), quoted in Stokes et al. (2013, 229).

107. Sundquist (1983).

108. Shefter (1994).

109. Shefter (1994); Wilson (1962).

110. Shefter (1994, 84).

111. Shefter (1994, 84).

112. Folke, Hirano, and Snyder (2011, 569).

113. Folke, Hirano, and Snyder (2011); Shefter (1994). Before the 1930s, only nine states enacted civil service reforms, and some of those were weakened shortly after passage. Seven states passed reforms in the 1930s, another seven passed them in the 1940s, and the following two decades brought passage in eight and twelve additional states, respectively.

114. Folke, Hirano, and Snyder (2011, 569) note: "Specifically, in 1939 an amendment to the Social Security Act required states to enact merit-based personnel systems for state and local government employees working in welfare, health, and unemployment compensation agencies as a condition for receiving federal grants-in-aid. A few states enacted more sweeping reforms around this time, but most did not."

115. Shefter (1994, 83).

116. Milkis (1993, 11).

117. TPOs subsume the concept of machines but are not reducible to them. A TPO is "any organization at the level of county, city, city ward, township, or other local jurisdiction" that is largely autonomous, durable, hierarchical, concerned with nomination of candidates to public office, and operated primarily through material incentives. A machine is "a TPO in control of a city or county government" (Mayhew, 1986, 21). All local machines are TPOs, but not all TPOs are machines. Even those that are not, however, should be expected to depress programmaticism through the same mechanism as machines. Thus, their inclusion should not distort the analysis in this chapter.

118. Erie (1988); Stokes et al. (2013). See also Banfield and Wilson (1965).

119. Examining state-level data from 1885 to 1995, Folke, Hirano, and Snyder (2011) show that patronage was electorally effective for state legislatures and state executive office. The effect is large, especially for entrenched parties (those that have controlled the legislature for a long time).

120. Erie (1988).

121. Folke, Hirano, and Snyder (2011); Klingner (2006).

122. Hilton (2019, 572–73).

123. Hilton (2016); Ignazi (1996).

124. Hall (2003); Hilton (2016).

125. Hilton (2016, 143).

126. Shefter (1994).

127. As Shefter (1994, 87) notes, "The presidential task forces that drafted New Frontier and Great Society legislation argued that municipal bureaucracies did not command the resources, the talent, or the initiative that was necessary to solve the 'urban crisis,'" at the forefront of the federal agenda in the 1960s.

128. Shefter (1994, 87).

129. Hilton (2016).

130. For more on the McGovern-Fraser Commission, see Cohen et al. (2008, chapter 6); Hershey (2017, chapter 10); and Center (1974).

131. Hilton (2016, 149).

132. See Layman, Carsey, and Horowitz (2006).

133. Of course, this trend was not universal. There were some stragglers (e.g., Nassau County, NY; Newark, NJ; San Antonio, TX). The discussion section at the end of the chapter addresses this issue.

134. Stokes et al. (2013, 232) argue that American clientelism's "final demise came with reform mayors in the 1950s in Philadelphia, Jersey City, and Boston; the early 1960s in New York; the mid-1970s in Chicago; and later still in Albany and Baltimore." This is essentially consistent with observations cited above.

135. Shefter (1994, 89).

136. Kuo (2018, 7) argues, "The relative weakness of party organization and relative strength of business organizations gave economic interest a powerful voice in the state-building process. While parties successfully reduced patronage and clientelism, they created opportunities for new forms of clientelistic politics through regulatory and rule-making institutions."

137. Stokes et al. (2013, 230).

138. Stokes et al. (2013, 230). See also Bickers and Stein (2000); and Levitt and Snyder (1995). Stokes et al. (2013, 230) elaborate:

> Research into distributive politics in contemporary United States discerns programmatic politics, as when a change of partisan control of congress changes spending patterns in ways predictable from the parties' ideologies; pork barrel politics, as when spending on sports and recreation facilities rises with the electoral vulnerability of the assemblyman or woman, and nonconditional benefits to individuals, as when spending on food stamps rises with the incumbent party's vote share in a congressional district. But no clientelism.

They later note that "Even in instances of nonprogrammatic distributive politics, such as the FEMA and (perhaps) Faith Based Initiative examples discussed earlier [in the book], the parties in power lack the capacity of the machines of old to hold voters to account" (232).

139. Daniel J. Hopkins, Daniel J. Coffey, Daniel J. Galvin, Gerald Gamm, John Henderson, Joel W. Paddock, and Eric Schickler, 2022, "Select American State Party Platforms, 1846-2017," Harvard Dataverse, V1. https://doi.org/10.7910/DVN/KNOSHL.

140. Daniel J. Coffey, 2019. "State Party Platform Project." http://statepartyplatforms.org, accessed June 27, 2023.

141. McCarty, Poole, and Rosenthal (2006).

142. A simpler version of this analysis with polarization as a dependent variable originally appeared in Krimmel (2013). McCarty (2016) extends the analysis, analyzing multiple years and adding some additional control variables. Here, I add measures of modernization. I examine only one year because McCarty shows that the negative relationship between TPO scores and polarization holds in a model that pools years for which state-level polarization data were available at the time (1996–2008).

143. Boris Shor and Nolan McCarty, 2012, "Replication Data for: Ideological Mapping of American Legislatures," Harvard Dataverse, V2, https://doi.org/10.7910/DVN/RCMM6E.

144. Skowronek (1982).

145. Shefter (1994); Stokes et al. (2013).

146. Stokes et al. (2013).

147. Stokes et al. (2013); Wolfinger (1972, inter alia).

Chapter 4. National Party Institutions and Programmaticism, 1856–1950

1. For a discussion of the dramatic drop in Democratic platform length between 1984 and 1988, see chapter 5.

2. Kevin McDermott, "National Democrats Convene in St. Louis to Draft Party Platform," *St. Louis Post-Dispatch*, June 25, 2016.

3. These speeches were identified through a research assistant's review of the convention transcripts. Many thanks to Claudia Chung for exemplary research assistance.

4. These archival documents were collected from several presidential libraries.

5. Slavery was also an issue on which Republicans had trouble putting forth a strong, precise course of action. While they were clearly opposed to southern "slave power," they could not agree on a specific antislavery platform (Foner, 1970). Petitions, an alternative form of political advocacy, were an important force in persuading Abraham Lincoln on this issue (Carpenter, 2021).

6. See speeches by John Thurston, temporary chairman of the convention, and H. B. Jones, chairman of the National Committee, *Official Proceedings of the 1888 Republican National Convention*, Chicago, Illinois, June 19–23 and 25. All RNC proceedings are from the Library of Congress collection Electing the President: Proceedings of the Republican National Conventions, 1856–1988.

7. *Proceedings of the 1860 Democratic National Convention*, Charleston, April 24, 1860, 16. All DNC proceedings are from the Library of Congress collection Electing the President: Proceedings of the Democratic National Conventions, 1832–1988.

8. Lee (2016b).

9. *Proceedings of the First Three Republican National Conventions of 1856, 1860, and 1864*, May 16, 1860, 92.

10. *Proceedings of the First Three Republican National Conventions*, 92. The Thayer and Greeley quotes are found on pp. 93 and 94, respectively.

11. Greeley represented Oregon at the convention but had previously represented New York's 6th District in Congress.

12. *Proceedings of the National Union Convention*, June 7, 1864, 58; also appears in *Proceedings of the First Three Republican National Conventions*, 227.

13. The earliest example I found was a set of resolutions written by the National Council of the Union League of America in 1868. The resolutions were referred to the Committee on Resolutions but then also read to the floor while members were waiting for the committee to finish its work. Being read into the record didn't mean that they were adopted by the convention, just that the delegates heard the resolutions.

14. For example, there was an argument in 1884 about whether it was appropriate to read a statement from the Woman's Christian Temperance Union on the floor or whether it should just be referred to the Committee on Resolutions. They ended up reading it and then referring it to the committee.

15. The minority report's recommendation was as follows: "The Republican party authorizes the use of both gold and silver as equal standard money, and pledges its power to secure the free and unlimited coinage of gold and silver at our mints at the ratio of sixteen parts of silver to one of gold." *Official Proceedings of the Eleventh Republican National Convention*, June 18, 1896, 86.

16. The delegates were Henry Teller of Colorado, F. T. DuBois of Idaho, Frank Cannon of Utah, Charles Hartman of Montana, R. F. Pettigrew of South Dakota, and A. C. Cleveland of Nevada.

17. *Official Proceedings of the Eleventh Republican National Convention*, June 18, 1896, 101.

18. *Official Proceedings of the Democratic National Convention*, August 29, 1864, 26.

19. *Official Proceedings of the National Democratic Convention*, July 10, 1872, 45.

20. *Official Proceedings of the National Democratic Convention*, June 2, 1892, 89.

21. Transcript of the Meeting of the Democratic National Committee, January 16, 1896.

22. *Official Proceedings of the Democratic National Convention*, July 9, 1896, 196.

23. From approximately 1800 to 1933, the federal government's main functions involved administrative matters, subsidies, tariffs, public lands, patents, and currency. Overall, the federal government had relatively few responsibilities, while "the states did most of the fundamental governing, and the states were in particular responsible for those aspects of government that require directly coercive techniques," like regulation (Lowi, 1990, 194).

24. Cotter and Bibby (1980, 3–4).

25. *Proceedings of the Democratic National Committee*, March 5, 1931; appendix to *Official Report of the Proceedings of the Democratic National Convention*, 1932, 499. See also Cotter and Bibby (1980, 4).

26. *Proceedings of the Democratic National Committee*, March 5, 1931, 400; "Democrats Will Open Headquarters in City," *Washington Post*, May 1, 1929.

27. *Proceedings of the Democratic National Committee*, March 5, 1931, 424.

28. *Proceedings of the Democratic National Committee*, March 5, 1931, 411.

29. See, e.g., Key (1949).

30. APSA Committee on Political Parties (1950); Overacker (1941).

31. Asked, "Why is it that the Postmaster General's job has always been the national chairman?," Farley answered, "Oh, I don't know. It's been true since before Jackson's time, I guess." The interviewer followed up: "I suppose it's because of patronage." Farley responded, "I imagine so—and because of the contacts that go with it." James A. Farley, oral history interview, May 10, 1957, Columbia University, New York, 37.

32. Farley oral history, 8.

33. Cotter and Bibby (1980, 7).

34. Samuel C. Brightman, oral history interview, December 7–8, 1966, Harry S. Truman Presidential Library and Museum, Independence, MO, 31.

35. APSA (1950, 48), quoting *Proceedings of the Democratic National Committee*, 1919.

36. Neale Roach, oral history interview, January 21 and October 2, 1969, Truman Library, 2; see also Cotter and Bibby (1980, 5).

37. Roach oral history, 2–3

38. Roach oral history.

39. The RNC had operating expenses of $60,500 in 1933, $216,676 in 1934, and $159,977 in 1935 (Overacker, 1937, 475).

40. According to Overacker (1937), the waning of activity after the 1940 election was largely a consequence of the Hatch Act, which limited parties' expenditures per year, spurring a decentralization of party spending.

41. Thomson (1939, 307).

42. Speech of Joseph Robinson, permanent chairman of the Democratic Convention, 1936, *Official Report of the Proceedings of the Democratic National Convention*, June 23–27, 1936.

43. Quotation comes from Rep. Martin, *Official Report of the Proceedings of the Twenty-Second Republican National Convention*, June 26, 1940, 96.

44. *Official Proceedings of the Republican National Convention*, 1932, 86; *Official Proceedings of the Republican National Convention*, 1948, 43.

45. *Proceedings of the Democratic National Committee*, February 26, 1919, appendix to *Proceedings of the 1920 Democratic National Convention*, 511.

46. Thomson (1939, 308).

47. Thomson (1939, 309).

48. Thomson (1939, 311–12).

49. John D. M. Hamilton, oral history interview, February 11, and May 31, 1967, Herbert Hoover Presidential Library, West Branch, IA, 22.

50. Hamilton oral history, 23

51. Hamilton oral history, 25–26. Bridges (1939, 299–300) analyzes the situation similarly, arguing that there was a disconnect between Republicans in Congress, who "were cool to the idea," and the "rank and file," who "showed a great deal of interest in the Hoover proposal."

52. Bridges (1939, 300).

53. Hamilton oral history, 25.

54. Hamilton oral history, 27. News articles also depict the Glenn Frank Committee as a compromise. See, e.g., "GOP Program Heads Meet with Frank," *Hartford Courant*, May 12, 1938, 11; and "Program Goes to Republicans Late in June," *New York Herald Tribune*, May 13, 1939, 3.

55. Bridges (1939, 299).

56. Bridges (1939, 300).

57. Cleaves A. Jones, "British Hear G.O.P. Aims," *Los Angeles Times*, March 2, 1938, 2.

58. "Frank Urges Faith in Free Enterprise," *New York Times*, January 13, 1938, 1.

59. "Frank's Board Reaching Out to Tap Opinion," *New York Herald Tribune*, July 17, 1938.

60. Cleaves A. Jones, "Glenn Frank Maps G.O.P. Campaign," *Los Angeles Times*, March 1, 1938.

61. Geoffrey Parsons, Jr. "'Government By Hunch' Hit in Program of Republicans," *New York Herald Tribune*, March 1, 1938.

62. Bridges (1939, 299).

63. Bridges (1939, 305).

64. "Frank to Query Rank and File on Party Issues," *New York Herald Tribune*, May 13, 1938.

65. S. J. Woolf, "Dr. Frank Scans America's Political Horizons," *New York Times*, May 15, 1938.

66. "Program Report Given Republicans," *New York Times*, November 30, 1938.

67. Bridges (1939, 301).

68. "Frank is Loath to 'Draft 1940 Platform in '38,'" *New York Herald Tribune*, July 31, 1938.

69. Bridges (1939, 303).

70. Bridges (1939, 304).

71. "Program Goes to Republicans Late in June."

72. "Republicans Offer Basis for Platform to Redeem Nation from New Deal," *New York Herald Tribune*, February 19, 1940, 1.

73. Dewey made 134 appearances.

74. Speech reprinted in Goldzwig (2008).

75. John E. Barriere, oral history interview, December 20, 1966, Truman Library, 15–16.

76. Dr. Johannes Hoeber, oral history interview, September 13, 1966, Truman Library.

77. Kenneth M. Birkhead, oral history interview, July 7, 1966, Truman Library, 28.

78. William L. Batt Jr., oral history interview, July 26–27, 1966, Truman Library; Goldzwig (2008).

79. Birkhead oral history, 36.

80. Batt oral history, 4.

81. To put this $80,000 figure in context, the following are a few examples of DNC expenditures for 1944: $44,454.04 for the chairman's office, $59,364.39 for the Women's Division, and $757,344.09 for radio. Their total expenditures in 1944 amounted to $1,864,866.22 (Overacker, 1945). To my knowledge, detailed information on budget and expenditures is not available for 1948, but these figures from 1944 should nonetheless help contextualize the $80,000 allocated for the Research Division in 1948.

82. Batt oral history, 7.

83. Hoeber oral history, 17.

84. Batt oral history. For examples of Files on the Facts documents, see folder Research Division—Fact Sheets, 1948–1952, box 27, David Lloyd Papers, Truman Library.

85. Batt oral history, 62.

86. Brightman oral history, 108.

87. Hoeber oral history; Anthony Leviero, "Something New Is Added at the White House," *New York Times*, August 1, 1948, E3.

88. Batt was on the National Board and was chairman in Philadelphia for both organizations.

89. Birkhead oral history, 27.

90. Birkhead oral history, 44.

91. Hoeber oral history.

92. Birkhead oral history, 24.

93. Hoeber oral history, 13–14. Birkhead also uses the term "interlopers" in his oral history to describe their reception by the rest of the DNC. Barriere, another member of the Research Division, expresses a similar impression in his oral history.

94. Birkhead oral history, 37–38.

95. Birkhead oral history, 39.

96. Hoeber oral history, 10, 59.

97. Hoeber oral history, 46.

98. For example, concern was expressed by David Lloyd, who went from his position in the Research Division to become an administrative assistant to the president. From that position, he tried along with a few others to keep this effort going in service of the 1950 campaign.

99. Brightman oral history; Heersink and Peterson (2017); R. N. Smith (1982).

100. APSA Committee on Political Parties (1950, 81).

101. APSA Committee on Political Parties (1950, 29).

102. APSA Committee on Political Parties (1950, 38).

103. Casey (1944), quoted in APSA Committee on Political Parties (1950, 48–49).

104. *Official Report of the Proceedings of the Fourteenth Republican National Convention*, June 18, 1908, 125.

105. In 1912, the Wisconsin delegate who presented the minority report was Walter C. Owen. In 1916 and 1920, it was Edwin J. Gross.

106. *Official Proceedings of the Eighteenth Republican National Convention*, June 11, 1924, 118.

107. *Official Report of the Proceedings of the Twentieth Republican National Convention*, June 15, 1932, 126.

108. *Official Report of the Proceedings of the Twenty-Second Republican National Convention*, June 26, 1940, 135.

109. The Committee on Resolutions ended up adopting an antiwar plank.

110. *Official Proceedings of the Twenty-Fourth Republican National Convention*, June 23, 1948, 186–87.

111. *Proceedings of the Democratic National Convention*, 1904, 239.

112. *Proceedings of the Democratic National Convention*, 1908, 159.

113. An amendment on presidential term limits was introduced in 1940, and an amendment suggesting an international air force was introduced in 1944. Both were rejected by voice vote.

114. *Official Report of the Proceedings of the Democratic National Convention*, June 28, 1928, 203.

115. *Proceedings of the Democratic National Convention*, 1928, 183.

116. Keyserling notes that even though he was no longer working for Wagner directly after 1937, he "was the one that [Wagner] always called back on the important jobs, including his platform writing and also the legislation." Leon H. Keyserling, oral history interview, May 3, 1971, Truman Library, 38.

117. Keyserling oral history, 35.

118. Keyserling oral history, 35–36.

119. This section benefited especially from the outstanding research assistance of Annie Iezzi.

120. Galvin (see, e.g., 2010); Klinkner (1994).

121. For a rich analysis of the domestic impact of the fall of democracies abroad, see Katznelson (2013).

122. Thomson (1939, 312).

Chapter 5. National Party Institutions and Programmaticism, 1950–2020

1. "U.S. Its 'Precinct,'" *Kansas City Star*, January 29, 1950, newspaper clipping, folder SHAKC, box 155, Democratic National Committee Files, Truman Library.

2. Galvin (2010); Klinkner (1994). See also Cotter and Bibby (1980); Galvin (2014); Heersink (2023).

3. See the online appendix for graphs. In new work, Boris Heersink (2023) uses carefully coded *New York Times* articles to show how RNC and DNC activities (and attention thereto) have changed over time. The trend is not simple or smooth, but there are more articles about RNC/DNC activities at the end of the period under study (2016) than at the beginning (1913).

4. See, e.g., Boris Heersink and Jeffrey A. Jenkins, "Who Can Get Trump to Tone It Down? Reince Priebus Is Trying," *Washington Post*, July 13, 2015.

5. Schlozman and Rosenfeld (n.d.).

6. APSA (1950, 40), citing Merriam 1921; Merriam and Gosnell 1949.

7. APSA (1950, 40), citing Merriam 1921; Merriam and Gosnell 1949.

8. Press release, April 23, 1950, folder NDCC, box 211, Democratic National Committee Files, Truman Library.

9. Press release, January 26, 1952; folder Press Releases—Democratic National Committee (8/22/51 to 2/4/52) (folder 6), box 213, Democratic National Committee Files, Truman Library.

10. Press release, January 3, 1952, folder Press Releases—Democratic National Committee (8/22/51 to 2/4/52) (folder 6), box 213, Democratic National Committee Files, Truman Library.

11. This figure comes from an August 20, 1952, executive session of the Democratic National Committee and refers to the prior six months. Transcript, Proceedings, Executive Committee, Democratic National Committee, August 20, 1952, folder Transcript, Executive Committee Meeting, August 20, 1952, box 222, Democratic National Committee Records, Truman Library. The Research Division accounted for $52,345 of $101,254 in new expenses. The second highest was $9,805 for "additional equipment, supplies, and materials."

12. Notes, Program of the Research Division of the Democratic National Committee, folder Democratic National Committee: Research Division, 1952, box 158, Democratic National Committee Files, Truman Library.

13. Report to members of the Democratic National Committee and state chairmen, January 20, 1953, folder Chairman's Report to the Committee, January 20, 1953, box 219, Democratic National Committee Records, Truman Library.

14. Notes, Program of the Research Division of the Democratic National Committee, folder Democratic National Committee: Research Division, 1952, box 158, Democratic National Committee Files, Truman Library.

15. Report to members of the Democratic National Committee and state chairmen, January 20, 1953.

16. Report to members of the Democratic National Committee and state chairmen, September 4, 1953, folder Chairman's Report to the Committee, September 4, 1953, box 219, Democratic National Committee Records, Truman Library.

17. Report to the Democratic National Committee, May 4, 1954, folder Chairman's Report to the Committee, May 4, 1954, box 219, Democratic National Committee Records, Truman Library.

18. Report of Chairman Mitchell, December 4, 1954, meeting of the DNC, appendix to *Official Proceedings of the Democratic National Convention, 1956*, 624. The member of Congress to which he referred was Clarence Cannon.

19. *The National Advisory Council: A Program of the Democratic National Committee*, pamphlet, folder ECMW, box 156, Democratic National Committee Files, Truman Library.

20. Report to members of the Democratic National Committee and state chairmen, September 4, 1953.

21. "Opposition, Party; Democrats Lament Lack of Big Rocks to Toss at GOP Administration; Find Ike's Middle-of-Road Course Covers Key Goals They Have Long Plugged," January 6, 1954, folder Democratic National Committee: Democratic Party as an Opposition Party, box 157, Democratic National Committee Files, Truman Library.

22. Paul Butler, "A Democratic National Convention in 1954?" presentation at the Meeting of the Executive Committee of the DNC, March 31 to April 1, 1953, folder "A Democratic National Convention in 1954?" box 219, Democratic National Committee Files, Truman Library.

23. Rosenfeld (2018, 29).

24. Rosenfeld (2018, 23).

25. Rosenfeld (2018, 29) notes: "A committee appointed to consider the idea [of a 1954 convention] dismissed it on logistical grounds."

26. G. Roberts (1987).

27. Klinkner (1994, 20-21).

28. Drexel A. Sprecher oral history, August 17, 1972, 12.

29. Sprecher oral history, 13.

30. Sprecher oral history, 9–11.

31. Statement by Paul M. Butler, calling first meeting of Council, December 18, 1956, box 34, folder Democratic National Committee Advisory Council—authorization, purposes, and organization, Charles S. Murphy Papers, Truman Library.

32. The Advisory Council of the Democratic National Committee Plan of Operations, May 6, 1957, box 692, folder Index—Democratic Advisory Council, Harry S. Truman Post-Presidential Papers, Truman Library.

33. Rosenfeld (2018, 31).

34. These states had low TPO scores (either 1 or 2) (Mayhew, 1986).

35. Klinkner (1994, 23).

36. *Official Report of the Proceedings of the 1960 Democratic National Convention,* July 11–15, 1960, 15.

37. Quoted in Klinkner (1994, 25).

38. Klinkner (1994, 25).

39. *The Democratic Task During the Next Two Years: A Policy Statement by the Democratic Advisory Council,* December 7, 1958, booklet, folder Democratic Advisory Council, 1958, box 21, Truman Library; Index, February 1959, box 34, folder Democratic National Committee Advisory Council—index, Charles S. Murphy Papers, Truman Library.

40. Quoted in Rosenfeld (2018, 39).

41. Memo from Charles Tyroler II to Members of the Advisory Committee on Economic Policy, November 21, 1958, box 34, folder Democratic National Committee Advisory Council—working papers, January—November 1958, Murphy Papers, Truman Library.

42. Walter Lippmann, "Debate on Defense," *New York Herald Tribune,* June 25, 1959, folder Democratic Advisory Council, 1959 (3 of 3), box 21, David D. Lloyd Papers, Truman Library.

43. Klinkner (1994, 38).

44. Statement by the Democratic Advisory Council on the Little Rock School Controversy, September 15, 1957, box 34, folder Democratic National Committee Advisory Council—policy statements, Murphy Papers, Truman Library.

45. Brightman oral history, 134.

46. C. W. McKay Jr. to Hon. Byron Skelton, July 17, 1959, box 62, folder Democratic National Committee—Paul Butler; Truman Post-Presidential Papers, Truman Library.

47. Richard L. Strout, "A Voice for the 'Out' Party," *Christian Science Monitor,* November 19, 1959, folder Democratic Advisory Council, 1959 (2 of 3), box 21, David D. Lloyd Papers, Truman Library.

48. Quoted in Rosenfeld (2018, 30).

49. *Proceedings of the 1960 Democratic National Convention*, 14.

50. Advisory Council Plan of Operations, May 6, 1957.

51. Statement on Its Purposes by the Democratic Advisory Council, January 4, 1957, box 34, folder Democratic National Committee Advisory Council—authorization, purposes, and organization, Murphy Papers, Truman Library.

52. *Democratic Task During the Next Two Years.*

53. Charles S. Murphy to Hon. Harry S. Truman, August 7, 1957, box 62, folder Democratic National Committee—Paul Butler, Truman Papers, Truman Library.

54. John M. Bailey oral history, April 27, 1966, 129.

55. Cohen et al. (2008).

56. Quoted in Rosenfeld (2018, 150–51).

57. Rosenfeld (2018, 150).

58. Rosenfeld (2018, 112).

59. Rosenfeld (2018, 112–13).

60. At this time, the term *me too* referred to a style of politics in which the parties faintly echoed each other rather than establishing their own distinct positions. It was often used particularly to describe Republicans going along with New Deal politics. The phrase was not associated with a culture of sexual harassment and violence against women, as it is today.

61. Rosenfeld (2018, 81).

62. Report of Chairman Guy George Gabrielson to the Republican National Committee Meeting, February 6, 1950, box 14, folder 1950 (Republican National Committee), Bertha S. Adkins Papers, Dwight D. Eisenhower Presidential Library, Abeline, KS.

63. *Republican National Finance Committee Bulletin* No. 2, January 31, 1950, box 14, folder 1950 (Republican National Committee), Adkins Papers, Eisenhower Library.

64. Proceedings: Policy Committee, Republican National Committee, January 18–19, 1950, box 14, folder Proceedings: Policy Committee, Republican National Committee, 1950, Adkins Papers, Eisenhower Library.

65. News release, report of Chairman Guy George Gabrielson to the Republican National Committee, February 6, 1950, box 14, folder 1950 (Republican National Committee), Adkins Papers, Eisenhower Library.

66. Report to the Policy Committee on the Policy Letters and Group Resolutions Received by the Republican National Committee, January 17, 1950, box 14, folder Proceedings: Policy Committee, Republican National Committee, 1950, Adkins Papers, Eisenhower Library.

67. Charles H. Percy to Senator Thruston B. Morton, October 1, 1959, box 3, folder Memos to Committee Members, Cornelius P. Cotter Papers, Eisenhower Library.

68. Memo from Neil Cotter to Members of the Republican Committee on Program and Progress, March 20, 1959, box 3, folder Memos to Committee Members, Cotter Papers, Eisenhower Library.

69. Percy to Morton, October 1, 1959.

70. Percy to Morton, October 1, 1959.

71. Program and Progress Percy Reports, January 25, 1960, box 5, folder Summation of Committee Activities Cornelius P. Cotter, Cotter Papers, Eisenhower Library.

72. Percy to Morton, October 1, 1959.

73. The exact wording of the questions was as follows:

(1) What are the enduring principles by which Republicans must guide themselves now and in the future? (2) What, in your opinion, are the chief dogmas we must discard? (3) Trying to look ahead ten or fifteen years, what are the great problems you foresee for the United States and the Republican Party? (4) In the same period, what are the greatest opportunities you foresee for the United States and the Republican Party? (5) Have you any other observations you think would be helpful to this Committee in its attempt to state principles and objectives as well as analyze problems and opportunities?

Charles Percy to Herbert Hoover, undated, box 3, Memos to Committee Members, Cotter Papers, Eisenhower Library.

74. See folder Republican Committee on Program and Progress: Correspondence, 1959 (2); box 17, Adkins Papers, Eisenhower Library, folder Letters through Percy office to Cornelius P. Cotter, box 1, Cotter Papers, Eisenhower Library.

75. Charles Percy to Thruston E. Morton, April 23, 1959, box 3, folder Memos to Committee Members, Cotter Papers, Eisenhower Library.

76. Program and Progress Percy Reports, box 5, folder Summation of Committee Activities Cornelius P. Cotter, Cotter Papers, Eisenhower Library.

77. Meeting summary, Republican Committee on Program and Progress, April 18–19, 1959, folder Agenda and Discussion Papers, box 3, Cotter Papers, Eisenhower Library.

78. Program and Progress Percy Reports.

79. "Special Report: Percy Report Used for GOP Campaign Material," February 16, 1960, folder Republican Committee on Program and Progress: Correspondence, 1959 (3), box 17, Adkins Papers, Eisenhower Library.

80. *Congressional Quarterly*, February 16, 1960.

81. Special Report: Percy Report Used for GOP Campaign Material.

82. Memo, Chuck Percy to Members, Republican Committee on Program and Progress, November 24, 1959, folder Republican Committee on Program and Progress, Correspondence, 1959 (3), box 17, Adkins Papers, Eisenhower Library.

83. Roscoe Drummond, "Percy Policy Study Called Eminently Good Beginning," *New York Herald Tribune*, October 7, 1959, 25.

84. Program and Progress Percy Reports.

85. Rosenfeld (2018, 85).

86. See, e.g., folder Republican Party—Vol. II (2), box 701, Republican National Committee Files, Eisenhower Library.

87. Alcorn oral history, 1957, 40.

88. Kenneth B. Keating; "A New Republican Offensive," June 29, 1962, folder Republican Party Activities, 1961–62, box 18, Adkins Papers, Eisenhower Library.

89. Research Division, Republican National Committee, June 7, 1963, folder Republican Party Activities, 1963–1965, box 18, Adkins Papers, Eisenhower Library.

90. Klinkner (1994, 85–86).

91. Raymond Moley, "Two Good Years for Ray Bliss," *Canton Repository*, April 9, 1967, box 27, folder Republican National Committee (5); and report by the Chairman 1966 to the Republican National Committee, January 23, 1967, box 27, folder Republican National Committee (6), Eisenhower Post-Presidential Papers, 1967 Principal File, Eisenhower Library.

92. Declaration for the Republican Coordinating Committee meeting at the Willard Hotel, March 3, 1965, folder 1964–1965—Joint Senate and House Republican Leadership—Republican Coordinating Committee (1), box 15, Robert Humphreys Papers, Eisenhower Library.

93. Ray C. Bliss to Dwight D. Eisenhower, May 18, 1965, folder Republican Coordinating Committee (Bliss, Ray), box 7, Eisenhower Post-Presidential Papers, 1965 Principal File, Eisenhower Library.

94. Report by the Chairman 1966, January 23, 1967.

95. The six task forces in 1966 were The Conduct of Foreign Relations; Federal Fiscal and Monetary Policies; Functions of the Federal, State, and Local Governments; Job Opportunities; Human Rights and Responsibilities; and Problems of Aging. The two created at the December 1966 meeting were Crime and Delinquency and National Defense. Report by the Chairman 1966, January 23, 1967.

96. Memo, Ray Bliss to Members of the Republican Coordinating Committee, March 18, 1967, box 27, folder Republican National Committee (5), Eisenhower Post-Presidential Papers, 1967 Principal File, Eisenhower Library.

97. Report by the Chairman 1966, January 23, 1967.

98. Report by the Chairman 1966, January 23, 1967.

99. Report by the Chairman 1966, January 23, 1967.

100. Klinkner (1994, 85).

101. Klinkner (1994, 85); memo, Ray C. Bliss to Republican Coordinating Committee, March 2, 1968, folder R(3), box 44, Eisenhower Post-Presidential Papers, 1968 Principal File, Eisenhower Library.

102. Report by the Chairman 1966, January 23, 1967.

103. Report by the Chairman 1966, January 23, 1967.

104. Klinkner (1994, 147).

105. Klinkner (1994, 148).

106. Rosenfeld (2018, 206).

107. As discussed in chapter 2, quasi-sentences are text strings delineated by periods or semicolons (whereas sentences are delineated by periods only). This is the same unit used to analyze the content of platforms in chapter 1.

108. The subcommittees were (1) Agriculture; (2) Business and Economic Policy; (3) Civil Rights and Immigration; (4) Foreign Policy; (5) Government Affairs; (6) Labor and Human Welfare; (7) National Defense; (8) National Resources and Public Works; (9) Taxation and Fiscal Policy; and (10) Veterans' Affairs.

109. *Official Proceedings of the Twenty-Sixth Republican National Convention*, August 20, 1956, 190.

110. *Official Proceedings of the Twenty-Sixth Republican National Convention*, August 20, 1956, 191.

111. *Official Proceedings of the Twenty-Sixth Republican National Convention*, August 20, 1956, 191.

112. David (1971, 303).

113. *Official Report of the Proceedings of the Twenty-Seventh Republican National Convention*, July 27, 1960, 222.

114. *Official Report of the Proceedings of the Twenty-Seventh Republican National Convention,* July 27, 1960, 222–23.

115. David (1971, 305).

116. *Official Report of the Proceedings of the Twenty-Seventh Republican National Convention,* July 27, 1960, 224.

117. *Official Report of the Proceedings of the Twenty-Seventh Republican National Convention,* July 27, 1960, 230.

118. Press release, "Four experts to address Platform Committee," June 24, 1964, folder GOP Platform Committee Organizations, box 190, Democratic National Committee Files, First Series, Lyndon B. Johnson Presidential Library, Austin, TX.

119. *Official Report of the Proceedings of the Twenty-Eighth Republican National Convention,* July 14, 1964, 189.

120. *Official Report of the Proceedings of the Twenty-Eighth Republican National Convention,* July 14, 1964, 190.

121. *Official Report of the Proceedings of the Twenty-Ninth Republican National Convention,* August 6, 1968.

122. David (1971, 306).

123. *Official Report of the Proceedings of the Twenty-Ninth Republican National Convention,* August 6, 1968, 239.

124. *Official Report of the Proceedings of the Twenty-Ninth Republican National Convention,* August 6, 1968, 238.

125. *Official Proceedings of the Thirty-First Republican National Convention,* August 17, 1976, 289.

126. The subcommittees were (1) Economics, Business, and Agriculture; (2) Governmental Concerns; (3) Human Resources; (4) Community and National Development; (5) Energy, Environment, and Natural Resources; (6) Human Rights and Responsibilities; and (7) Foreign Policy and National Defense.

127. *Official Proceedings of the Thirty-First Republican National Convention,* August 17, 1976, 290.

128. *Official Report of the Thirty-Second Republican National Convention,* July 15, 1980, 215.

129. *Official Report of the Proceedings of the Thirty-Third Republican National Convention,* August 20–23, 1984, 250.

130. *Official Report of the Proceedings of the Thirty-Third Republican National Convention,* August 20–23, 1984, 342.

131. *Official Report of the Proceedings of the Thirty-Third Republican National Convention,* August 20–23, 1984, 252.

132. Resolution Regarding the Republican Party Platform, https://prod-cdn-static.gop.com /docs/Resolution_Platform_2020.pdf, accessed May 27, 2022.

133. See, e.g., Geoff Colvin, "The Republican Party Turns Its Platform into a Person: Donald Trump," *Fortune,* August 25, 2020, https://fortune.com/2020/08/25/gop-convention-rnc-platform-republican-party-2020-donald-trump/; Tom Wheeler, "The 2020 Republican Party Platform: 'L'etat, c'est moi.'" *Brookings,* August 25, 2020, https://www.brookings.edu/blog /up-front/2020/08/25/the-2020-republican-party-platform-letat-cest-moi/; Tom Porter, "Republicans Will Not Adopt a New Platform at This Week's Convention and Will Instead Pledge

to 'Enthusiastically' Support Trump," *Business Insider*, August 24, 2020, https://www.business-insider.com/gop-platform-at-rnc-pledge-trump-support-2020-8.

134. Matthew Dessem, "Republicans Announce Their 2020 Platform Consists of Supporting Whatever Trump Wants," *Slate*, August 23, 2020, https://slate.com/news-and-politics/2020/08/republicans-declare-their-2020-platform-is-to-support-whatever-trump-wants-to-do.html.

135. David Frum, "The Platform the GOP Is Too Scared to Publish," *Atlantic*, August 25, 2020, https://www.theatlantic.com/ideas/archive/2020/08/new-gop-platform-authoritarianism/615640/.

136. Ronn Blitzer, "GOP Announces No New 2020 Platform, Party to 'Enthusiastically Support' Trump Agenda." *Fox News*, August 24, 2020, https://www.foxnews.com/politics/gop-no-new-2020-platform-trump-agenda.

137. Sub-Committee on Platform and Resolutions, Democratic platform, July 1952 (2 folders), box 2, Murphy Papers, Truman Library.

138. E.g., Proceedings of Subcommittee on Platform and Resolutions, July 19, 1952, transcript, p. 1046 folder Proceedings of Subcommittee on Platform and Resolutions, July 19, 1952 (2 of 2), box 217, Democratic National Committee Files, Truman Library.

139. Democratic National Convention, July 17, 1952, transcript, folder Democratic National Convention July 17, 1952 (3 of 3), box 218, Democratic National Committee Files, Truman Library.

140. *Proceedings of the Democratic National Convention*, 1964, Committee on Resolutions and Platform Panel No. 2, August 17, 1964, folder Proceedings of DNC Platform Panel 2 August 17 '64, box 291, Democratic National Committee Files, Series 1, LBJ Library.

141. Democratic National Convention, July 17, 1952, transcript.

142. Democratic National Convention, July 17, 1952.

143. *Proceedings of the Democratic National Convention*, 1960.

144. "Democrats Set Hearings on Platform: 300 Witnesses Apply to Testify," *Chicago Tribune*, August 16, 1968 and "Platform Writers Feel Pressure From Johnson," *Philadelphia Bulletin*, August 20, 1968, folder DNC '68 Platform: Committee, Program, etc., box 14, Democratic National Committee Files, Series 1, LBJ Library.

145. Hilton (2021, 100–101).

146. *The Official Proceedings of the Democratic National Convention*, 1976, 227.

147. *Proceedings of the 1984 Democratic National Convention*, 249.

148. Walters (1990, 436).

149. Quoted in Walters (1990, 436).

150. Walters (1990, 436).

151. For more on differences in the openness of Democratic and Republican platform-writing processes, see Weinberg (1977).

152. Walters (1990).

153. Maisel (1993–1994).

154. Maisel (1993–1994, 681).

155. Videos of these hearings are available for public viewing on C-SPAN, www.c-span.org.

156. Fine (1994b, 856–57).

157. Democratic Study Group Pamphlet, September 1963, folder Democratic Study Group Sponsored and Supported, box 18, Democratic National Committee Files, Series 1, LBJ Library.

Chapter 6. Party Competition and American Democracy

1. Aldrich, Berger, and Rohde (2002); Brady and Han (2006, 2007); Hetherington (2009); Pierson and Schickler (2020).

2. Lack of historical data has been identified as a significant impediment to the study of programmaticism (Kitschelt and Wilkinson, 2007b; Luna, Rosenblatt, and Toro, 2014).

3. Acemoglu and Robinson (2012); Fox (1994); Fukuyama (2014); Kuo (2018); Trounstine (2008).

4. Stokes et al. (2013).

5. Merton (1968); Schmidt (1977).

6. Keefer (2007); Kitschelt and Wilkinson (2007a); Stokes (2007).

7. Hofstadter (1969, 4).

8. Hofstadter (1969, 4).

9. There are, of course, many ways to think about democracy, which vary, among other ways, in their level of detail—here, Dahl's conceptualization has more requirements than a minimalist definition like the one offered by Adam Przeworski (1991) ("Democracy is a system in which parties lose elections")—and in their focus on procedural requirements, as in Dahl's definition, or on outcomes, as in work by Acemoglu and Robinson (2006). See also, e.g., Diamond (2002) and Schumpeter (1942). I find Dahl's work most useful for present purposes because it offers a practical standard, or at least the beginning of one, by which we can evaluate the extent to which issues are reasonably subject to party competition. Paradoxically, party competition needs certain limitations in order to facilitate a free state.

10. Dahl (1972, 3).

11. Levitsky and Ziblatt (2019, 9).

12. Levitsky and Ziblatt (2019, 9). For the purposes of this book, in other words, parties should not be racing to compete over every issue.

Appendix

1. For more on supervised topic models, see Hillard, Purpura, and Wilkerson (2007); Kwon et al. (2007) and Laver, Benoit, and Garry (2003).

2. In this quotation, M. Roberts et al. were referring specifically to STMs, but the point applies more broadly to unsupervised topic models.

3. Grimmer and Stewart (2013), in their comparison, "provide one direct test to ensure that the output from an unsupervised model is just as valid, reliable, and useful as the categorization schemes from supervised methods" (25).

4. If one chooses not to use covariates, STM is equivalent to using the CTM (Blei and Lafferty, 2007). For technical details on STM, including additional differences between STM and LDA, see M. Roberts et al. (2014). I have focused here primarily on comparing STM to LDA because they are both mixed-membership models, but it's important to note that STM

also builds on single-membership models that allow topic prevalence to vary over time and document author (Grimmer, 2010; Quinn et al., 2010). I prefer to use STM here because a mixed-membership model offers richer information about how platform sentences may relate to multiple topics, and enables inclusion of a covariate for topic content as well as prevalence. This is critical, as it seems very likely that Democrats and Republicans will use different language to speak about the same topic.

5. One might be concerned that using covariates in estimating the STM would interfere with one's ability to test hypotheses about the relationship between covariates and topics afterward. Specifically, one might be concerned that using a piece of metadata (e.g., party) at the topic estimation stage might cause false positives in analyzing the influence of party on platform contents. That is, joint estimation might cause spurious correlations, making it look like there is a relationship between covariates and topics when there really is not. M. Roberts et al. (2014) examine this possibility and find that such concerns are unfounded (see their appendix). In fact, they find that STM can also be used in experimental settings to estimate treatment effects in open-ended survey responses (M. Roberts et al., 2014). In such cases, the treatment condition serves as a covariate in topic estimation and in a subsequent analysis examining the impact of the treatment on responses.

6. For a list of papers using STM, see the website associated with the *stm* R package: www.structuraltopicmodel.com.

7. Catalinac examines Japanese election manifestos from 1986 to 2009.

8. In this environment, text before and after a semicolon in a sentence would be treated as two separate quasi-sentences. The use of quasi-sentences follows the practices of the Comparative Agendas Project for textual data.

9. I experimented with various levels for the minimum threshold. Using the general standard recommended by Grimmer and Stewart (2013) of 1% of documents (also used by Hopkins and King 2010) resulted in an excessive loss of words (from 15,588 after other preprocessing to 258 after applying this minimum threshold). Even halving this standard, setting the minimum threshold at 0.5% of documents (as in Quinn et al. 2010), left only 541 terms in the corpus. It makes sense that a high threshold would not work well for platforms, since they are meant to be encyclopedic statements covering many topics. Clearly, a much lower minimum threshold is needed. Indeed, Grimmer and Stewart (2013) argue that the appropriate standard will vary for different corpora. Examining the number of words removed by each minimum threshold from 0 to 100, I found that the curve is very steep between 0 and 20, and flattens out considerably around 40 (see the online appendix). I ran sets of models (with K ranging from 20 to 30 in increments of 1) with minimum thresholds of 1 (which removes documents that appear only once), 10, 20, 30, and 40. All these models include party and year (estimated with a spline) as prevalence covariates with an interaction, and party as a content covariate. For an explanation of why I chose this model and range for K, see the online appendix, which includes an illustration of the average semantic coherence score across topics for each model. Exclusivity scores are not calculated because exclusivity is built into the STM with content covariates. Semantic coherence clearly tends to improve in moving from a threshold of 1 to 10. Beyond that, it is very similar across different thresholds. I proceed with the threshold set at 20, the middle of the range, which leaves 2,549 words in the corpus.

10. Indeed, as explained in a highly influential article by Grimmer and Stewart (2013, 6): "A simple list of words, which we call *unigrams*, is often sufficient to convey the general meaning of a text." Scholars have experimented with clusters of two words (bigrams) and beyond (ngrams) (Jurafsky and Martin, 2009). This complicates the analysis with dubious payoff. As Lucas et al. (2015) explain in their appendix, "Because the space of ordered word pairs (bigrams) and ordered word triples (trigrams) is significantly higher than using a single word, this procedure is often coupled with some method of selecting the most relevant phrases (Gentzkow and Shapiro, 2010; Jensen et al., 2012). This process can often engender subtle difficulties in interpretation (see for example the critique of trigrams in Spirling (2012))." Given the unfeasibility of reviewing ngrams when the volume of documents is very large, this seems not worth the time or risk. As Grimmer and Stewart state, "In practice, for common tasks, like measuring sentiment, topic modeling, or search, *ngrams* do little to enhance performance."

11. I use the *stm* package's s() function, "which selects a fairly flexible b-spline basis" (M. Roberts, Stewart, and Tingley, 2019, 9).

12. I chose 20 as a floor because it is implausible that a lower level would cover the range of major topics in American politics over more than one and a half centuries, and 40 as a ceiling because this is far greater than the number of major topics identified by the CAP, and more than 40 would almost certainly be unwieldy.

13. For a discussion of these metrics and a plot showing how they change along with different levels of K and model specifications, see the online appendix.

14. Many thanks to Annie Iezzi for exceptional research assistance on this task as well as with other parts of the project.

15. At some levels of K, there were multiple topics for these categories, but these categories were always or almost always there. One might question the extent to which American dream constitutes a real policy issue area. But looking at associated words and sentences, it encompasses things that are central to American politics, like manifest destiny and social mobility. This militated in favor of its inclusion. Moreover, it emerged as a consistent topic across levels of K.

16. For example, one such topic was about the institution of the presidency, another was about general disagreement in Congress, etc.

17. I display only topics relating to issue areas. Other topics, like the one about the institution of the presidency, are not included because they are not relevant to my analysis.

18. These data were originally coded by Christina Wolbrecht (n.d.). They were then added to the Policy Agendas Project's data repository, which then became part of the CAP. Coding for the American Institutions Project was begun by John S. Lapinski and Ira Katznelson, financed by NSF Grant SES 0318280; it was subsequently expanded by David A. Bateman.

19. Proksch, Slapin, and Thies (2011, 119) succinctly summarize the mechanics of Wordfish: Wordfish assumes that word frequencies are generated by a Poisson process. The systematic component of this process contains four parameters: document (party) positions, document (party) fixed effects, word weights (discriminating parameters), and word fixed effects. Word fixed effects capture the fact that some words need to be used much more often than others in a language. Such words (e.g., conjunctions or articles) may serve a grammatical purpose but have no substantive or ideological meaning. The document-fixed-effect parameters control for the possibility that some documents in the analysis may be significantly longer than others. Of greatest interest are the

parameters capturing the positions of the party documents, and the word discrimination parameters. We identify the model by transforming all estimated positions to have a mean of 0 and a standard deviation of 1. This relative identification can be made absolute by prescribing a direction for the position (e.g., constraining the LDP to be to the right of the JCP in a particular year).

For more detail, see Proksch, Slapin, and Thies (2011); Slapin and Proksch (2008); and Proksch and Slapin (2009).

20. Among the fourteen topics for which the percentage exceeding the 0.1 threshold was greater than the percentage designated as the top topic, the difference between these two ranged from 0.02% to 1.02%, with a mean of 0.52%.

21. Including any platform sentence that exceeds the 0.1 threshold for a topic makes no difference for six topics, as the only sentences that exceed this threshold are those for which the topic was already designated as the top topic in these cases. For the remaining fourteen topics, it adds a small number of sentences.

22. As in the full platform graph, the year 1988 has been excluded because it is a significant outlier. The trend is similar, but more difficult to see because of the altered scale, when 1988 is included, as shown in the online appendix.

BIBLIOGRAPHY

Abramowitz, Alan, I. 2006. "Comments on Chapter Two: Disconnected, or Joined at the Hip?" In *Red and Blue Nation? Characteristics and Causes of America's Polarized Politics*, ed. Pietro S. Nivola and David W. Brady. Stanford, CA: Brookings Institution Press, 49–71.

Abramowitz, Alan I., and Kyle L. Saunders. 2008. "Is Polarization a Myth?" *Journal of Politics* 70(2):542–55.

Acemoglu, Daron, and James A. Robinson. 2006. *Economic Origins of Dictatorship and Democracy*. New York: Cambridge University Press.

Acemoglu, Daron, and James A. Robinson. 2012. *Why Nations Fail: The Origins of Power, Prosperity, and Poverty*. New York: Crown.

Adams, Greg. 1997. "Abortion: Evidence of an Issue Evolution." *American Journal of Political Science* 41(3):718–37.

Adler, E. Scott, and John Wilkerson. 2020. *Congressional Bills Project*. NSF 00880066 and 00880061. University of Washington, http://www.congressionalbills.org/.

Aldrich, Howard E. 1979. *A Study of Public Works Investment in the United States, 1879–1970*. Washington, DC: CONSAD Research Corporation.

Aldrich, John H. 1994. *Why Parties?: The Origin and Transformation of Political Parties in America*. Chicago: University of Chicago Press.

Aldrich, John H., Mark M. Berger, and David W. Rohde. 2002. "The Historical Variability in Conditional Party Government, 1877–1994." In *Party, Process, and Political Change in Congress*, ed. David Brady and Mathew McCubbins. Stanford, CA: Stanford University Press, 17–35.

Alesina, Alberto, Reza Baqir, and William Easterly. 1999. "Public Goods and Ethnic Divisions." *Quarterly Journal of Economics* 114(4):1243–84.

Alesina, Alberto, and Edward Ludwig Glaeser. 2004. *Fighting Poverty in the US and Europe: A World of Difference*. Oxford: Oxford University Press.

APSA Committee on Political Parties. 1950. "Toward a More Responsible Two-Party System: A Report of the Committee on Political Parties." *American Political Science Review* 44(3):1–99.

Arthur, W. Brian. 1994. *Increasing Returns and Path Dependence in the Economy*. Ann Arbor: University of Michigan Press.

Baland, Jean-Marie, and James A. Robinson. 2008. "Land and Power: Theory and Evidence from Chile." *American Economic Review* 98:1737–65.

Baldwin, Kate. 2013. "Why Vote with the Chief? Political Connections and Public Goods Provision in Zambia." *American Journal of Political Science* 57(4):794–809.

Baldwin, Kate, and John D. Huber. 2010. "Economic versus Cultural Differences: Forms of Ethnic Diversity and Public Good Provision." *American Political Science Review* 104(4): 644–62.

Banfield, Edward C., and James Q. Wilson. 1965. *City Politics*. New York: Cambridge University Press.

Bateman, David A., Ira Katznelson, and John S. Lapinski. 2018. *Southern Nation: Congress and White Supremacy after Reconstruction*. Princeton, NJ: Princeton University Press.

Bates, Robert H. 1974. "Ethnic Competition and Modernization in Contemporary Africa." *Comparative Political Studies* 6(4):457–84.

Bawn, Kathleen, Martin Cohen, David Karol, Seth Masket, Hans Noel, and John Zaller. 2012. "A Theory of Political Parties: Groups, Policy Demands and Nominations in American Politics." *Perspectives on Politics* 10(3):571–97.

Baylor, Christopher. 2017. *First to the Party: The Group Origins of Political Transformation*. Philadelphia: University of Pennsylvania Press.

Benoit, Kenneth, and Michael Laver. 2006a. "Benchmarks for Text Analysis: A Response to Budge and Pennings." *Electoral Studies* 26(1):130–35.

Benoit, Kenneth, and Michael Laver. 2006b. *Party Policy in Modern Democracies*. London: Routledge.

Benoit, Kenneth, Kohei Watanabe, Haiyan Wang, Stefan Muller, Patrick O. Perry, Bejamin Lauderdale, and William Lowe. n.d. "quanteda.textmodels: Scaling Models and Classifiers for Textual Data."

Bensel, Richard. 2004. *The American Ballot Box in the Mid-Nineteenth Century*. New York: Cambridge University Press.

Bickers, Kenneth N., and Robert M. Stein. 2000. "The Congressional Pork Barrel in a Republican Era." *Journal of Politics* 62(4):1070–86.

Blei, David M. 2012. "Probabilistic Topic Models." *Communications of the ACM* 55(4): 77–84.

Blei, David M., and John D. Lafferty. 2007. "A Correlated Topic Model of Science." *Annals of Applied Statistics* 1(1):17–35.

Blei, David M., Andrew Ng, and Michael Jordan. 2003. "Latent Dirichlet Allocation." *Journal of Machine Learning Research* 3:993–1022.

Bloch Rubin, Ruth. 2017. *Building the Bloc: Intraparty Organization in the U.S. Congress*. Cambridge: Cambridge University Press.

Blodgett, Geoffrey T. 1962. "The Mind of the Boston Mugwump." *Mississippi Valley Historical Review* 48(4):614–34.

Blodgett, Geoffrey, T. 1980. "The Mugwump Reputation, 1870 to the Present." *Journal of American History* 66(4):867–87.

Bone, Hugh. 1958. *Party Committees and National Politics*. Seattle: University of Washington Press.

Bone, Hugh. 1971. *American Politics and the Party System*. New York: McGraw-Hill.

Brady, David, John Ferejohn, and Laurel Harbridge. 2006. "Polarization and Public Policy: A General Assessment." In *Red and Blue Nation?: Consequences and Correction of America's Polarized Politics*, ed. Pietro S. Nivola and David W. Brady. Stanford, CA: Brookings Institution Press, 72–85.

Brady, David, and Hahrie Han. 2006. "Polarization Then and Now: A Historical Perspective." In *Red and Blue Nation?: Consequences and Correction of America's Polarized Politics*, ed. Pietro S. Nivola and David W. Brady. Stanford, CA: Brookings Institution Press, 119–73.

Brady, David, and Hahrie Han. 2007. "A Delayed Return to Historical Norms: Congressional Party Polarization after the Second World War." *British Journal of Political Science* 37(3):505–31.

Bridges, Ronald. 1939. "The Republican Program Committee." *Public Opinion Quarterly* 23(3): 299–309.

Brown, M. Craig, and Charles N. Halaby. 1987. "Machine Politics in America, 1870–1945." *Journal of Interdisciplinary History* 17:587–612.

Budge, Ian, and Richard I. Hofferbert. 1990. "Mandates and Policy Outputs: U.S. Party Platforms and Federal Expenditures." *American Political Science Review* 84(1):111–31.

Budge, Ian, David Robertson, and Derek Hearl, eds. 1987. *Ideology, Strategy and Party Change: Spatial Analyses of Post-War Election Programmes in 19 Democracies*. Cambridge: Cambridge University Press.

Budge, Ian, Hans-Dieter Klingemann, Andrea Volkens, Judith Bara, and Eric Tannenbaum. 2001. *Mapping Policy Preferences: Estimates for Parties, Electors and Governments, 1945–1998*. Oxford: Oxford University Press.

Burgess, Robin, Remi Jedwab, Edward Miguel, Ameet Morjaria, and Gerard Padró i Miquel. 2015. "The Value of Democracy: Evidence from Road Building in Kenya." *American Economic Review* 105(6):1817–51.

Bustikova, Lenka, and Cristina Corduneanu-Huci. 2017. "Patronage, Trust, and State Capacity: The Historical Trajectories of Clientelism." *World Politics* 69(2):277–326.

Butler, Jon. 2000. *Becoming America: The Revolution before 1776*. Cambridge, MA: Harvard University Press.

Calvo, Ernesto, and Maria Victoria Murillo. 2004. "Who Delivers? Partisan Clients in the Argentine Electoral Market." *American Journal of Political Science* 48:742–57.

Calvo, Ernesto, and Maria Victoria Murillo. 2019. *Non-Policy Politics: Richer Voter, Poorer Voter, and the Diversification of Parties' Electoral Strategies*. New York: Cambridge University Press.

Carmines, Edward G., and James A. Stimson. 1989. *Issue Evolution: Race and the Transformation of American Politics*. Princeton, NJ: Princeton University Press.

Carpenter, Daniel P. 2001. *The Forging of Bureaucratic Autonomy: Reputations, Networks, and Policy Innovation in Executive Agencies, 1862–1928*. Princeton, NJ: Princeton University Press.

Carpenter, Daniel P. 2003. "The Multiple and Material Legacies of Stephen Skowronek." *Social Science History* 27(3):465–74.

Carpenter, Daniel, P. 2021. *Democracy by Petition: Popular Politics in Transformation, 1790–1870*. Cambridge, MA: Harvard University Press.

Castles, Francis G., and Peter Mair. 1984. "Left-Right Political Scales: Some Expert Judgments." *European Journal of Political Science* 12(1):73–88.

Catalinac, Amy. 2016. "From Pork to Policy: The Rise of Programmatic Campaigning in Japanese Elections." *Journal of Politics* 78(1):1–18.

Catalinac, Amy. 2018. "Positioning under Alternative Electoral Systems: Evidence from Japanese Candidate Election Manifestos." *American Political Science Review* 112(1):31–48.

Center, Judith A. 1974. "1972 Democratic Convention Reforms and Party Democracy." *Political Science Quarterly* 89(2):325–50.

Chabal, Patrick, and Jean-Pascal Daloz. 1999. *Africa Works*. London: James Currey.

Chandra, Kanchan. 2004. *Why Ethnic Parties Succeed: Patronage and Ethnic Head Counts in India*. New York: Cambridge University Press.

Chandra, Kanchan. 2007. "Counting Heads: A Theory of Voter and Elite Behavior in Patronage Democracies." In *Patrons, Clients, and Policies: Patterns of Democratic Accountability and Political Competition*, ed. Herbert Kitschelt and Steven I. Wilkinson. New York: Cambridge University Press, 84–109.

Chauchard, Simon. 2018. "Electoral Handouts in Mumbai Elections: The Cost of Political Competition." *Asian Survey* 58(2):341–64.

Cheeseman, Nic, Juan Pablo Luna, Herbert Kitschelt, Dan Paget, Fernando Rosenblatt, Kristen Sample, Sergio Toro, Jorge Valladares Molleda, Sam van der Staak, and Yi-ting Wang. 2014a. Introduction to *Politics Meets Policies: The Emergence of Programmatic Political Parties*, ed. Nic Cheeseman, Juan Pablo Luna, Herbert Kitschelt, Dan Paget, Fernando Rosenblatt, Kristen Sample, Sergio Toro, Jorge Valladares Molleda, Sam van der Staak and Yi-ting Wang. Stockholm: International Institute for Democracy and Electoral Assistance, xi–xv.

Cheeseman, Nic, Juan Pablo Luna, Herbert Kitschelt, Dan Paget, Fernando Rosenblatt, Kristen Sample, Sergio Toro, Jorge Valladares Molleda, Sam van der Staak, and Yi-ting Wang. 2014b. *Politics Meets Policies: The Emergence of Programmatic Political Parties*. Stockholm: International Institute for Democracy and Electoral Assistance.

Cheeseman, Nic, and Dan Paget. 2014. "Programmatic Politics in Comparative Perspective." In *Politics Meets Policies: The Emergence of Programmatic Political Parties*, ed. Nic Cheeseman, Juan Pablo Luna, Herbert Kitschelt, Dan Paget, Fernando Rosenblatt, Kristen Sample, Sergio Toro, Jorge Valladares Molleda, Sam van der Staak and Yi-ting Wang. Stockholm: International Institute for Democracy and Electoral Assistance, 75–98.

Chubb, Judith. 1981. "The Social Bases of an Urban Political Machine: The Case of Palermo." *Political Science Quarterly* 96:107–25.

Chubb, Judith. 1982. *Patronage, Power, and Poverty in Southern Italy*. Cambridge: Cambridge University Press.

Clark, Peter B., and James Q. Wilson. 1961. "Incentive Systems: A Theory of Organizations." *Administrative Science Quarterly* 6(2):129–66.

Clinton, Joshua D., and John Lapinski. 2008. "Laws and Roll Calls in the U.S. Congress, 1891–1994." *Legislative Studies Quarterly* 33(4):511–541.

Cohen, Marty, David Karol, Hans Noel, and John Zaller. 2008. *The Party Decides: Presidential Nominations Before and After Reform*. Chicago, IL: University of Chicago Press.

Collier, Ruth Berins, and David Collier. 1991. *Shaping the Political Arena: Critical Junctures, the Labor Movement, and Regime Dynamics in Latin America*. Princeton, NJ: Princeton University Press.

Cotter, Cornelius, and John F. Bibby. 1980. "Institutional Development of Parties and the Thesis of Party Decline." *Political Science Quarterly* 95:1–27.

Cox, Gary W. 1987. *The Efficient Secret*. New York: Cambridge University Press.

Cox, Gary W., and J. Morgan Kousser. 1981. "Turnout and Rural Corruption: New York as a Test Case." *American Journal of Political Science* 25(4):646–63.

Cox, Gary W., and Mathew D. McCubbins. 1993. *Legislative Leviathan: Party Government in the House*. Berkeley: University of California Press.

Cox, Gary W., and Mathew D. McCubbins. 2005. *Setting the Agenda: Responsible Party Government in the U.S. House of Representatives*. New York: Cambridge University Press.

Cruz, Cesi, and Philip Keefer. 2010 "Programmatic Political Parties and Public Sector Reform." Presented at the Annual Meeting of the American Political Science Association, September 2–5, Washington, DC.

Cruz, Cesi, and Philip Keefer. 2015. "Political Parties, Clientelism, and Bureaucratic Reform." *Comparative Political Studies* 46(14):1942–73.

Dahl, Robert A. 1972. *Polyarchy: Participation and Opposition*. New Haven, CT: Yale University Press.

David, Paul T. 1971. "Party Platforms as National Plans." *Public Administration Review* 31(3):303–15.

Diamond, Larry. 2002. "Elections without Democracy: Thinking about Hybrid Regimes." *Journal of Democracy* 13(2):21–35.

Diaz-Cayeros, Alberto, Federico Estévez, and Beatriz Magaloni. 2016. *The Political Logic of Poverty Relief: Electoral Strategies and Social Policy in Mexico*. New York: Cambridge University Press.

Dixit, Avinash, and John Londregan. 1996. "The Determinants of Success of Special Interests in Redistributive Politics." *Journal of Politics* 58:1132–55.

Eder, Nikolaus, Marcelo Jenny, and Wolfgang C. Müller. 2017. "Manifesto Functions: How Party Candidates View and Use Their Party's Central Policy Document." *Electoral Studies* 45:75–87.

Engs, Robert F. 2002. *The Birth of the Grand Old Party: The Republicans' First Generation*. Philadelphia: University of Pennsylvania Press.

Erie, Steven P. 1988. *Rainbow's End: Irish Americans and the Dilemmas of Urban Machine Politics, 1840–1945*. Berkeley: University of California Press.

Farhang, Sean, and Ira Katznelson. 2005. "The Southern Imposition: Congress and Labor in the New Deal and Fair Deal." *Studies in American Political Development* 19:1–30.

Farrell, John A. 2001. *Tip O'Neill and the Democratic Century: A Biography*. New York: Little, Brown.

Feinstein, Estelle. 1975. "Toward a Meaning for Mugwumpery." *Reviews in American History* 3(4):467–71.

Fine, Terri Susan. 1994a. "Interest Groups & the Framing of the 1988 Democratic & Republican Party Platforms." *Polity* 26(3):517–30.

Fine, Terri Susan. 1994b. "Lobbying from Within: Government Elites and the Framing of the 1988 Democratic and Republican Party Platforms." *Presidential Studies Quarterly* 24(4):855–63.

Fiorina, Morris P. 2006. *Culture War? The Myth of a Polarized America*. New York: Pearson Longman.

Fiorina, Morris P., and Matthew S. Levendusky. 2006. "Disconnected: The Political Class versus the People." In *Red and Blue Nation?: Characteristics and Causes of America's Polarized Politics*, ed. Pietro S. Nivola and David W. Brady. Stanford, CA: Brookings Institution Press, 72–85.

Folke, Olle, Shigeo Hirano, and James M. Snyder. 2011. "Patronage and Elections in U.S. States." *American Political Science Review* 105(3):567–85.

Foner, Eric. 1970. *Free Soil, Free Labor, Free Men: The Ideology of the Republican Party before the Civil War*. New York: Oxford University Press.

Fox, Jonathan. 1994. "The Difficult Transition from Clientelism to Citizenship: Lessons from Mexico." *World Politics* 46:151–84.

Frye, Timothy, Ora John Reuter, and David Szakonyi. 2019. "Hitting Them with Carrots: Voter Intimidation and Vote Buying in Russia." *British Journal of Political Science* 49:857–81.

Frymer, Paul. 2017. *Building an American Empire: The Era of Territorial and Political Expansion*. Princeton, NJ: Princeton University Press.

Fukuyama, Francis. 2014. *Political Order: From the Industrial Revolution to the Globalization of Democracy*. New York: Farrar, Straus, Giroux.

Gabel, Matthew J., and John D. Huber. 2000. "Putting Parties in Their Place: Inferring Left-Right Ideological Positions from Party Manifestos Data." *American Journal of Political Science* 44(1):94–103.

Galvin, Daniel J. 2010. *Presidential Party Building: Dwight D. Eisenhower to George W. Bush*. Princeton, NJ: Princeton University Press.

Galvin, Daniel J. 2014. "The Transformation of the National Party Committees." In *CQ Guide to U.S. Political Parties*, ed. Barry Burden, Marjorie Hershey, and Christina Wolbrecht. Thousand Oaks, CA: Congressional Quarterly Press.

Geese, Lucas. 2019. "Immigration-Related Speechmaking in a Party-Constrained Parliament: Evidence from the 'Refugee Crisis' of the 18th German Bundestag (2013–2017)." *German Politics* 29(2):201–22.

Gentzkow, Matthew, and Jesse M. Shapiro. 2010. "What Drives Media Slant? Evidence from U.S. Daily Newspapers." *Econometrica* 78(1):35–71.

Gerring, John. 1998. *Party Ideologies in America: 1828–1996*. New York: Cambridge University Press.

Gingerich, Daniel W., and Luis Fernando Medina. 2013. "The Endurance and Eclipse of the Controlled Vote: A Formal Model of Vote Brokerage under the Secret Ballot." *Economics and Politics* 25(3):453–80.

Goldzwig, Steven R. 2008. *Truman's Whistle-Stop Campaign*. College Station: Texas A&M University Press.

Greenstone, J. David. 1969. *Labor in American Politics*. Chicago: University of Chicago Press.

Greif, Avner, and David D. Laitin. 2004. "A Theory of Endogenous Institutional Change." *American Political Science Review* 98:633–52.

Grimmer, Justin. 2010. "A Bayesian Hierarchical Topic Model for Political Texts: Measuring Expressed Agendas in Senate Press Releases." *Political Analysis* 18:1–35.

Grimmer, Justin, and Brandon M. Stewart. 2013. "Text as Data: The Promise and Pitfalls of Automatic Content Analysis Methods for Political Texts." *Political Analysis* 21(3):1–31.

Grossmann, Matt, and David A. Hopkins. 2016. *Asymmetric Politics: Ideological Republicans and Group Interest Democrats*. New York: Oxford University Press.

Guardado, Jenny, and Leonard Wantchekon. 2018. "Do Electoral Handouts Affect Voting Behavior?" *Electoral Studies* 53:139–49.

Gutchen, Robert. 1961. "Local Improvements and Centralization in Nineteenth-Century England." *Historical Journal* 4(1):85–96.

Habyarimana, James, Macartan Humphreys, Daniel N. Posner, and Jeremy Weinstein. 2007. "Why Does Ethnic Diversity Undermine Public Goods Provision?" *American Political Science Review* 101(4):709–25.

Hale, Henry E. 2007. "Correlates of Clientelism: Political Economy, Politicized Ethnicity, and Post-Communism Transition. In *Patrons, Clients, and Policies: Patterns of Democratic Accountability and Political Competition*, ed. Herbert Kitschelt and Steven I. Wilkinson. New York: Cambridge University Press, 227–50.

Hall, Simon. 2003. "On the Tail of the Panther: Black Power and the 1967 Convention of the National Conference for New Politics." *Journal of American Studies* 37(1):59–78.

Hartz, Louis. 1955. *The Liberal Tradition in America: An Interpretation of American Political Thought Since the Revolution*. New York: Harcourt, Brace.

Heersink, Boris. 2023. *National Party Organizations and Party Brands in American Politics: The Democratic and Republican National Committees, 1912–2016*. New York: Oxford University Press.

Heersink, Boris, and Brenton D. Peterson. 2017. "Truman Defeats Dewey: The Effect of Campaign Visits on Election Outcomes." *Electoral Studies* 49:49–64.

Herd, Pamela, and Donald Moynihan. 2019. *Administrative Burden: Policymaking by Other Means*. New York: Russell Sage Foundation.

Hershey, Marjorie Randon. 2017. *Party Politics in America*. New York: Routledge.

Hetherington, Marc. 2009. "Putting Polarization in Perspective." *British Journal of Political Science* 39:413–48.

Hicken, Allen. 2011. "Clientelism." *Annual Review of Political Science* 14(1):289–310.

Hicken, Allen, and Noah L. Nathan. 2020. "Clientelism's Red Herrings: Dead Ends and New Directions in the Study of Nonprogrammatic Politics." *Annual Review of Political Science* 23:277–94.

Hillard, Dustin, Stephen Purpura, and John Wilkerson. 2007. "Computer-Assisted Topic Classification for Mixed-Methods Social Science Research." *Journal of Information Technology and Politics* 4(4):31–46.

Hilton, Adam. 2016. "Searching for a New Politics: The New Politics Movement and the Struggle to Democratize the Democratic Party, 1968–1978." *New Political Science* 32(2): 141–59.

Hilton, Adam. 2019. "The Politics Insurgents Make: Reconstructive Reformers in U.S. and U.K. Postwar Party Development." *Polity* 51(3):559–96.

Hilton, Adam. 2021. *True Blues: The Contentious Transformation of the Democratic Party*. Philadelphia: University of Pennsylvania Press.

Hofstadter, Richard. 1969. *The Idea of a Party System: The Rise of Legitimate Opposition in the United States, 1780–1840*. Berkeley: University of California Press.

Hood, M. V. III, Quentin Kidd, and Irwin L. Morris. 1999. "Of Byrd[s] and Bumpers: Using Democratic Senators to Analyze Political Change in the South, 1960–1995." *American Journal of Political Science* 43:465–87.

Hopkins, Daniel, and Gary King. 2010. "A Method of Automated Nonparametric Content Analysis for Social Science." *American Journal of Political Science* 54(1):229–47.

Huber, John, and Ronald Inglehart. 1995. "Expert Interpretations of Party Space and Party Locations in 42 Societies." *Party Politics* 1(1):73–111.

Ichino, Nahomi, and Noah L. Nathan. 2013. "Crossing the Line: Local Ethnic Geography and Voting in Ghana." *American Political Science Review* 107(2):344–61.

Ignazi, Piero. 1996. "The Crisis of Parties and the Rise of New Political Parties." *Party Politics* 2(4):549–66.

Ingle, Stephen. 2008. *The British Party System*. 4th Ed. New York: Routledge.

Iyengar, Shanto, Guarav Sood, and Yphtach Lelkes. 2012. "Affect, Not Ideology: A Social Identity Perspective on Polarization." *Public Opinion Quarterly* 76(3):405–31.

Jacobson, Gary. 2000. "Party Polarization in National Politics: The Electoral Connection." In *Polarized Politics: Congress and the President in a Partisan Era*, ed. Jon R. Bond and Richard Fleisher. Washington, DC: CQ Press, 9–30.

James, Scott C. 2006. "Patronage Regimes and American Party Development from 'The Age of Jackson' to the Progressive Era." *British Journal of Political Science* 36(1):39–60.

Jenkins, Jeffrey A. 2004. "Partisanship and Contested Election Cases in the House of Representatives, 1789–2002." *Studies in American Political Development* 18:112–35.

Jensen, Jacob, Ethan Kaplan, Suresh Naidu, and Laurence Wilse-Samson. 2012. "Political Polarization and the Dynamics of Political Language: Evidence from 130 Years of Partisan Speech." *Brookings Papers on Economic Activity* 2012 2:1–81.

Jurafsky, Dan, and James Martin. 2009. *Speech and Natural Language Processing: An Introduction to Natural Language Processing, Computational Linguistics, and Speech Recognition*. Upper Saddle River, NJ: Prentice Hall.

Karol, David. 2009. *Party Position Change in American Politics: Coalition Management*. New York: Cambridge University Press.

Katznelson, Ira. 2005. *When Affirmative Action Was White: An Untold History of Racial Inequality in Twentieth-Century America*. New York: Norton.

Katznelson, Ira. 2013. *Fear Itself: The New Deal and the Origins of Our Time*. New York: Norton.

Keefer, Philip. 2007. "Clientelism, Credibility, and the Policy Choices of Young Democracies." *American Journal of Political Science* 51(4):804–21.

Keefer, Philip. 2006. "Programmatic Parties: Where Do They Come from and Do They Matter?" Presented at the Annual Meeting of the American Political Science Association, August 31–September 3, Philadelphia.

Keefer, Philip, and Razvan Vlaicu. 2007. "Democracy, Credibility, and Clientelism." *Journal of Law, Economics, and Organization* 24(2):371–406.

Keller, Morton. 1977. *Affairs of State: Public Life in Late Nineteenth-Century America*. Cambridge, MA: Harvard University Press.

Kennedy, David M. 2009. "What the New Deal Did." *Political Science Quarterly* 124(2):251–68.

Key, V. O. 1942. *Politics, Parties, and Pressure Groups*. New York: Crowell.

Key, V. O. 1949. *Southern Politics in State and Nation*. New York: Knopf.

Key, V. O. 1964. *Politics, Parties, and Pressure Groups*. 5th ed. New York: Crowell.

Kim, Sung Eun. 2018. "Media Bias against Foreign Firms as a Veiled Trade Barrier: Evidence from Chinese Newspapers." *American Political Science Review* 112(4):954–70.

King, Desmond S., and Rogers M. Smith. 2005. "Racial Orders in American Political Development." *American Political Science Review* 99(1):75–92.

King, Gary, Michael Laver, Richard Hofferbert, Ian Budge, and Michael D. McDonald. 1993. "Mandates and Policy Outputs: U.S. Party Platforms and Federal Expenditures." *American Political Science Review* 87(3):744–50.

Kingdon, John. 1984. *Agendas, Alternatives, and Public Policies.* Boston, MA: Little, Brown.

Kitschelt, Herbert. 2000. "Linkages between Citizens and Politicians in Democratic Polities." *Comparative Political Studies* 33:845–79.

Kitschelt, Herbert. 2007. "The Demise of Clientelism in Affluent Capitalist Democracies." In *Patrons, Clients, and Policies: Patterns of Democratic Accountability and Political Competition,* ed. Herbert Kitschelt and Steven I. Wilkinson. New York: Cambridge University Press, 298–321.

Kitschelt, Herbert, and Kent Freeze. n.d. "Programmatic Party System Structuration: Developing and Comparing Cross-National and Cross-Party Measures with a New Global Data Set." Working paper.

Kitschelt, Herbert, Kirk A. Hawkins, Juan Pablo Luna, Guillermo Rosas, and Elizabeth J. Zechmeister. 2010. *Latin American Party Systems.* New York: Cambridge University Press.

Kitschelt, Herbert, and Daniel M. Kselman. 2013. "Economic Development, Democratic Experience, and Political Parties' Linkage Strategies." *Comparative Political Studies* 46(11):1453–84.

Kitschelt, Herbert, and Yi-ting Wang. 2014. "Programmatic Parties and Party Systems: Opportunities and Constraints." In *Politics Meets Policies: The Emergence of Programmatic Political Parties,* ed. Nic Cheeseman, Juan Pablo Luna, Herbert Kitschelt, Dan Paget, Fernando Rosenblatt, Kristen Sample, Sergio Toro, Jorge Valladares Molleda, Sam van der Staak, and Yi-ting Wang. Stockholm: International Institute for Democracy and Electoral Assistance, 43–74.

Kitschelt, Herbert, and Steven I. Wilkinson. 2007a. "Citizen-Politician Linkages: An Introduction." In *Patrons, Clients, and Policies: Patterns of Democratic Accountability and Political Competition,* ed. Herbert Kitschelt and Steven I. Wilkinson. New York: Cambridge University Press, 1–49.

Kitschelt, Herbert, and Steven I. Wilkinson. 2007b. A Research Agenda for the Study of Citizen-Politician Linkages and Democratic Accountability." In *Patrons, Clients, and Policies: Patterns of Democratic Accountability and Political Competition,* ed. Herbert Kitschelt and Steven I. Wilkinson. New York: Cambridge University Press, 322–43.

Klingemann, Hans-Dieter. 1995. "Party Positions and Voter Orientations." In *Citizens and the State,* ed. Hans-Dieter Klingemann and Dieter Fuchs. Oxford: Oxford University Press, 183–205.

Klingemann, Hans-Dieter, Richard Hofferbert, and Ian Budge. 1994. *Parties, Policies, and Democracy.* Boulder, CO: Westview Press.

Klingner, Donald E. 2006. "Societal Values and Civil Service Systems in the United States." In *Civil Service Reform in the States: Personnel Policy and Politics at the Subnational Level,* ed. J. Edward Kellough and Lloyd G. Nigro. Albany: State University of New York Press, 11–33.

Klinkner, Philip. 1994. *The Losing Parties: Out-Party National Committees, 1956–1993.* New Haven, CT: Yale University Press.

Koter, Dominika. 2013. "King Makers: Local Leaders and Ethnic Politics in Africa." *World Politics* 65(2):187–232.

Krimmel, Katherine. 2013. "Special Interest Partisanship: The Transformation of American Political Parties." PhD diss., Columbia University.

Krimmel, Katherine. 2017. "The Efficiencies and Pathologies of Special Interest Partisanship." *Studies in American Political Development* 31(1):149–69.

Krimmel, Katherine, Jeffrey Lax, and Justin Phillips. 2016. "Gay Rights in Congress: Public Opinion and (Mis)Representation." *Public Opinion Quarterly* 80(4):888–913.

Kuo, Didi. 2018. *Clientelism, Capitalism, and Democracy: The Rise of Programmatic Politics in the United States and Britain.* New York: Cambridge University Press.

Kwon, Namhee, Eduard Hovy, Liang Zhou, and Stuart Shulman. 2007. "Identifying and Classifying Subjective Claims." *Eighth National Conference on Digital Government Research.* Digital Government Society of North America, Philadelphia, May 20–23, 2007, p. 76–81. Philadelphia: Digital Government Society of North America.

Lapinski, John S. 2013. *The Substance of Representation: Congress, American Political Development, and Lawmaking.* Princeton, NJ: Princeton University Press.

Larson, Jennifer M., and Janet I. Lewis. 2017. "Ethnic Networks." *American Journal of Political Science* 61(2):350–64.

Laver, Michael, Kenneth Benoit, and John Garry. 2003. "Extracting Policy Positions from Political Texts Using Words as Data." *American Political Science Review* 97(2):311–32.

Laver, Michael, and Ian Budge. 1992. *Party, Policy, and Government Coalitions.* London: St. Martin's Press.

Laver, Michael, and John Garry. 2000. "Estimating Policy Positions from Political Texts." *American Journal of Political Science* 44:619–34.

Layman, Geoffrey, Thomas Carsey and Juliana Horowitz. 2006. "Party Polarization in American Politics: Characteristics, Causes, and Consequences." *Annual Review of Political Science* 9:83–110.

Lee, Frances E. 2016a. *Insecure Majorities: Congress and the Perpetual Campaign.* Chicago: University of Chicago Press.

Lee, Frances E. 2016b. "Patronage, Logrolls, and 'Polarization': Congressional Parties of the Gilded Age, 1876–1896." *Studies in American Political Development* 30:116–27.

Leuchtenburg, William E. 1963. *Franklin D. Roosevelt and the New Deal.* New York: Harper and Row.

Levi, Margaret. 1999. "A Model, a Method, and a Map: Rational Choice in Comparative and Historical Analysis." In *Comparative Politics: Rationality, Culture, and Structure,* ed. Mark I. Lichbach and Alan S. Zuckerman. Cambridge: Cambridge University Press, 19–41.

Levitt, Steven D., and James M. Snyder. 1995. "Political Parties and the Distribution of Federal Outlays." *American Journal of Political Science* 39(4):958–80.

Levitsky, Steven, and Daniel Ziblatt. 2019. *How Democracies Die.* New York: Penguin Random House.

Lewis, Jeffrey B., Keith Poole, Howard Rosenthal, Adam Boche, Aaron Rudkin and Luke Sonnet. 2023. *Voteview: Congressional Roll-Call Votes Database.* Accessed November 1, 2023. https://voteview.com/.

Lieberman, Robert. 2001. *Shifting the Color Line: Race and the American Welfare State.* Cambridge, MA: Harvard University Press.

Lipset, Seymour Martin, and Stein Rokkan. 1967. *Party Systems and Voter Alignments*. New York: Free Press.

Lizzeri, Alessandro, and Nicola Persico. 2004. "Why Did Elites Extend the Suffrage? Democracy and the Scope of Government, with an Application to Britain's 'Age of Reform.'" *Quarterly Journal of Economics* 119(2):705–63.

Lowe, Will, and Kenneth Benoit. 2013. "Validating Estimates of Latent Traits from Textual Data Using Human Judgment as a Benchmark." *Political Analysis* 21:298–313.

Lowi, Theodore J. 1972. "Four Systems of Policy, Politics, and Choice." *Public Administration Review* 32(4):298–310.

Lowi, Theodore J. 1990. "The Roosevelt Revolution and the New American State." In *Comparative Theory and Political Experience: Mario Einaudi and the Liberal Tradition*, ed. Peter Katzenstein, Theodore Lowi, and Sidney Tarrow. Ithaca, NY: Cornell University Press, 188–212.

Lucas, Christopher, Richard Nielsen, Margaret Roberts, Brandon Stewart, Alex Storer, and Dustin Tingley. 2015. "Computer-Assisted Text Analysis for Comparative Politics." *Political Analysis* 23(2):254–77.

Luebbert, Gregory M. 1991. *Liberalism, Fascism, or Social Democracy: Social Classes and the Political Origins of Regimes in Interwar Europe*. New York: Oxford University Press.

Luna, Juan Pablo, Fernando Rosenblatt, and Sergio Toro. 2014. "Programmatic Parties: A Survey of Dimensions and Explanations in the Literature." In *Politics Meets Policies: The Emergence of Programmatic Political Parties*, ed. Nic Cheeseman, Juan Pablo Luna, Herbert Kitschelt, Dan Paget, Fernando Rosenblatt, Kristen Sample, Sergio Toro, Jorge Valladares Molleda, Sam van der Staak, and Yi-ting Wang. Stockholm: International Institute for Democracy and Electoral Assistance, 1–42.

Luttmer, Erzo F. P. 2001. "Group Loyalty and the Taste for Redistribution." *Journal of Political Economy* 109(3):500–28.

Lyne, Mona M. 2007. "Rethinking Economics and Institutions: The Voter's Dilemma and Democratic Accountability." In *Patrons, Clients, and Policies: Patterns of Democratic Accountability and Political Competition*, ed. Herbert Kitschelt and Steven I. Wilkinson. New York: Cambridge University Press, 159–81.

Magaloni, Beatriz, Alberto Diaz-Cayeros, and Federico Estévez. 2007. "Clientelism and Portfolio Diversification: A Model of Electoral Investment with Applications to Mexico." In *Patrons, Clients, and Policies: Patterns of Democratic Accountability and Political Competition*, ed. Herbert Kitschelt and Steven I. Wilkinson. New York: Cambridge University Press, 182–205.

Mahoney, James, and Kathleen Thelen. 2010. "A Theory of Gradual Institutional Change." In *Explaining Institutional Change: Ambiguity, Agency, and Power*, ed. James Mahoney and Kathleen Thelen. New York: Cambridge University Press, 1–37.

Maisel, L. Sandy. 1993–1994. "The Platform-Writing Process: Candidate-Centered Platforms in 1992." *Political Science Quarterly* 108(4):671–98.

Makemson, Harlen. 2004. "A 'Dude and Pharisee': Cartoon Attacks on *Harper's Weekly* Editor George William Curtis and the Mugwumps in the Presidential Campaign of 1884." *Journalism History* 29(4):179–89.

Manning, Christopher, Prabhakar Raghavan, and Hinrich Schutze. 2008. *Introduction to Information Retrieval*. Cambridge: Cambridge University Press.

Mares, Isabela. 2015. *From Open Secrets to Secret Voting: Democratic Electoral Reforms and Voter Autonomy*. New York: Cambridge University Press.

Mares, Isabela, and Lauren E. Young. 2016. "Buying, Expropriating, and Stealing Votes." *Annual Review of Political Science* 19:267–88.

Mares, Isabela, and Lauren E. Young. 2018. "The Core Voter's Curse: Clientelistic Threats and Promises in Hungarian Elections." *Comparative Political Studies* 51(11):1441–71.

Mares, Isabela, and Lauren E. Young. 2019. *Conditionality and Coercion: Electoral Clientelism in Eastern Europe*. Oxford: Oxford University Press.

Masket, Seth E. 2011. *No Middle Ground: How Informal Party Organizations Control Nominations and Polarize Legislatures*. Ann Arbor: University of Michigan Press.

Masket, Seth E. 2016. *The Inevitable Party: Why Attempts to Kill the Party System Fail and How They Weaken Democracy*. New York: Oxford University Press.

Mason, Lilliana. 2018. *Uncivil Agreement: How Politics Became Our Identity*. Chicago: University of Chicago Press.

Mathews, Chris. 2013. *Tip and the Gipper: When Politics Worked*. New York: Simon and Schuster.

Mayhew, David. 1974. *Congress: The Electoral Connection*. New Haven, CT: Yale University Press.

Mayhew, David. 1986. *Placing Parties in American Politics*. Princeton, NJ: Princeton University Press.

McCarty, Nolan. 2016. "Reducing Polarization: Some Facts for Reformers." *University of Chicago Legal Forum* 2015(9):116–27.

McCarty, Nolan, Keith T. Poole, and Howard Rosenthal. 2006. *Polarized America: The Dance of Ideology and Unequal Riches*. Cambridge, MA: MIT Press.

McCarty, Nolan, and Eric Schickler. 2018. "On the Theory of Parties." *Annual Review of Political Science* 21:175–93.

McCormick, Richard P. 1966. *The Second American Party System: Party Formation in the Jacksonian Era*. Chapel Hill: University of North Carolina Press.

McFarland, Gerald W. 1963. "The New York Mugwumps of 1884: A Profile." *Political Science Quarterly* 78(1):40–58.

Medina, Luis Fernando, and Susan C. Stokes. 2007. "Monopoly and Monitoring: An Approach to Political Clientelism." In *Patrons, Clients, and Policies: Patterns of Democratic Accountability and Political Competition*, ed. Herbert Kitschelt and Steven I. Wilkinson. New York: Cambridge University Press, 68–83.

Merton, Robert. 1968. *Social Theory and Social Structure*. New York: Free Press.

Mettler, Suzanne. 1998. *Dividing Citizens: Gender and Federalism in New Deal Public Policy*. Ithaca, NY: Cornell University Press.

Miguel, Edward, and Mary Kay Gugerty. 2005. "Ethnic Diversity, Social Sanctions, and Public Goods in Kenya." *Journal of Public Economics* 89(11–12):2325–68.

Mickey, Robert. 2015. *Paths Out of Dixie: The Democratization of Authoritarian Enclaves in America's Deep South, 1944–1972*. Princeton, NJ: Princeton University Press.

Milkis, Sidney M. 1993. *The President and the Parties: The Transformation of the American Party System since the New Deal*. Oxford: Oxford University Press.

Miller, Warren E., and Donald E. Stokes. 1963. "Constituency Influence in Congress." *American Political Science Review* 57(1):45–56.

Morgan, Jana, and Nathan J. Kelly. 2017. "Social Patterns of Inequality, Partisan Competition, and Latin American Support for Redistribution." *Journal of Politics* 79(1): 193–209.

Morone, James. 2004. *Hellfire Nation: The Politics of Sin in American History*. New Haven, CT: Yale University Press.

Muhtadi, Burhanuddin. 2019. *Vote Buying in Indonesia: The Mechanics of Electoral Bribery*. Singapore: Palgrave Macmillan.

Müller, Wolfgang C. 2007. "Political Institutions and Linkage Strategies. In *Patrons, Clients, and Policies: Patterns of Democratic Accountability and Political Competition*, ed. Herbert Kitschelt and Steven I. Wilkinson. New York: Cambridge University Press, 251–75.

Nathan, Noah L. 2016. "Local Ethnic Geography, Expectations of Favoritism, and Voting in Urban Ghana." *Comparative Political Studies* 49(14):1896–1929.

Nathan, Noah L. 2019. *Electoral Politics and Africa's Urban Transition: Class and Ethnicity in Ghana*. New York: Cambridge University Press.

Noel, Hans. 2013. *Political Ideologies and Political Parties in America*. New York: Cambridge University Press.

North, Douglass C. 1990. *Institutions, Institutional Change, and Economic Performance*. New York: Cambridge University Press.

Oldfield, Duane M. 1996. *The Right and the Righteous: The Christian Right Confronts the Republican Party*. Lanham, MD: Rowman and Littlefield.

Oliveros, Virginia. 2021. *Patronage at Work: Public Jobs and Political Services in Argentina*. New York: Cambridge University Press.

O'Neill, Thomas P., with William Novak. 1987. *Man of the House: The Life and Political Memoirs of Speaker Tip O'Neill*. New York: Random House.

Orren, Karen, and Stephen Skowronek. 2004. *The Search for American Political Development*. New York: Cambridge University Press.

Orren, Karen, and Stephen Skowronek. 2017. *The Policy State: An American Predicament*. Cambridge, MA: Harvard University Press.

Overacker, Louise. 1937. "Campaign Funds in the Presidential Election of 1936." *American Political Science Review* 31:473–98.

Overacker, Louise. 1941. "Campaign Finance in the Presidential Election of 1940." *American Political Science Review* 35:701–27.

Overacker, Louise. 1945. "American Government and Politics: Presidential Campaign Funds, 1944." *American Political Science Review* 39:899–925.

Persson, Torsten, Guido Tabellini, and Francesco Trebbi. 2003. "Electoral Rules and Corruption." *Journal of the European Economic Association* 1(4):958–89.

Pierson, Paul. 2000a. "Increasing Returns, Path Dependence, and the Study of Politics." *American Political Science Review* 94(2):251–67.

Pierson, Paul. 2000b. "Not Just What, but When: Timing and Sequence in Political Processes." *Studies in American Political Development* 14(1):72–92.

Pierson, Paul, and Eric Schickler. 2020. "Madison's Constitution under Stress: A Developmental Analysis of Political Polarization." *Annual Review of Political Science* 23:37–58.

Polsby, Nelson W. 2005. *How Congress Evolves: Social Bases of Institutional Change*. New York: Oxford University Press.

Pomper, Gerald. 1968. *Elections in America*. New York: Dodd Mead.

Poole, Keith T., and Howard Rosenthal. 1997. *Congress: A Political-Economic History of Roll Call Voting*. New York: Oxford University Press.

Poole, Keith T., and Howard Rosenthal. 2007. *Ideology and Congress*. New Brunswick, NJ: Transaction.

Poole, Mary. 2006. *The Segregated Origins of Social Security: African Americans and the Welfare State*. Chapel Hill: University of North Carolina Press.

Posner, Daniel N. 2005. *Institutions and Ethnic Politics in Africa*. Cambridge: Cambridge University Press.

Post, Kenneth. 1963. *The Nigerian Federal Election of 1959*. Oxford: Oxford University Press.

Proksch, Sven-Oliver, and Jonathan B. Slapin. 2009. "How to Avoid Pitfalls in Statistical Analysis of Political Texts: The Case of Germany." *German Politics* 18(3):323–44.

Proksch, Sven-Oliver, and Jonathan B. Slapin. 2010. "Position Taking in European Parliament Speeches." *British Journal of Political Science* 40(3):587–611.

Proksch, Sven-Oliver, Jonathan B. Slapin, and Michael F. Thies. 2011. "Party System Dynamics in Post-war Japan: A Quantitative Content Analysis of Electoral Pledges." *Electoral Studies* 30:114–24.

Przeworski, Adam. 1991. *Democracy and the Market*. New York: Cambridge University Press.

Quadagno, Jill. 1996. *The Color of Welfare: How Racism Undermined the War on Poverty*. New York: Oxford University Press.

Quinn, Kevin M., Burt L. Monroe, Michael Colaresi, Michael H. Crespin, and Dragomir R. Radev. 2010. "How to Analyze Political Attention with Minimal Assumptions and Costs." *American Journal of Political Science* 54(1):209–28.

Ranney, Austin. 1962. *The Doctrine of Responsible Party Government: Its Origins and Present State*. Urbana: University of Illinois Press.

Reid, Joseph D., and Michael M. Kurth. 1988. "Public Employees in Political Firms: Part A. The Patronage Era." *Public Choice* 59:253–62.

Roberts, George C. 1987. *Paul M. Butler: Hoosier Politician and National Political Leader*. Lanham, MD: University Press of America.

Roberts, Jason M., and Steven S. Smith. 2012. "Procedural Contexts, Party Strategy, and Conditional Party Voting in the U.S. House of Representatives, 1971–2000." *American Journal of Political Science* 47(2):305–17.

Roberts, Margaret E., Brandon M. Stewart, and Edoardo M. Airoldi. 2013. "The Structural Topic Model and Applied Social Science." Presented at Advances in Neural Information Processing Systems Workshop on Topic Models: Computation, Application, and Evaluation, Lake Tahoe, Nevada, December 5–10.

Roberts, Margaret E., Brandon M. Stewart, and Dustin Tingley. 2019. "stm: An R Package for Structural Topic Models." *Journal of Statistical Software* 91(2):1–40.

Roberts, Margaret E., Brandon M. Stewart, Dustin Tingley, Christopher Lucas, Jetson Leder-Luis, Shana Kushner Gadarian, Bethany Albertson, and David G. Rand. 2014. "Structural Topic Models for Open-Ended Survey Responses." *American Journal of Political Science* 58(4):1064–82.

Rohde, David W. 1991. *Parties and Leaders in the Postreform House*. Chicago: University of Chicago Press.

Rosenfeld, Sam. 2018. *The Polarizers: Postwar Architects of Our Partisan Era*. Chicago: University of Chicago Press.

Rothschild, Jacob, Adam J. Howat, Richard M. Shafranek, and Ethan C. Busby. 2019. "Pigeonholing Partisans: Stereotypes of Party Supporters and Partisan Polarization." *Political Behavior* 41(1):423–43.

Royed, Terry. 1996. "Testing the Mandate Model in Britain and the United States: Evidence from the Reagan and Thatcher Eras." *British Journal of Political Science* 26(1):45–80.

Schattschneider, E. E. 1942. *Party Government*. New York: Holt, Rinehart and Winston.

Schattschneider, E. E. 1948. "Pressure Groups versus Political Parties." *Annals of the Academy of Political and Social Science* 259:17–23.

Schattschneider, E. E. 1960. *The Semi-Sovereign People*. New York: Holt, Rinehart and Winston.

Scheiner, Ethan. 2007. "Clientelism in Japan: The Importance and Limits of Institutional Explanations." In *Patrons, Clients, and Policies: Patterns of Democratic Accountability and Political Competition*, ed. Herbert Kitschelt and Steven I. Wilkinson. New York: Cambridge University Press, 276–97.

Schickler, Eric. 2001. *Disjointed Pluralism: Institutional Innovation and the Development of the U.S. Congress*. Princeton, NJ: Princeton University Press.

Schlozman, Daniel, and Sam Rosenfeld. 2024. *The Hollow Parties: The Many Pasts and Disordered Present of American Party Politics*. Princeton, NJ: Princeton University Press.

Schlozman, Daniel, and Sam Rosenfeld. 2019. "The Hollow Parties." In *Can America Govern Itself?*, ed. Frances Lee and Nolan McCarty. New York: Cambridge University Press, 120–51.

Schmidt, Steffen, ed. 1977. *Friends, Followers, and Factions: A Reader in Political Clientelism*. Berkeley: University of California Press.

Schumpeter, Joseph A. 1942. *Capitalism, Socialism, and Democracy*. New York: Harper and Brothers.

Scott, James C. 1969. "Corruption, Machine Politics, and Political Change." *American Political Science Review* 63:1142–58.

Shefter, Martin. 1977. "Party and Patronage: Germany, England, and Italy." *Politics and Society* 7(4):403–51.

Shefter, Martin. 1994. *Political Parties and the State: the American Historical Experience*. Princeton, NJ: Princeton University Press.

Sheingate, Adam. 2003. "Political Entrepreneurship, Institutional Change, and American Political Development." *Studies in American Political Development* 17(2):185–203.

Sheingate, Adam. 2014. "Institutional Dynamics and American Political Development." *Annual Review of Political Science* 17:461–77.

Skocpol, Theda. 1992. *Protecting Soldiers and Mothers: The Political Origins of Social Policy in the United States*. Cambridge, MA: Harvard University Press.

Skowronek, Stephen. 1982. *Building a New American State: The Expansion of National Administrative Capacities, 1877–1920*. New York: Cambridge University Press.

Slapin, Jonathan B., and Sven-Oliver Proksch. 2008. "A Scaling Model for Estimating Time-Series Party Positions from Texts." *American Journal of Political Science* 52(3):705–22.

Smith, Richard Norton. 1982. *Thomas E. Dewey and His Times*. New York: Simon and Schuster.

Smith, Rogers M. 1993. "Beyond Tocqueville, Myrdal, and Hartz: The Multiple Traditions in America." *American Political Science Review* 87(3):549–66.

Stigler, George J. 1972. "Economic Competition and Political Competition." *Public Choice* 13:91–106.

Stokes, Susan C. 2005. "Perverse Accountability: A Formal Model of Machine Politics with Evidence from Argentina." *American Political Science Review* 99:315–26.

Stokes, Susan C. 2007. "Political Clientelism." In *Oxford Handbook of Comparative Politics*, ed. Charles Boix and Susan Stokes. New York: Oxford University Press, 604–27.

Stokes, Susan C., Thad Dunning, Marcelo Nazareno, and Valeria Brusco. 2013. *Brokers, Voters, and Clientelism: The Puzzle of Distributive Politics*. New York: Cambridge University Press.

Summers, Mark. 1987. *The Plundering Generation: Corruption and the Crisis of the Union, 1849–1861*. New York: Oxford University Press.

Sundquist, James L. 1983. *Dynamics of the Party System: Alignment and Realignment of Political Parties in the United States*. Washington, DC: Brookings Institution.

Tarrow, Sidney. 1967. *Peasant Communism in Southern Italy*. New Haven, CT: Yale University Press.

Thelen, Kathleen. 1999. "Historical Institutionalism in Comparative Politics." *Annual Review of Political Science* 2:369–404.

Thomas, Samuel J. 2001. "Holding the Tiger: Mugwump Cartoonists and Tammany Hall in Gilded Age New York." *New York History* 82(2):155–82.

Thomson, C. A. H. 1939. "Research and the Republican Party." *Public Opinion Quarterly* 3(2):306–13.

Trounstine, Jessica. 2008. *Political Monopolies in American Cities: The Rise and Fall of Bosses and Reformers*. Chicago: University of Chicago Press.

Truman, David. 1951. *The Governmental Process: Political Interests and Public Opinion*. New York: Knopf.

Van Riper, Paul P. 1958. *History of the United States Civil Service*. Evanston, IL: Row, Peterson.

Van De Walle, Nicolas. 2007. "Meet the New Boss, Same as the Old Boss? The Evolution of Political Clientelism in Africa." In *Patrons, Clients, and Policies: Patterns of Democratic Accountability and Political Competition*, ed. Herbert Kitschelt and Steven I. Wilkinson. New York: Cambridge University Press, 50–67.

Wallis, John Joseph. 1974. "Employment, Politics, and Economic Recovery during the Great Depression." *Review of Economics and Statistics* 69(3):516–20.

Walters, Ronald W. 1990. "Party Platforms as Political Process." *PS: Political Science and Politics* 3(2):436–38.

Wang, Yi-ting, and Kiril Kolev. 2019. "Ethnic Group Inequality, Partisan Networks, and Political Clientelism." *Political Research Quarterly* 72(2):329–41.

Wantchekon, Leonard. 2003. "Clientelism and Voting Behavior: Evidence from a Field Experiment in Benin." *World Politics* 55(3):399–422.

Ward, Deborah E. 2005. *The White Welfare State: The Racialization of U.S. Welfare Policy*. Ann Arbor: University of Michigan Press.

Weinberg, Martha Wagner. 1977. "Writing the Republican Platform." *Political Science Quarterly* 92(4):655–62.

Weitz-Shapiro, Rebecca. 2012. "What Wins Votes: Why Some Politicians Opt Out of Clientelism." *American Journal of Political Science* 56(3):568–83.

Weitz-Shapiro, Rebecca. 2014. *Curbing Clientelism in Argentina: Politics, Poverty, and Social Policy*. New York: Cambridge University Press.

Wilkinson, Steven I. 2007. "Explaining Changing Patterns of Party-Voter Linkages in India." In *Patrons, Clients, and Policies: Patterns of Democratic Accountability and Political Competition*, ed. Herbert Kitschelt and Steven I. Wilkinson. New York: Cambridge University Press, 110–40.

Wilson, James Q. 1962. *The Amateur Democrat: Club Politics in Three Cities*. Chicago: University of Chicago Press.

Wolbrecht, Christina. 2000. *The Politics of Women's Rights: Parties, Positions, and Change*. Princeton, NJ: Princeton University Press.

Wolfinger, Raymond E. 1972. "Why Political Machines Have Not Withered Away and Other Revisionist Thoughts." *Journal of Politics* 34:365–98.

Wright, Gavin. 1974. "The Political Economy of New Deal Spending: An Econometric Analysis." *Review of Economics and Statistics* 56(1):30–38.

X.Y.Z. 1894. "The Opportunity of the Mugwump." *Sewanee Review* 3(1):1–9.

Yakter, Alon. 2019. "The Heterogeneous Effect of Diversity: Ascriptive Identities, Class and Redistribution in Developed Democracies." *European Journal of Political Research* 58(3):820–44.

INDEX

Page numbers in *italics* refer to figures and tables.

abolitionism, 74

abortion, 2, 19

Advisory Committee on Policies and
  Platforms (ACPP), 122–23

Advisory Committee on Political
  Organization (ACPO), 153

affective polarization, 8

Alcorn, Meade, 162, 165

Aldrich, John, 29

American Federation of Labor (AFL), 128

American Institutions Project, 199, 204

American Political Science Association
  (APSA), 87; parties' professionalization
  backed by, 135–36, 149; parties' similarities criticized by, 3, 105, 107, 149;
  responsible party government backed
  by, 10–11, 12, 55

Americans for Democratic Action (ADA),
  134

American Veterans Committee (AVC), 134

analytical history, 67–96, 191

Argentina, 39

Arrington, Richard, 181

Australia, 43

Australian (secret) ballot, 42, 46–47, 51, 82

Austria, 42, 43, 45

Bailey, John, 159

Banfield, Edward C., 95

Bankhead, William, 123

Barkley, Alben, 103

Barrasso, John, 103

Batt, Bill, 133, 134, 135

Bawn, Kathleen, 29

Beer, Samuel, 160

Belgium, 43, 45

Benoit, Kenneth, 207

Bibby, John F., 146

Biden, Joe, 1

Birkhead, Kenneth, 133, 134

Black Lives Matter, 178

Blaine, James G., 75, 112

Bliss, Ray, 166, 167, 168

Bone, Hugh, 146

Brazil, 38, 39

Bridges, Ronald, 126, 129

Brightman, Samuel, 122, 134, 135, 157

Brock, Bill, 168–69

Brown, M. Craig, 72, 85

Brown, Watt T., 121

Bryan, William Jennings, 80

Budge, Ian, 212

Bunche, Ralph, 128

bureaucracy, 44–45, 50–51, 84

Bureau of the Budget, 80

Bush, George H. W., 182

Bushnell, C. S., 112

Butler, Paul, 152–55, 157–58, 160, 165, 179, 183

Canada, 73

Carpenter, Daniel P., 223n33

Cartter, D. K., 112

Casey, Ralph D., 136

Cheeseman, Nic, 55, 213–14n13

PRINCETON STUDIES IN
AMERICAN POLITICS

Historical, International, and Comparative Perspectives

Paul Frymer, Suzanne Mettler, and Eric Schickler,
Series Editors

Ira Katznelson, Martin Shefter, and Theda Skocpol,
Founding Series Editors

A NOTE ON THE TYPE

This book has been composed in Arno, an Old-style serif typeface in the classic Venetian tradition, designed by Robert Slimbach at Adobe.

GPSR Authorized Representative: Easy Access System Europe - Mustamäe tee 50, 10621 Tallinn, Estonia, gpsr.requests@easproject.com

www.ingramcontent.com/pod-product-compliance
Lightning Source LLC
Chambersburg PA
CBHW020841270326
41928CB00006B/504